PRINCIPLES AND POLITICS IN
CONTEMPORARY BRITAIN

Principles and Politics in Contemporary Britain

Mark Garnett

LONGMAN
London and New York

Addison Wesley Longman Limited
Edinburgh Gate
Harlow
Essex CM20 2JE, England
and Associated Companies throughout the world.

Published in the United States of America
by Longman Publishing, New York

© Addison Wesley Longman Ltd 1996

First published 1996

ISBN 0 582 28924–6 PPR

British Library Cataloguing-in-Publication Data

A catalogue record for this book is
available from the British Library

Library of Congress Cataloging-in-Publication Data

Garnett, Mark, 1963–
    Principles and politics in contemporary Britain / Mark Garnett.
        p.   cm.
    Includes bibliographical references and index.
    ISBN 0–582–28924–6
    1. Political parties—Great Britain.   2. Great Britain—Politics
and government—1964–1979.   3. Great Britain—Politics and
government—1979–
    JN1121.G39   1996
    324.241′009′045—dc20
                                                            95–46261
                                                            CIP

Set in 10/11 Times by 5
Produced through Longman Malaysia, TCP.

CONTENTS

LIST OF ABBREVIATIONS

ACAS	Advisory Conciliation and Arbitration Service
AES	Alternative Economic Strategy
ALF	Animal Liberation Front
ASI	Adam Smith Institute
CAP	Common Agricultural Policy
CBI	Confederation of British Industry
CDS	Campaign for Democratic Socialism
CLPD	Campaign for Labour Party Democracy
CND	Campaign for Nuclear Disarmament
CPRS	Central Policy Review Staff
CPS	Centre for Policy Studies
CRD	Conservative Research Department
CSA	Campaign for a Scottish Assembly
DEA	Department of Economic Affairs
DOE	Department of the Environment
DTI	Department of Trade and Industry
DUP	Democratic Unionist Party
EC	European Community
EC/EEC	European Economic Community
EMS	European Monetary System
ERM	Exchange Rate Mechanism
EU	European Union
FOE	Friends of the Earth
GLC	Greater London Council
IEA	Institute of Economic Affairs
IMF	International Monetary Fund
IRA	Irish Republican Army
LCC	Labour Co-ordinating Committee
LSC	Labour Solidarity Campaign
MP	Member of Parliament
NATO	North Atlantic Treaty Organisation
NEB	National Enterprise Board
NEC	National Executive Committee
NEDC	National Economic Development Council
NF	National Front
NHS	National Health Service
NICRA	Northern Ireland Civil Rights Association
NUM	National Union of Mineworkers

NUPRG	New Ulster Political Research Group
OMOV	One Member One Vote
PLP	Parliamentary Labour Party
RFMC	Rank and File Mobilising Committee
RSPCA	Royal Society for the Prevention of Cruelty to Animals
SCLV	Socialist Campaign for Labour Victory
SDLP	Social Democratic and Labour Party
SDP	Social Democratic Party
SEA	Single European Act
SLP	Scottish Labour Party
SNP	Scottish Nationalist Party
SPD	Social Democratic Party (Germany)
SWP	Socialist Workers' Party
TUC	Trades Union Congress
UK	United Kingdom
USA	United States of America
UUP	Ulster Unionist Party
VAT	Value Added Tax
VFS	Victory for Socialism
WLM	Women's Liberation Movement

ACKNOWLEDGEMENTS

It would have been impossible to write this book without constructive criticism, and I am indebted to several people who gave up their time to read chapters, or discuss vital issues. Parts of the book were read by Ian Gilmour, David Marquand, William Wallace, and Gerry Taylor. The whole manuscript was read with great care and patience by Philippa Sherrington. Tony Benn, Michael Foot and Robert Garner were also generous in answering my questions, and I would like to thank the two anonymous referees for their invaluable suggestions. Without the guidance and encouragement of Bernard Crick and Iain Hampsher-Monk this book would not have been written. I am also grateful to Chris Harrison and Jane Toettcher at Longman for their enthusiastic support, and to all those who have helped in the production process. Good natured political discussions with my family have been too rare recently, and I hope that the book will supply the deficiency. My other inspiration has been the Thatcherites of all parties – may they prosper as they deserve. If errors of fact or interpretation remain, they are entirely my own responsibility.

Principles and politics

This book offers readers an introduction to the nature and role of principles in UK politics since 1970. Its main focus is the effect of principles on the activities of political parties, although it also takes account of non-parliamentary movements and public opinion. Until the 1980s, books on this theme were extremely rare; there are numerous studies which concentrate on principles and politics in isolation from each other, but few have attempted a sustained account of the relationship between the two. In part, this neglect has arisen from the view that politicians in the UK are primarily interested in action rather than belief, but it also owes something to the academic division of labour between political science and political theory. There are signs that this unfortunate schism may be ending, and interest in the role of principles has also been encouraged by an often-passionate debate about 'Thatcherism'. This book aims to develop this interest further, by showing that Thatcherism was not as unusual as commentators have implied. Principles did not suddenly begin to influence policy-makers after the Conservative Party victory in 1979. All that changed when Mrs Thatcher became Prime Minister was that the UK government now had a leader whose declarations of principle were impossible to ignore.

Since books on this theme have been so rare, there is a need to establish some ground rules. For example, what kind of evidence are we looking for? If we are hoping to find most politicians indulging in abstract philosophical speculations we will not proceed very far; democratic systems are inhospitable to those who refuse to acknowledge that theory and practice are related yet distinct. Even Mrs Thatcher could not hope to transfer her ideas from the pages of F. A. Hayek into legislation without some tactical rewriting. On the other hand, it is in the interest of politicians to be seen as basing their policies on coherent ideas; they are often so good at rationalising their statements and actions that there is a danger of interpreting *everything* as the product of principle. In other words, there is a need to find a discriminating balance between an unrealistic demand for 'pure' ideas and a naive acceptance of self-serving pleas.

This task is complicated by the fact that politicians are often unaware of the extent of their debt to theorising. J. M. Keynes once quipped that people who claim to be free from any influence usually turn out to be 'the slaves of some defunct economist'; this may have been a deliberate overstatement, but his remark contains an element of truth (Keynes, 1936, 383). Unfortunately the nature of this influence has yet to be investigated in detail. Ideas pass into practice through complex filters, and it is a serious mistake to scan the pages of *Hansard* in a search for direct quotations from illustrious political and economic thinkers. For one thing, the theorists who enjoy most prominence in academic studies are not necessarily the ones who appeal most to practitioners; Michael Foot's socialism, for example, has been influenced more by Jonathan Swift and William Hazlitt than by Karl Marx or even William Morris. Secondly, the views of politicians and voters do not need to have been inspired by their own reading in order to qualify as ideas. Margaret Thatcher originally developed her principles from the teachings of her father and her experiences as a housewife; the writings of Milton Friedman and F. A. Hayek were important to her, since they gave her beliefs additional clarity and intellectual respectability, but her presuppositions were established by the time that she came to study these writers carefully. Just as politics departments are unnaturally divided into 'theorists' and 'scientists', many commentators have simply assumed that people are either 'thinkers' or 'doers' (Bradley, 1981, 173–4). This kind of approach is bound to lead to distorted analysis. In short, for the purpose of this book political thoughts which are innovative, mundane or simply muddle-headed are regarded as equally valid subjects for investigation, whatever their origin. We can explain why we think that some principles are more convincing, original or appropriate than others, but this should not mean that those who fail our tests should be excluded from the discussion.

Sometimes politicians do acknowledge a direct debt to theorists (whether 'defunct' or living); this makes things easier, although we still need to study the way in which the theory has been used. Normally the only way of reaching useful conclusions about principles and politics is to examine the underlying tendency of policies and statements. This approach inevitably involves the concept of *ideology*. Ideology is a warmly contested subject, and in a brief discussion the best that one can do is to provide a working definition, and then apply it consistently. Some will argue that many of the ideas discussed in this book should not be graced (or disgraced) with the name of ideology, preferring to draw distinctions (for instance) between ideologies and 'doctrines'. In part, this arises out of the chequered history of ideology. For much of the time since it was coined in the late eighteenth century, people have used the term as a synonym for either distorted thinking (the Marxist view), or for extremism (the approach taken by many conservatives and liberals). Instead of helping us to understand politics, both of these interpretations are designed to discredit opposing beliefs; as such, they are themselves products of ideological thought, which inadvertently tell us a great deal about those who apply them. The essential point is that ideology should be used as a tool for analysis; in a book of this nature, it is also important to ensure that the text does not collapse beneath the weight of definitions and distinctions. For this reason, the all-embracing term of ideology has been retained, with a definition that can provide a clear basis for analysis.

The best approaches to ideology are those which at least have no bias built into them. The interpretation followed here is illustrated by Andrew Vincent in his book *Modern Political Ideologies*. For Vincent, 'ideologies are bodies of concepts, values and symbols which incorporate conceptions of human nature and thus indicate what is possible or impossible for humans to achieve' (Vincent, 1995, 16). Most people have views about human nature, however vague or confused they might be. Our ideas on the subject may or may not find expression in any political actions, however trivial; there is plenty of evidence, for example, that people's views on the subject are frequently at odds with the platform of the parties they vote for (Heath et al., 1991, 217). Since the major UK parties are broad coalitions, it often happens that even senior politicians find themselves espousing policies which run counter to their real beliefs. All that this proves to the student of ideology is the party labels are inadequate guides to the real beliefs of voters and political actors.

Ideology and political action

This approach implies that ideology is an inescapable aspect of political life, rather than a curse that should be eradicated. Ideologies can inspire rigid, programmatic thinking but this says more about the temperament of the individual than the nature of the ideology. Only an unusual minority among the population wishes to reshape society in accordance with a blueprint; this is true of an even smaller proportion of those who feel the additional pressures of crucial decision-making. Ideologies are both *descriptive* and *prescriptive*; they make sense of complex realities, and suggest what believers ought to do if they want prosperity to continue, or the world set right again. Those who accept the diagnosis provided by an ideology can either follow this advice or decide not to do anything – that is, we might think that the logical course of action dictated by our beliefs is not practicable in a hostile environment. This is the way some Marxists might be feeling in the mid-1990s, just as some economic liberals probably felt resigned to impotence in (say) 1974. In these cases, inaction does not necessarily denote a total lack of ideological commitments; after all, if these people did not subscribe to their ideologies then they would not feel so depressed about the situation. This means that the student is constantly required to make judgements about the complex relationship between ideology, personality and circumstances. These judgements might be challenged, but if views of human nature are the common standard by which beliefs are evaluated then at least different interpretations will be appealing to the same evidence.

Since practical politics is a process of adaptation, it is quite unusual to find direct expression about human nature in public discourse. The general rule is that these ideological presuppositions will be implicit. The politicians who make regular and clear appeals to a particular vision of human nature (as Margaret Thatcher does) are those whose ideological impulse is most pronounced. Other politicians might seem to be driven only by circumstances, changing their policies so quickly that they seem to be inspired by nothing more lofty than a desire to win or cling to office. Close examination will often reveal some base-line of principle even in these cases. Fortunately a knowledgeable democracy will demand that apparent 'conversions' should be justified, which means that the analyst generally has more evidence on which to base a judgement in these cases (Garnett, 1994, 97–108).

The present study does not take the professed ideological loyalties of politicians at face value. In an emotive activity like politics, it is wrong to simply accept what participants say about themselves; instead of endorsing their chosen labels, their beliefs need to be examined carefully if we are to make sense of their behaviour. Like ideology as a whole, the nature of particular beliefs is contested, and it is quite possible for members of the same ideological family to quarrel over the details of policy. The logical structure of ideologies might point to particular conclusions, but the tactical route to these ends can vary dramatically among a group of believers. However, these controversies can go only so far; for example, socialist premises might suggest diverse short-term proposals, but when politicians disagree about the premises themselves the student is forced to decide who is 'right'. Some specialists believe that this approach is quite mistaken, and that a search for the 'essential' premises which characterise different ideologies is futile (Greenleaf, 1983, 11–14). Yet if two people wholly agree on the best kind of social arrangements, and one calls herself a conservative while the other claims to be a life-long liberal, there is a need to clarify matters if our political vocabulary is to remain meaningful. This is tacitly accepted even by W. H. Greenleaf, who criticises the attempt to establish the 'core' principles of each ideology but ends up establishing categories of his own which are open to similar objections. Fortunately there is broad agreement about the general outlines of each ideological tradition; commentators disagree about how they work out in practice, but this difficulty will be reduced as further studies appear.

During the period since 1970, questions about the traditional ideologies of British political parties have become common features of political disputes. For many years the Labour Party debated the nature of socialism. The fact that it no longer does so is eloquent testimony to the changes since 1979, and currently the leadership faces the problem of how to replace it while remaining broadly consistent with Labour's historic aims. The relationship between the Liberal Party and the Social Democratic Party (SDP), and their eventual semi-merger, was bedevilled by differing interpretations of the liberal and social-democratic traditions. Perhaps the most spectacular of all recent controversies is the continuing argument over what constituents 'true' conservatism. The most famous contribution to this quarrel was Sir Keith Joseph's confession of 1975 that he had been 'converted' to conservatism only in the previous year. In Joseph's words, before 1974 'I had thought that I was a conservative but I can see now that I was not really one at all' (Halcrow, 1989, 56–60). In short, Joseph realised that it was possible for people to be wrong about the nature of their own beliefs – a sound justification for 'second-guessing' by less partial observers. His outburst also shows that people who feel that they have changed their minds often find it necessary to explain their ideas in more detail than those who think that they have remained consistent. The ironic twist to this unusual piece of self-criticism is that Joseph's actual views seem not to have changed at all. His actions as a high-spending minister in Edward Heath's government had transgressed the economic liberal principles which he had always favoured; as a result, he felt that a public confession was required if he was to re-establish his ideological credibility. So not even apparently candid witnesses like Sir Keith can be entirely trusted when they talk about themselves.

In keeping with the rest of the subject, ideological terminology can be confusing. In Sir Keith's case, we are dealing with the claim that a member of the Conservative Party is not necessarily a 'conservative'. Unfortunately, established usage means that we have to persevere in spite of this problem. In the following pages, 'conservative' is used to refer to a particular ideology;

'Conservative' denotes membership of the political party. A similar distinction must be drawn between 'liberal' and 'Liberal'. It is likely that whatever labels we apply, confusion is bound to arise. For example, during the late 1980s the news media regularly used the single word 'conservative' to characterise the Stalinist opponents of Mikhail Gorbachev, and Christian fundamentalists in the United States. In the context of the UK, it served to describe free-market liberals and strong advocates of state action within the Conservative Party. In fact, only the last-named group advocated policies which can be readily squared with the traditional approach of British conservatism. Conservatism is perhaps the most slippery of ideological terms; it is unusually sensitive to cultural contexts, and it might be argued that it is a specifically English phenomenon (fortunately this is not a debate which need concern us directly). Still, the inadequate terminology at the disposal of broadcasters can never excuse the unnecessary confusion which these accounts must have caused. Provided that labels are used with consistency they should not get in the way of a more satisfactory picture of ideological debates.

The structure of the book is both thematic and chronological. It traces the development of ideas within British parties since 1970. Attention focuses on principles in proportion to their actual influence on politics, rather than the extent to which they draw on original or profound thought. Of course not all of the influential ideas since 1970 have been associated with party-political activity. This has been especially true since the mid-1980s as the attraction of major parties has declined; this development is dealt with in Chapter 8. The time-scale is convenient, but also covers some important changes in British political thinking. It ends in mid-1995, but it is hoped that the previous discussion will provide a framework on which readers can base an understanding of future developments. The more that people try to interpret events from the recent past, the better chance we have of understanding the present. Some scholars of contemporary history protest that conclusions can be only provisional until all the relevant documents have been released, but historical conclusions are inevitably provisional to some extent, and we can never be sure that the whole range of evidence has been consulted. The continuing topicality of the period under review will provoke argument, and this might help readers to speculate about the underlying issues and themes.

Summary

Several key points arise from this discussion. The present study is an attempt to identify the underlying ideas which informed British politics between 1970 and 1995. It focuses on ideologies, which are taken to be systems of thought which arise from different views of human nature. Although categorisation of these beliefs cannot be precise, most people's views can be placed within distinct ideological 'families'. Ideologies provide explanations for current events, and suggest ways of dealing with the situation. Whether or not these courses of action are followed depends on various factors, but the most important consideration is the strength of a person's ideological commitment. Politicians are not usually given to pronouncements about human nature, but an ideological profile can be drawn up from the assumptions and behaviour of most political actors. These profiles can override the claims of politicians, which are often contradicted by the evidence. The conclusions of outside observers may be challenged, but the most important thing is to establish criteria which allow us to judge competing interpretations. Ideology is too important a subject to be simply left to the ideologues. There is no assumption that the principles espoused by all political actors arise from clear and consistent premises about human nature. However, most people do have ideological views of some kind, and in general politicians can be expected to have entered public life with some notions of the best kind of social organisation to accommodate human nature as they see it.

This leads to one final remark. If we all have our own ideas about human nature, then evidence of commitment of some kind is bound to creep into our writing, however careful we are. The search for 'value-free' accounts of human activities is therefore misplaced. This is one reason why no survey of British politics since 1970 can escape unchallenged, although it applies equally to work on any period. An important advantage of the study of ideology, however, is that it should make us more aware of our own views; a sympathetic understanding of competing ideas may cause us to be a little more sceptical, or it might reinforce our opinion that we are right. In either case, our self-knowledge will have been increased, and whatever our degree of participation we can hope to add something to the quality of contemporary political debate.

List of works cited

Bradley, Ian (1981), 'Intellectual Influences in Britain: Past and Present', in Arthur Seldon (ed.) *The Emerging Consensus*, Institute of Economic Affairs

Garnett, Mark (1994), 'An Essay on Inconsistency in Politics', *Government and Opposition*, volume 29, number 1

Greenleaf, W. H. (1983), *The British Political Tradition: Volume II, The Ideological Heritage*, Methuen

Halcrow, Morrison (1989), *Keith Joseph: A Single Mind*, Macmillan

Heath, Anthony, Evans, Geoff, Field, Julia, and Witherspoon, Sharon (1991), *Understanding Political Change: The British Voter 1964–1987*, Pergamon

Keynes, John Maynard (1936), *The General Theory of Employment, Interest and Money*, Macmillan

Vincent, Andrew (1995), *Modern Political Ideologies*, Blackwell

Selected further reading: parties, principles and post-war history

Adams, Ian (1993), *Political Ideology Today*, Manchester University Press.

Annan, Noel (1991), *Our Age: The Generation that Made Post-War Britain*, Fontana.

Ball, Terence, and Dagger, Richard (1991), *Political Ideologies and the Democratic Ideal*, HarperCollins.

Barker, Rodney (1994), *Politics, Peoples and Government: Themes in British Political Thought since the Nineteenth Century*, Macmillan.

Barnett, Corelli (1986), *The Audit of War: The Illusion and Reality of Britain as a Great Power*, Macmillan.

Bellamy, Richard (1992), *Liberalism and Modern Society: An Historical Argument*, Polity.

Crick, Bernard (1973), 'On Theory and Practice', in his *Political Theory and Practice*, Allen Lane.

Crick, Bernard (1987), *Socialism*, Open University Press.

Eccleshall, Robert (1990), *English Conservatism since the Restoration*, Allen and Unwin.

Eccleshall, Robert, Geoghegan, Vincent, Jay, Richard, et al. (1994), *Political Ideologies: An Introduction*, Routledge, 2nd edition.

Freeden, Michael (1978), *The New Liberalism: An Ideology of Social Reform*, Oxford University Press.

Garner, Robert, and Kelly, Richard (1993), *British Political Parties Today*, Manchester University Press.

Goodwin, Barbara (1993), *Using Political Ideas*, John Wiley, 3rd edition.

Gray, John (1986), *Liberalism*, Open University Press.

Haywood, Andrew (1992), *Political Ideologies: An Introduction*, Macmillan.

Kavanagh, Dennis (1992), 'Debate: The Post-War Consensus', *Contemporary Record*, volume 3, number 2.

Leach, Robert (1991), *British Political Ideologies*, Philip Alan.

McLellan, David (1995), *Ideology*, Open University Press, 2nd edition.

Middlemas, Keith (1979), *The Politics of Industrial Society: The Experience of the British System since 1911*, André Deutsch.

Morgan, Kenneth (1992), *The People's Peace: British History 1945–1990*, Oxford University Press.

Plamenatz, John (1970), *Ideology*, Pall Mall.

Seliger, Martin (1976), *Ideology and Politics*, Allen and Unwin.

Tivey, Leonard, and Wright, Anthony (ed.) (1992), *Political Thought since 1945: Philosophy, Science, Ideology*, Edward Elgar.

CHAPTER 1

A decade of discontent? The Labour Party, 1970–79

Background

In 1964, Harold Wilson's Labour Party came into office with ambitious plans and a slender parliamentary majority of four seats over all other parties. In contrast to the Conservatives, who had allegedly 'wasted' their years of power since 1951, Wilson confronted the electorate as the apostle of dynamic change. Under Labour, he promised, technology would be harnessed for the good of the people; renewed economic strength would be used to create 'a fairer order of society' (Wilson, 1974, 17).

Although the further general election called in 1966 rewarded Labour with a majority of ninety-five, by 1970 most commentators agreed that the hopes of 1964 had not been realised. With hindsight, the most surprising thing about the 1970 election is that Labour were clear favourites to win. After the result, opponents and supporters of the Wilson government were certainly not short of possible explanations for the defeat. Unhappy post-mortems like this were soon to become a regular feature of Labour Party politics.

Labour's difficulties did not begin in 1964, however. In many respects they were built into the party at its foundation in 1900. At that time, it was recognised that instead of relying on the Liberal Party for parliamentary support, organised labour needed its own elected representatives. Yet this initial incentive for unity could not disguise the contrasting ideas held within the fledgling party. Although the vast majority of party members were committed to peaceful, as opposed to revolutionary, change, some had a clear vision of a socialist society and a determination to bring it about. Such activists mingled uneasily with others who either disliked theorising of any kind, or were broadly content with things as they were. The party was not socially uniform, containing both working-class trade unionists and middle-class intellectuals, notably those associated with the Fabian Society. These class differences did not coincide precisely with differences of principle, but they were not calculated to assist the long-term prospects for unity within the party. From the outset, then, the Labour Party was a coalition (or a 'broad church', as its members preferred to say). Over the years, as Labour's popularity grew and the Liberal Party declined, the diversity of principles held by its members tended to increase rather than diminish. In a party system where Labour seemed to be the only electable alternative to the Conservatives, ambitious politicians who might have been congenial recruits for a strong Liberal Party have decided that joining Labour is their only realistic option. Significantly, Harold Wilson was a member of the Liberal Party for part of his undergraduate career.

After the First World War, the party adopted a programme and constitution which seemed to represent a conclusive move towards a coherent socialist position. The programme (*Labour and the New Social Order*) denounced the 'monstrous inequalities' produced by capitalism, and promised that a Labour government would do nothing to prop up such an unjust system. In its place, the party would promote 'deliberately planned co-operation in production and distribution', with the intention of producing 'a healthy equality of material circumstances' for all human beings (Coates, D, 1975, 14). The constitution included Clause IV, section 4, which committed Labour to remove the means of production, distribution and exchange from private hands. In pursuit of these goals, *Labour and the New Social Order* spoke of the immediate nationalisation of transport, mining and electricity, and promised that nationalisation of land would not be far away.

Despite these radical aspirations, the first Labour government, formed by Ramsay MacDonald in 1924, made very little progress towards a socialist society. Admittedly, this was a short-lived minority administration, and it could be argued that, as a relatively new party, Labour would need experience of power before it could realise its intentions. The second MacDonald government, however, was a different matter. In 1931, faced with an economic slump and the prospect of cuts in unemployment benefit, the Cabinet resigned. This failure to shape a positive response to what could be interpreted as the inevitable final crisis of capitalism would have been bad enough; what made matters worse was Ramsay MacDonald's decision, encouraged by King George V, to remain in office with Conservative support. In the eyes of Labour loyalists, MacDonald's action transformed him from hero to traitor. As the immediate shock wore off, his past record was reinterpreted; the suggestion that he had never really been a socialist seemed to be proved by his long-standing appreciation of aristocratic society. While MacDonald remained true to his party, his social life was tolerated; after 1931, it was remembered as a sure sign that he had always wanted to go over to the enemy. The suspicion that party leaders might be tempted to repeat such a betrayal has remained alive ever since.

In particular, this concern was aroused by moderates who, like MacDonald, strayed into upper-class company.

The 1945–51 government of Clement Attlee has generally been regarded as the most successful Labour administration. Even this legacy, however, has promoted divisions. Labour's nationalisation of basic industries such as coal, steel and electricity could be regarded either as a useful step towards the fulfilment of the dreams of 1918, or as a completed programme which marked the proper boundaries of state ownership. In 1959 Hugh Gaitskell, the then Labour leader, unsuccessfully urged the party to take the latter view. He wanted the abandonment of Clause IV, on the grounds that Labour's constitutional attachment to complete nationalisation of the means of production gave a misleading and counter-productive impression. After Gaitskell's failure, the party remained opposed on paper to the private ownership of industry, although its leader's belief in the 'mixed economy' was widely shared. Among his opponents in 1959 was Harold Wilson, who always wished to avoid divisions within the party. This stance left Wilson well placed to succeed Gaitskell, and he won the leadership after the latter's death in 1962.

Socialists and social democrats

Socialists

Although Labour's divisions (like those of other parties) are often simply denoted by the terms 'left', 'right' and 'centre', even commentators who use the words usually admit that they are little better than convenient shorthand which does not tell us enough about the *nature* of the beliefs in question. As early as 1968 Samuel Brittan argued persuasively that these labels are both confusing and damaging; the choice between left and right in UK politics generally is a 'Bogus Dilemma' (Brittan, 1968). The importance of differing loyalties and personality clashes within the modern Labour Party adds to the normal problems of providing a tidy ideological map; Henry Drucker has also argued that the 'ethos' of the party should be examined along with its 'doctrine' (Drucker, 1979). Bearing in mind these complications, however, in a brief survey primarily concerned with questions of belief it is still possible to illustrate the party's divisions through the categories of 'socialist' and 'social democrat'.

Herbert Morrison, the main architect of the Attlee government's nationalisation programme, once famously defined socialism as whatever the Labour Party did. Similarly, it has been a regular tactic of Conservative leaders to simply call Labour 'the socialist party', in the hope that this word alone would be enough to discredit it. On the same principle, Margaret Thatcher once called Neil Kinnock 'a crypto-communist'. Clearly these approaches to the question need to be set aside, and even though complete precision is impossible, some broad fundamental principles can be identified.

Besides the feelings of those like Harold Wilson who wished to avoid unnecessary splits, Gaitskell's defeat over Clause IV demonstrated the strong emotional pull of socialist ideas on the Labour Party of 1959–60. Socialists oppose private ownership of the means of production because the profit motive entails the exploitation of workers whose labour is only partly rewarded. Also, the capitalist system encourages people to regard one another as competitors; for socialists, this competition impoverishes human nature, which can thrive only in a system of harmonious co-operation. The distribution of rewards under capitalism is also markedly unjust; indeed, cunning and deceit are rewarded more often than genuinely commendable traits such as generosity. Socialists are committed to a thorough transformation of capitalist society, involving a decisive shift of power from employers to workers. The vast majority of socialists within the Labour Party have always believed that this goal can be achieved through parliamentary action. Revolutionary writers such as Karl Marx have often been admired, but more for their ethical commitment to a fairer society than for their advocacy of revolutionary action. Hence, British socialists normally describe themselves as 'democratic socialists', and their beliefs stem from a conviction that a socialist society would be morally superior to the capitalist alternative.

Between 1964 and 1970 the truly socialist element within the Labour Party, which included Members of Parliament (MPs) such as Ian Mikardo, Frank Allaun and Judith Hart, was unable to exert significant influence on policy. Perhaps the main reason for this was its lack of a recognised charismatic leader. Aneurin (Nye) Bevan, founder of the National Health Service (NHS) and a superb rallying orator, had died in 1960. Although Bevan's friends shared the general distrust of Harold Wilson, most were content to see him elected as Gaitskell's successor. Wilson had at one time been closely associated with the 'Bevanites', and resigned from the Cabinet with Bevan in 1951 over the introduction of National Health charges. In the absence of a more reliable alternative candidate throughout the 1960s, the socialist grouping within the Labour Party (mainly those associated with the newspaper *Tribune*) were by no means the most dangerous of many plotters against Wilson's authority.

Recriminations began even before Labour lost the 1970 election. In the *Political Quarterly* the moderate Reg Prentice, who had served in the Wilson government, claimed that the party had not been socialist enough. As Prentice's subsequent career showed, this allegation could also be levelled against him. Yet Prentice spoke for many socialists when he identified the government's 'surrender to anti-trade union prejudices' in its 1969 White Paper *In Place of Strife* as the worst blot on its record (Prentice, 1970). The White Paper was a carrot-and-stick approach to the unions; certain rights were protected in return for a clamp-down on unofficial strikes, enforced through twenty-eight-day cooling off periods and pre-strike ballots. Barbara Castle, the Employment Secretary, won support for her proposals from Wilson, Chancellor Roy Jenkins and the Minister of Technology, Tony Benn, but there was a widespread feeling within the labour movement that unions were being used as a scapegoat for the government's own failings. The Home Secretary James Callaghan led a Cabinet attack on the measures, and legislation was abandoned in exchange for a voluntary (albeit 'solemn and binding') agreement between government and unions. Although socialists could applaud this as a victory for workers, they could only wonder why the Labour leadership had chosen to tackle the issue in the first place.

The 1964–70 government gave socialists little to celebrate in other areas. In 1964 a Department of Economic Affairs (DEA) was set up to challenge the supremacy of the Treasury, which had always been regarded as a powerful obstacle to socialist policies. Yet apart from a desire to maintain the impression of a dynamic government, the main inspiration behind the creation of this department was Harold Wilson's desire to provoke hostility between his main internal rivals, George Brown (who headed the new department) and the then Chancellor, James Callaghan. The DEA produced a National Plan which owed more to the goal of industrial efficiency than the dismantling of capitalism, and even this was abandoned in 1966. In foreign affairs, socialists were unhappy with Wilson's apparent eagerness to please the US President Lyndon Johnson, despite his country's war against North Vietnam. Wilson also seemed helpless in the face of defiance from the racist Rhodesian government led by Ian Smith. Against this record, the renationalisation of the steel industry in 1967 was too meagre a bone to satisfy socialists.

Social democrats

Since the fall of the Attlee government in 1951, the main intellectual impetus within the Labour Party undoubtedly came from its 'revisionist' wing. Most of the revisionists continued to identify themselves as socialists until the 1970s, but it would be more accurate to describe them as social democrats. The most prominent contribution to the social democratic case was Anthony Crosland's book *The Future of Socialism*, first published in 1956. Crosland argued that recent developments in industry meant that Britain was no longer a truly capitalist nation. Although the question of ownership was still important, control of industry had passed from shareholders to managers, and other questions were now more relevant if a just society was to be created. In particular, governments could act to redistribute wealth and guarantee real equality of opportunity. Complete equality of rewards was not possible, but in a fairer society incomes would gradually flatten out. For Crosland, nationalisation could be justified only as a means to the end of a morally fair social order; this particular means was now outdated, and socialists needed to readjust to changed realities (Crosland, 1964).

Crosland's ideas, then, represented at least a major revision or updating of socialism. For his numerous supporters, the continued attachment of the Labour Party to the principle of nationalisation was an irrational nuisance. The persuasiveness of Crosland's views depended crucially on the consistent achievement of high economic growth-rates. Without this, wealth distribution would meet with resistance from the rich. Growth would be heavily dependent upon the performance of the private sector; if this was threatened by the prospect of nationalisation, shareholders would be reluctant to provide necessary investment. Apart from threatening the achievement of high growth-rates, nationalisation had never been very popular with the electorate. During this period of Cold War politics, the association of state ownership with the Soviet Union was hardly likely to bring extra support for any British party. Since Hugh Gaitskell agreed with Crosland, it is not surprising that he was so keen to abandon Clause IV in the late 1950s. His move coincided with the decision of the German Social Democratic Party (SPD) to renounce any lingering allegiance to Marxist ideas at its 1959 Bad Godesberg Congress (Padgett and Paterson, 1991, 29).

Although in practice the immediate goals of the social democrats did not seriously conflict with those of their socialist colleagues, Crosland's view that capitalism had been reformed was regarded by socialists as naive at best. Crosland admitted that class divisions were important, but he did not share the socialist view that owners of capital and their representatives throughout the British establishment would fight stubbornly to retain their advantages. As Aneurin Bevan justifiably claimed, the controversy within the Labour Party was 'between those who want the mainsprings of economic power transferred to the community and those who believe that private enterprise should still remain supreme but that its worst characteristics should be modified by liberal ideas of justice and equality' (Greenleaf,

1983, 470). In short, socialists thought that Crosland's proposals would merely throw a veil of decency over a system which was itself irredeemably unfair. For socialists, only the nationalisation of at least the 'commanding heights' of the British economy could ensure a just society. Under Hugh Gaitskell, the bitterness generated by this internal debate led to the formation of the Campaign for Democratic Socialism (CDS), which was opposed by the smaller Victory for Socialism (VFS). Crosland privately urged Gaitskell to expel the 'hard-boiled extreme left' from the party; the depth of hatred felt for the socialists among Gaitskell's friends can be measured by the fact that it was originally proposed to call the CDS 'Victory for Sanity' (Dorril and Ramsay, 1992, 22–9).

As Bevan hinted, social democracy owes as much to the liberal tradition as it does to socialism. Towards the end of the nineteenth century, liberal thinkers (notably Thomas Hill Green) had concluded that in an increasingly complex and anonymous industrial society, individuals needed state support to ensure that they were given a fair chance of a meaningful life. Green and his followers thus retained the liberal focus on the individual, but recognised that the old attachment to the free market must be modified by collective action in view of its tendency to fail. This point had been emphasised by Britain's economic decline at the end of the nineteenth century, and was graphically illustrated by the poor health of working-class volunteers for the Boer War. Green's ideas were an important inspiration for the social reforms of the Liberal Asquith government (1906–16). Ultimately they lay behind the economic and social proposals of John Maynard Keynes and William Beveridge, which did so much to shape politics after the Second World War. The social democrats' admiration for Keynes and Beveridge integrated them within this 'collectivist' liberal tradition (see also Chapter 3). The fact that Roy Jenkins, a leading social democrat, had written an appreciative biography of Asquith could only increase the socialist suspicion that the social democrats were concerned to humanise capitalism rather than to work seriously for fundamental changes. To add to their misgivings, Jenkins shared Ramsay MacDonald's penchant for aristocratic society.

In Harold Wilson's Cabinets between 1964 and 1970, social democrats were powerfully represented. Jenkins rapidly advanced to the Home Office, before succeeding Callaghan as Chancellor in 1967. Crosland himself held posts in the DEA, the Department of Education and the Board of Trade; he ended up as Secretary of State for Local Government and Regional Planning. Other social democrats, including Shirley Williams, Roy Hattersley, David Marquand, William Rodgers, David Owen and John Mackintosh, made up for their lack of high office with ability and enthusiasm.

Rightly or wrongly the 1964–70 government was identified as predominantly social democratic in its leanings.

In spite of this popular perception, few social democrats were entirely content with Labour's record in government. At the Home Office, Roy Jenkins consistently supported 'permissive' private members' legislation on issues such as abortion and homosexuality; moves to outlaw racial and sexual discrimination were equally welcome to social democrats. Yet their most urgent priorities, concerning education and wealth distribution, were not realised. The relative position of the poor improved very marginally, if at all, during these years, and in 1968 proposals to raise the school leaving age were selected as early victims of Jenkins' spending cuts. Anthony Crosland requested local education authorities to plan for the phasing out of selective schooling in 1965, but ironically more progress towards this aim was made under Edward Heath's Conservative government (with Margaret Thatcher at the Department of Education). Finally, growth in the UK economy remained sluggish at an average rate of 2.2 per cent, well below the forecast included in the ill-fated National Plan, and languishing behind the prosperity experienced in countries of the European Economic Community (EEC). The key assumption of *The Future of Socialism* – that high levels of growth would be achieved, and reduce the pain of wealth distribution – was found to have been over-optimistic in practice.

What went wrong?

By 1970, socialists and social democrats were at least united in their disappointment. The burden of explanation, however, fell more heavily on the social democrats. For them, the problem had lain in Harold Wilson's failure to devalue the pound sterling on taking office in 1964, or at least in 1966 (Marquand, 1992, 155–65). In defence of sterling's exchange value, Wilson had consistently chosen to deflate the economy, and to sacrifice social democratic priorities such as the school leaving age. The high interest rates established to uphold the pound choked off industrial investment, and an over-valued currency made British exports uncompetitive. Wilson clearly did not want to continue Labour's reputation as the party of devaluation (which it had earned at the time of the Attlee government, of which he was a member). For the social democrats, this label was preferable to becoming known as a party which reneged on its promises.

Wilson himself subsequently claimed that 'economic constraints' had thwarted 'the social revolution to which we were committed'.

Under the circumstances, 'we achieved far more than most would have expected' (Wilson, 1974, 17–18). Wilson's memoirs blamed his government's record on the mess left behind by the Conservatives, particularly the severe balance of payments deficit. This defence did not impress many Labour supporters. Throughout his premiership, Wilson had posed as a conciliator between Labour's two main ideological groupings. As a result, his fall from office left him vulnerable to assault from both sides. Whatever energy was left to ministers after their frequent bouts of crisis management expended itself in bitter faction-fighting, which Wilson's own suspicions only exacerbated. With neither the socialists nor the social democrats in obvious control of the party's direction, the most serious friction occurred within, rather than between, the factions. Since Wilson carefully avoided identification with any consistent ideological position, he could count only on an element of personal loyalty within the Cabinet which wore very thin over the years. Often the question seemed not to be whether Wilson would fall, but who from each faction would be best placed to challenge for the leadership when he was toppled. Personal ambitions thus helped to reinforce the impression that the government lacked any firm principles of any kind.

In opposition, 1970–74

Between the defeat of June 1970 and the return to office in February 1974 the Labour Party adopted a recognisably socialist programme. This happened for several reasons. First, whatever their own feelings, the social democratic wing of the party was more compromised by the failure of the previous government. Wilson had not been one of them, but he was perceived as standing closer to their views than he did to socialism. If this handicap were not enough for them, they soon found themselves distracted by the controversy which developed when it became clear that the United Kingdom's application for membership of the EEC was not going to be vetoed by France, as it had been in 1963 and 1967. For social democrats, the prosperous community offered a promising solution for the growth problem of the 1960s. By contrast, many socialists regarded it as a capitalist club, which would divert attention from the wider human community and deprive Britain of the sovereign power it would need if a transformation of society were to be successfully implemented. On this issue the social democratic position was defeated within the party, and Roy Jenkins resigned from the deputy leadership in 1972 when the party committed itself to holding a referendum on EEC membership.

While the social democrats were occupied with this issue, other forces were working on behalf of the socialists. The election of what was perceived to be a right-wing Conservative government led to a polarisation of politics. A growing sense of militancy developed inside the trade unions as they fought against the Conservative Industrial Relations Act (Ferris, 1972). In the late 1960s there had been a notable shift towards radicalism in the trade union hierarchy; Hugh Scanlon, once a member of the Communist Party, replaced a moderate at the head of the Engineers' Union, while Jack Jones, who had fought for the Republicans in the Spanish Civil War, was elected leader of the Transport Workers. With the trade union 'block vote' exerting significant leverage over the Labour Party Conference, this shift in opinion was transmitted to sections of the party. The student unrest experienced throughout Western Europe and the United States in the late 1960s also acted to renew interest in socialist alternatives to unimaginative government policies; notably in Britain, it inspired a group of young 'New Left' academics to write *May Day Manifesto 1968* (Williams, 1968). After his defeat Harold Wilson was not in a position to temper this mood. Thus, although important books by Roy Jenkins and Anthony Crosland showed that social democracy had not lost its intellectual edge in the early 1970s, the socialist momentum was irresistible (Jenkins, 1972; Crosland, 1974). Finally, a newly-radicalised Tony Benn held the chairmanship of the party in 1971–72, and, freed from the need to maintain loyal silence during the difficult years of Labour government, the *Tribune* group increased its membership and began to make itself heard (Warde, 1982, 171–6).

These factors culminated in what has been called Labour's 'most radical programme since the war' – *Labour's Programme 1973*, approved by its annual conference held in Blackpool (Whitehead, 1985, 120). The centrepiece of the programme was the proposed extension of state ownership. Although Harold Wilson blocked a specific plan to nationalise twenty-five of Britain's largest companies, a National Enterprise Board (NEB) was to be set up, with powers to invest throughout the economy. Planning agreements were to be drawn up with private sector firms, and worker participation in management was advocated. These policies were designed to combat the modern development which socialists identified as the greatest menace to their ideals – the growth of the multinational firm, able to avoid the impact of socialist policies by simply transferring their operations to another country. Economic and social equality was to be a priority of the next Labour government, and along with wealth, power over all forms of production would be shifted significantly towards working people and their families.

Back in office, 1974–79

The Heath government's confrontation with the miners brought about the early general election of February 1974 (see Chapter 2). On the key issue of relations with the unions, Labour was very well placed. Since the brief quarrel over *In Place of Strife* the election of Mr Heath had presented Labour and the unions with a unifying enemy. The rekindled friendship was cemented through meetings of the Trades Union Congress (TUC) and the Labour Party leadership which agreed to a list of proposals known as the 'Social Contract'. The unions were granted concessions over pensions, housing and child benefits; subsidies and other price controls would help to keep down living costs. In addition, the unions received a promise that the Conservative Industrial Relations Act would be repealed, and an Advisory Conciliation and Arbitration Service (ACAS) set up to defuse labour disputes. Unlike the 1964–70 administration, the next Labour government would not impose statutory limitations on wages, but the union contribution to the deal was clearly intended to be a responsible attitude towards free collective bargaining. As far as they went, these policies coincided with short-term socialist aspirations. Overall, even though the socialists within the Labour Party did not get everything that they had wanted in the manifesto for February 1974, their reasons for satisfaction can be detected in the evidence that Roy Jenkins did not think that his party deserved to win this particular election (Jenkins, 1994, 364).

The Labour Party was undoubtedly helped in February 1974 by its perceived harmony with the trade unions. Yet its chances of forming a successful government were thrown into doubt by the election result which turned the Conservatives out of office. Between February and October 1974, when Labour asked the country for a stronger mandate, it governed without a majority. Even after October, its parliamentary position was worse than it had been in 1964 – the overall majority was only three seats. Labour also inherited a precarious economic situation, worse than the one they were faced with ten years earlier. The world-wide rise in commodity prices in 1973, followed by the near-quadrupling of the cost of oil between October 1973 and January 1974, helped to produce a massive balance of payments deficit, and a year-on-year inflation rate of 13 per cent at the time of the February election. Unemployment had risen sharply in the early years of the Heath government, and although the urgent measures subsequently taken to combat it brought the figure down, the underlying problems of the UK economy remained.

In fact, Labour's combination of electoral and economic constraints probably would have been enough to spike the idealistic 1973 programme, even if the leadership had been wholeheartedly behind it. Only something more radical, which bravely ignored the Treasury view of economic realities, might have worked to the satisfaction of socialists; after the publication of Stuart Holland's *The Socialist Challenge* (1975), such a platform began to emerge in the shape of the Alternative Economic Strategy (AES), which advocated selective import controls as a means of protecting a real socialist experiment in Britain. By that time, however, there was little reason to imagine that the leadership would contemplate such a course. Any changes from the approach of Labour's first few months in power would be in a very different direction.

Despite the ominous background, Wilson's third government actually made a promising start for both socialists and social democrats. These groups agreed that the worst off in society should not bear the heaviest cost for the restoration of Britain's damaged prospects. Denis Healey's first budget included significant increases for pensioners, and other benefits were raised. The scope of Value Added Tax (VAT) was extended, but food subsidies were increased. Allowances were lifted, to ensure that 1.5 million people escaped income tax entirely, but the basic rate was raised by 3 per cent, and a reform of the tax structure left the rate on the highest earned incomes at 83 per cent. The Chancellor's promise in opposition to target the rich was fulfilled by the introduction of a 98 per cent band for the greatest 'unearned' incomes. These down-payments on the Social Contract were supplemented by a July mini-budget which reduced the rate of VAT from 10 to 8 per cent, introduced rate relief, increased food subsidies and encouraged employment in depressed regions. In the mean time the hated Industrial Relations Act had been repealed, and the miners' strike ended with a 29 per cent settlement.

Criticism from the *Tribune* group was understandably muted at this time, but for socialists these policies were only the icing – significant nationalisation would be the cake. Unfortunately, they were never able to taste it. Concessions wrested from the Labour leadership in the weakness of opposition could be easily evaded when they were back in office. Although the Industry ministry was entrusted to the sympathetic Tony Benn and Eric Heffer, the vaunted Industry Act did not become law until December 1975, and even then represented a watered-down version of the original proposals. The NEB had a theoretical budget of £1 billion, which was far below socialist expectations. Instead of buying a significant share of profitable enterprises, the Board seemed to be designed as a prop for failing concerns – a view reinforced when a non-socialist businessman, Sir Don Ryder, was appointed as its chairman. Whatever faith socialists might still have had in the policy by 1975 was crushed when Harold

Wilson grasped the occasion of the 'Yes' vote in the European Referendum to sack the anti-marketeer Tony Benn. Eric Heffer had already left office over the same issue. Eric Varley, Benn's replacement, had no comparable zest for nationalisation. Of the planning agreements which were an essential accompaniment to the socialist programme, only one was actually signed with a private company. This was the American-owned Chrysler car manufacturer, which received bountiful cash hand-outs in return for co-operation, before selling their British operation to Peugeot without consulting the government.

Soon after Benn's unceremonious removal to a less appetising assignment at Energy, the government took action to control wage rises which were now easily outstripping inflation. According to the Labour leadership, this could result only in workers 'pricing themselves out of jobs', and British industry becoming still less competitive. Certainly overseas confidence in Britain was low, and the pound was under pressure again. In April of the same year, Denis Healey had begun to unravel the Social Contract, cutting food and housing subsidies and raising taxes with less discrimination against the rich than he had previously contrived. This was an inauspicious time to begin asking the TUC to keep its side of the bargain struck before the 1974 election, but the government negotiated a flat rate limit of £6 to run for a year from August 1975 (higher earners were to have their pay frozen). This at least looked egalitarian, as the low paid did comparatively well out of it; Hugh Scanlon and Jack Jones, the union leaders most closely associated with the Social Contract, urged their members to accept it. In subsequent years, however, percentage increases were restored, ending with a 5 per cent limit for Stage IV of the incomes policy in 1978. Although the trade union leaders had loyally supported the pay policy up until that time, the patience of their members had been pushed too far. The result was a succession of strikes which quickly became collectively honoured with the Shakespearian title 'The Winter of Discontent'; this was followed by the fall of the Callaghan government, defeated first in a House of Commons vote of confidence, then at the ensuing general election of 3 May 1979.

The IMF loan

Although the Labour Party remained in office until 1979, it effectively lost any independent powers in December 1976, when it agreed to strict International Monetary Fund (IMF) economic instructions in return for a loan to support the ailing pound on the foreign exchange markets. This represented the culmination of a process of retrenchment which had begun in April 1975. Harold

Wilson escaped from the government's difficulties by resigning on 16 March 1976, just after his sixtieth birthday; the arrival of James Callaghan as his successor in Downing Street only made the government more determined to row back from the high public spending of its first year.

Between the two general elections of 1974, the Labour Party had defied the international trend towards economic deflation in the wake of the oil price rise. Once this risky strategy had failed to win Labour a secure majority in October 1974 it was quickly ditched. In a famous speech to the 1976 party conference, Callaghan signalled that, far from sticking to even watered-down socialism, the government would now even turn its back on the economics of the liberal Keynes. Skilfully implying that the government was not responsible for the economic crisis, Callaghan told the conference that the Keynesian approach had failed instead; the strategy of increasing government spending to reduce unemployment during a recession had simply led to higher unemployment in the long run. It was now time to try something different. Since Keynesian economics had been an essential element of social democratic thinking, this speech is often regarded as marking the end of a post-war social democratic 'consensus'.

Callaghan's speech had been written by his son-in-law, Peter Jay, a convert to the 'monetarist' doctrine that inflation rises only when governments allow the amount of money in the economy to grow too fast. In the circumstances of 1976, monetarist theory dictated a severe reduction in government spending. Like all good converts, Jay grossly simplified the situation to discredit his former beliefs. Since Keynes had been well aware of the dangers represented by excessive inflation, his own reaction to the recession caused by the oil price explosion would surely have been more cautious than that of the Wilson government. The fact that the Labour government had actually increased public expenditure in obedience to its electoral needs rather than to Keynes' theories seemed to get lost in Jay's analysis. As early as 1970, in fact, it had been claimed that the style of politics needed to put Keynes' ideas into practice was 'beyond the comprehension of the Labour Party' (Bogdanor, 1970, 113). Jay's speech-writing efforts served only to demonstrate the truth of that remark.

The cuts proposed by the Chancellor did not pass through the Cabinet unchallenged. For the social democrats, Anthony Crosland had already been grumbling in private about the 'illiterate and reactionary attitude to public expenditure' now being followed at the Treasury (Crosland, S, 1982, 355). From the socialist wing, Tribunites such as Michael Foot campaigned hard, and Tony Benn put the case for the AES, with import and credit controls. However, despite his friendship with Callaghan,

Crosland was sidelined from economic policy at the Foreign Office, and Benn had been under a cloud since 1975. The Prime Minister, in alliance with the Chancellor, got his way. The precarious parliamentary position of the party turned the idea of a determined rebellion in the House of Commons into an invitation for Margaret Thatcher to form a government; since Thatcher refused to distinguish between socialists and social democrats (loathing them both equally) this was not a tempting prospect. The *Tribune* group in particular staged protests against the IMF measures, but when it came to votes of confidence they were forced to direct their resentment into different channels. By 1978 supporters of the AES had formed the Labour Co-ordinating Committee (LCC), which produced an alternative manifesto for the party in 1979 (Seyd, 1987, 91–5). However, the full impact of such factions was not to affect the Labour Party until they had fallen from power.

By the autumn of 1976 unemployment exceeded 1.5 million, although it later fell back slightly. The government's freedom of manoeuvre was even further constricted when a pact was forged with the Liberal Party, without which it would have lost a vote of confidence in March 1977 (see Chapter 3). Callaghan also had to devote precious parliamentary time to devolution legislation for Wales and Scotland, in a bid to secure the support of nationalist parties. The party presented an increasingly unreal appearance, as socialists passed conference motions for radical policies (including the abolition of the House of Lords), while the government stuck to no principle more elevated than a hand-to-mouth struggle for survival. Although the party's standing in the opinion polls recovered during the run up to the Winter of Discontent, Callaghan's decision to delay the election looks in hindsight like a merciful one; sufficient damage had been done to morale without the prospect of another similar period in office for Labour.

What went wrong – this time?

Socialists had no hesitation in allocating blame for the mis-adventures of the 1974–79 Labour governments. They had not been socialist enough. This time the verdict could not be delivered by Reg Prentice, who had joined the Conservative Party in 1976 after a long battle in his constituency with people whom he could never accuse of insufficient loyalty to socialism. Others were on hand to identify the culprits. According to Tony Benn, the 1979 defeat 'followed thirty years of anti-socialist revisionism preached from the top of the Labour Party' (Benn, 1980, 213). In a contribution to the Institute for Workers' Control volume

What Went Wrong?, Ken Coates stigmatised the same foe (Coates, K, 1979, 7–33). Social democracy, or 'revisionism', had failed; socialism had never been given a chance. During the period from 1970, socialist hopes had been raised only to be cruelly dashed. The logical conclusion seemed to be that if the Labour Party would not act to transform society, then socialists should act to transform the Labour Party. After Harold Wilson had vetoed the commitment to nationalise the twenty-five companies in 1973, a group of activists set up the Campaign for Labour Party Democracy (CLPD), committed to making MPs accountable to constituency activists for their parliamentary actions, and to holding the leadership to conference decisions. Significantly, in 1973 the ban on 'prescribed organisations' (which usually meant Marxist ones) within the party was lifted, and the following year a Trotskyite, Andy Bevan, was named as the Labour Party's Youth Officer. It was during the IMF crisis that Tony Benn first read Marx's *Communist Manifesto* – curiously enough, just after he had first dipped into Hitler's *Mein Kampf*. He also consulted the Cabinet minutes from the MacDonald crisis of 1931, and was struck by the parallels (Benn, 1990, 634–94).

Whether or not a full-blooded socialist programme would have fared better, the idea that social democracy should be exclusively blamed for Labour's plight is untenable. As we have seen, Labour gained office in 1974 armed with socialist policies; when crisis struck, socialism was replaced not by social democracy but by what David Coates has called 'unbridled managerialism' (Coates, D, 1980, 33). Of the leading social democrats from 1964–70, Anthony Crosland died early in 1977, while Roy Jenkins resigned from the Cabinet in September 1976 after being offered the presidency of the European Commission. None of the major Labour figures of this time – Wilson, Callaghan and Healey – was a socialist, but although Healey in particular was strongly attracted by continental social democracy it would be stretching a point too far to claim that any of these party leaders acted in accordance with Croslandite principles.

Social democracy certainly faced a crisis during the mid-1970s, and the problems were not confined to the United Kingdom. Under Helmut Schmidt, the German SPD also had to postpone ambitious reforms during this difficult period (Padgett and Paterson, 1991, 149–50). As David Marquand has pointed out, social democracy was always vulnerable because of its liberal ancestry, which burdened it with a built-in contradiction between its collectivist economic strategy and a preference for individualism in its ethics (Marquand, 1987, 323). Yet this was not the primary reason for its problems during the 1970s. The same forces within the world economy, along with the continuing failure of British industrialists to invest – factors which Anthony Crosland had largely overlooked when writing *The Future of Socialism* – knocked both social democrats and the government from their preferred courses. This is not to say that these preferences were identical. Social democratic elements within the party such as the 'Manifesto' group of MPs and readers of the journal *Socialist Commentary* had more reason to support the government than to oppose it, but their attitude was hardly one of positive enthusiasm. It arose partly because they feared letting Mrs Thatcher into Downing Street, and partly because possible successors to Jenkins and Crosland, such as David Owen and Roy Hattersley, were making their way through the Cabinet ranks, hopefully to positions from where they could exercise more effective influence over policy. In any case, while Crosland had been angry enough to join socialists in their criticism of the IMF terms, other social democrats were not prepared to create a common front against the leadership with their most hated political opponents.

To compound their misery, these tactical choices left the social democrats vulnerable to their socialist critics when the blame for 1974–79 was shared out. In presenting their analysis, the socialists pulled off a masterful stroke; the defeat was turned into an opportunity to settle ideological scores with their revisionist foes. It would not be unfair to say that for some of them this opportunity more than compensated for the return of a Conservative government which, after all, might finally expose the unacceptable nature of capitalism. With the campaign for 'democracy' within the Labour Party gathering momentum, the 1972 deselection of Dick Taverne from his Lincoln seat by socialists in his constituency party stood as a warning to any social democrats who refused to repent for their failings. Many of them concluded after 1979 that they could hope to restore their position only by forming a separate party. This, of course, laid them open to the most destructive of Labour Party insults – 'MacDonaldism'.

Conclusion

In terms of either socialist or social democratic priorities, the record of the 1964–70 and 1974–79 Labour governments cannot be seriously defended. At best, both sides might choose to assert that the governments were beaten by unfortunate circumstances – that Labour seems to be elected only when the Conservatives have left an impossible situation for anyone with consistent principles to deal with (Castle, 1993, 501). For the socialists, however, there was a certain degree of compensation; with 'managerialism' and social democracy wholly discredited, the predictable result of the

1979 defeat was a new shift of Labour towards a more socialist outlook (see Chapter 5).

The IMF loan of 1976, and the cuts in government spending which preceded and followed it, is often taken as the death blow to a post-war consensus which is usually defined as 'social democratic'. While this subject will also be pursued in later chapters, it can already be seen that this picture is a serious distortion of reality. The reasons for social democratic dissatisfaction with the 1964–70 governments have already been explored; Roy Jenkins claims that Labour deserved to have won the 1970 election, but as Chancellor during 1967–70 he was constrained to carry out deflationary policies which did very little for the cause of social justice. The 1974–79 government has even fewer claims on social democratic respect. All one can say is that the major decisions of these years were taken by leaders who preferred social democracy to socialism, but, as Anthony Crosland bitterly remarked towards the end of his life, 'Even if the Government survives, does it make such a difference if Labour measures can't be implemented? . . . this is the most right-wing Labour Government we've had for years' (Crosland, S, 1982, 376). Thirteen years after Callaghan's fall, David Marquand was not inclined to be nostalgic; he still rated the 1974–79 government as 'one of the worst of the century' (Marquand, 1992, 158). For the eleven post-war years in which Labour held power, at least, it would be wrong to speak of a distinctive social democratic bias.

Whatever the self-conscious pursuit of ideology in office may do to the well-being of a country, the experience of Labour during these years points to two important advantages which it gives to believers. First, it dictates policy choice, and thus prevents long agonising over decisions. It helpfully provides an authority to leaders which is independent from their own personalities, but in many cases this insurance is unnecessary because ideology can transform ordinary politicians into charismatics. Tony Benn was hardly 'ordinary' at any time, but he was regarded as a technocratic follower of Harold Wilson for most of the 1960s. Just before the time of Labour's 1970 defeat he was reinvigorated by speaking to radical audiences; his discovery of new socialist thinking made him a far more formidable operator, with a devoted following among a public which already had little respect for its politicians. Benn identified the importance of firm convictions when he watched Margaret Thatcher in the House of Commons on the day of her fall from office: 'Thatcher was brilliant. She always has her ideology to fall back on' (Benn, 1994, 614).

Secondly, ideology allows scope for the creation of myths. The principles which drive decision-making can also create a ready-made history, showing how good intentions were crushed by enemies or unlooked-for events. As long as the ideology has been correctly followed, something (or someone) else must have been at fault if the policies did not work. These advantages apply to any firmly-held ideological position, and not just to those which are widely regarded as 'extreme'. Socialists attributed the failure of the 1974–79 governments to the deliberate betrayal of mischievous leaders, while social democrats tended to blame the trade unions. Like all effective ideological myths, these rival explanations contain elements of truth as well as distortions; if most people sided with the social democratic view, this simply tells us that people were generally more sympathetic to the ideology of social democrats.

By refusing to devalue in 1964, and accepting the IMF cuts in 1976, James Callaghan and Harold Wilson both showed themselves willing to adopt policies which destroyed any realistic hopes among their progressive followers. At best, Wilson and Callaghan were well-meaning figures who delivered spending cuts with a smile of sympathy instead of a joyful grin. Whatever their priorities were, they cannot be made to fit with any of the coherent ideological options of the post-war years. As such, they ensured that their subsequent excuses for failure could not enjoy principled support. For all their mixed fortunes, theoretical defences for social democracy, socialism, 'One Nation' conservatism and Thatcherism could be produced without too much trouble throughout this period, but the approach taken by Wilson and Callaghan was not easily translated into a celebratory treatise. To paraphrase Margaret Thatcher, no one ever fought a crusade under the banner of 'managerialism'. Instead of proving the bankruptcy of social democracy, or even the failure of a consensus of any kind, the Wilson-Callaghan record indicates that no one could hope to succeed in the Labour Party under the testing circumstances of these years without conveying a sense of principled conviction to the electorate. Since Harold Wilson failed by this criterion, not even four election victories out of five could save him from years of ridicule for his efforts. When a more measured critique was finally written, it merely argued that Wilson was not as bad as people had thought (Pimlott, 1992). Wilson has been posthumously applauded for his undoubted ability to keep his party together, but the fact that principle was discounted under both himself and his successor has left an unenviable legacy for the party. Hindsight can make politics seem seductively easy, but it would surely have been better to have come off the fence in the ideological battle than to leave both socialists and social democrats feeling that their ideas would have worked if they had been given a fair trial. Since the Labour Party has always been associated with conflicts of ideas, it remains to be seen whether the record of the Conservative Party during this period suggests any different lessons.

List of works cited

Benn, Tony (1980), *Arguments for Socialism*, Penguin

Benn, Tony (1990), *Against the Tide: Diaries 1973–76*, Arrow

Benn, Tony (1994), *The End of an Era: Diaries 1980–90*, Arrow

Bogdanor, Vernon (1970), 'The Labour Party in Opposition, 1951–1964', in Vernon Bogdanor and Robert Skidelsky (eds) *The Age of Affluence 1951–1964*, Macmillan

Brittan, Samuel (1968), *Left and Right: The Bogus Dilemma*, Secker and Warburg

Castle, Barbara (1993), *Fighting All the Way*, Macmillan

Coates, David (1975), *The Labour Party and the Struggle for Socialism*, Cambridge University Press

Coates, David (1980), *Labour in Power? A Study of the Labour Government, 1974–1979*, Longman

Coates, Ken (1979), *What Went Wrong?*, Spokesman

Crosland, Anthony (1964), *The Future of Socialism*, Jonathan Cape

Crosland, Anthony (1974), *Socialism Now*, Jonathan Cape

Crosland, Susan (1982), *Tony Crosland*, Jonathan Cape

Dorril, Stephen, and Ramsay, Robin (1992), *Smear! Wilson and the Secret State*, Grafton

Drucker, Henry (1979), *Doctrine and Ethos in the Labour Party*, Allen and Unwin

Ferris, Paul (1972), *The New Militants: Crisis in the Trade Unions*, Penguin

Greenleaf, W. H. (1983), *The British Political Tradition: Volume II, The Ideological Heritage*, Methuen

Holland, Stuart (1975), *The Socialist Challenge*, Quartet

Jenkins, Roy (1972), *What Matters Now*, Fontana

Jenkins, Roy (1994), *A Life at the Centre*, Macmillan

Marquand, David (1987), 'British Politics, 1945–1987', in Peter Hennessy and Anthony Seldon (eds) *Ruling Performance: British Governments from Attlee to Thatcher*, Blackwell

Marquand, David (1992), *The Progressive Dilemma: From Lloyd George to Kinnock*, Heinemann, 2nd edition

Padgett, Stephen, and Paterson, William, (1991), *A History of Social Democracy in Postwar Europe*, Longman

Pimlott, Ben (1992), *Harold Wilson*, HarperCollins

Prentice, Reginald (1970), 'Not Socialist Enough', *Political Quarterly*, volume 41

Seyd, Patrick (1987), *The Rise and Fall of the Labour Left*, Macmillan

Warde, Alan (1982), *Consensus and Beyond: The Development of Labour Party Strategy since the Second World War*, Manchester University Press

Whitehead, Philip (1985), *The Writing on the Wall: Britain in the Seventies*, Michael Joseph

Williams, Raymond (ed.) (1968), *May Day Manifesto 1968*, Penguin

Wilson, Harold (1974), *The Labour Government 1964–70*, Penguin

Questions for discussion

- Would there be any justification for describing the Labour Party as 'socialist' between 1974 and 1979?
- Did Labour break a post-war 'consensus' between 1974 and 1979?

Selected further reading (see also Chapters 3 and 5)

Barratt Brown, Michael (1979), *From Labourism to Socialism: The Political Economy of Labour in the 1970s*, Spokesman.

Benn, Tony (1988), *Office Without Power: Diaries 1968–72*, Arrow.

Benn, Tony (1991), *Conflict of Interest: Diaries 1977–80*, Arrow.

Brittan, Samuel (1977), *The Economic Consequences of Democracy*, Temple Smith.

Bruce-Gardyne, Jock, and Lawson, Nigel (1976), *The Power Game: An Examination of Decision-Making in Government*, Macmillan.

Callaghan, John (1989), 'The Left: The Ideology of the Labour Party', in Leonard Tivey and Anthony Wright (eds) *Party Ideology in Britain,* Routledge.

Castle, Barbara (1980), *The Castle Diaries 1974–76*, Book Club edition.

Clarke, Peter (1978), *Liberals and Social Democrats*, Cambridge University Press.

Crick, Bernard (1987), *Socialism*, Open University Press.

Crossman, Richard (ed.) (1952), *New Fabian Essays*, Turnstile.

Durbin, Evan (1940), *The Politics of Democratic Socialism*, Routledge.

Foot, Paul (1968), *The Politics of Harold Wilson*, Penguin.

Foote, Geoffrey (1985), *The Labour Party's Political Thought: A History,* Croom Helm.

Harrison, Royden (1993), 'The Fabians: Aspects of a Very English Socialism', in Iain Hampsher-Monk (ed.) *Defending Politics: Bernard Crick and Pluralism*, British Academic Press.

Haseler, Stephen (1969), *The Gaitskellites*, Macmillan.

Hennessy, Peter (1992), *Never Again: Britain 1945–51*, Jonathan Cape.

Holmes, Martin (1985), *The Labour Government, 1974–79: Political Aims and Economic Reality*, Macmillan.

Howard, Anthony (ed.) (1979), *The Crossman Diaries*, condensed version, Magnum.

Jenkins, Mark (1979), *Bevanism: Labour's High Tide*, Spokesman.

Marquand, David (1976), *Ramsay MacDonald*, Jonathan Cape.

Marquand, David (ed.) (1982), *John P. Mackintosh on Parliament and Social Democracy*, Longman.

Miliband, Ralph (1961), *Parliamentary Socialism: A Study in the Politics of Labour*, Allen and Unwin.

Morgan, Kenneth (1984), *Labour in Power 1945–51*, Oxford University Press.

Morgan, Kenneth (1992), *Labour People: Leaders and Lieutenants, Hardie to Kinnock*, Oxford University Press.

Ponting, Clive (1989), *Breach of Promise: Labour in Power 1964–70*, Hamish Hamilton.

Saville, John (1973), 'The Ideology of Labourism', in Robert Benewick, Robert Berki and Bhikhu Parekh (eds) *Knowledge and Belief in Politics: The Problems of Ideology*, Allen and Unwin.

Shaw, Eric (1988), *Discipline and Discord in the Labour Party*, Manchester University Press.

Taylor, Robert (1980), *The Fifth Estate: Britain's Unions in the Modern World*, Pan.

Whitehead, Philip (1987), 'The Labour Governments, 1974–79', in Peter Hennessy and Anthony Seldon (eds) *Ruling Performance: British Governments from Attlee to Thatcher*, Blackwell.

Wilson, Harold (1964), *The New Britain: Selected Speeches 1964*, Penguin.

Wilson, Harold (1979), *Final Term: The Labour Government 1974–1976*, Weidenfeld and Nicolson.

Wright, Anthony (1986), *Socialism: Theory and Practices*, Oxford University Press.

Wyatt, Woodrow (1978), *What's Left of the Labour Party?*, Sidgwick and Jackson.

CHAPTER 2

From Selsdon Man to Grantham Woman: The Conservative Party, 1970–79

The Conservative Party has traditionally regarded unity and loyalty to its leader as important assets. This ethos has not meant that the party is immune from internal controversy; indeed, it has suffered significant splits in the nineteenth century (over repeal of the Corn Laws) and early in the twentieth century (concerning Tariff Reform). While some might attribute this sense of loyalty to the aristocratic roots of the party, it undoubtedly owes much to the fact that British politicians who have identified themselves with conservative principles over the years have broadly agreed on the meaning of these ideas. The paper wars which have enlivened the history of other ideologies have rarely distracted conservatives. At least, this was true until about 1970. Since then, the nature of conservatism has been as warmly disputed as any other variety of political belief. As a result, describing the impact of conservatism on British politics has become remarkably complicated, and equally sensitive.

Not the least of these complications is the fact that established usage demands that the same word 'conservative' is taken to denote both the ideology and the party. Some commentators try to solve this problem by simply merging the two things, so that whatever the Conservative Party does *is* conservatism at any given time. This is no more helpful that Herbert Morrison's claim that socialism is what the Labour Party does. One does not have to argue that ideologies should remain constant over time to take this view; a more conclusive objection is that modern British political parties tend to be coalitions of people with very different ideas. In the case of the Conservative Party, it is clear that when Margaret Thatcher became leader in 1975 the majority of her MPs disagreed with many of her pronouncements, and that this was still true when she resigned in 1990 (Norton, 1990). Given the fundamental nature of these disputes, it cannot be helpful to simply describe the respective positions as different 'strands' of conservatism. While investigating this awkward problem in the course of this chapter, a capital *C* will be used to designate the actions and beliefs of members of the Conservative Party, and a lower-case *c* whenever the ideology is meant. Obviously the two will often overlap, but not always.

It is easier to give examples of this confusion than to sort it out to everyone's satisfaction. For instance, when Herbert Spencer attempted to warn fellow liberals against excessive state interference in his book *The Man versus the State* (published 1884), he chose 'The New Toryism' as the title for his opening chapter. Spencer bitterly regretted that the Liberal Party of his time had 'lost sight of the truth that in past times Liberalism habitually stood for individual freedom *versus* State-coercion'. Tories could be excused for preferring the interests of the state to those of the individual, because this was what Tories had always done. Liberals, in his view, should have known better. So great was the new liberal propensity to use state power against the individual that 'it may by and by really happen that the Tories will be defenders of liberties which the Liberals, in pursuit of what they think the popular welfare, trample under foot' (Spencer, 1969, 67, 81). Incidentally, Spencer's use of the capital *L* to denote liberalism is instructive here. Although one must beware of reading too much into a very different context, it seems to reflect an assumption that liberal thinking and Liberal Party actions are always the same thing, yet *The Man versus the State* would not have been written if Spencer was confident about this continuing to be the case.

Spencer's message was a very serious one, although many of his readers must have thought that he was exaggerating his point for added effect. Whatever the Liberal Party might be up to at a particular time, the Tories would never be reliable friends of liberty in Spencer's individualist sense – that is, they would never accept that freedom should be regarded as the most important goal of political action. One hundred years later, however, his words seemed to have come literally true. In 1984, Margaret Thatcher's Conservative Party posed as the liberators of the individual, while the Liberal Party (in alliance with the SDP) consistently rejected Thatcher's rhetoric about rolling back the overmighty state. So who was right about conservatism – nineteenth-century liberals who thought of it as an anti-individualistic creed, or the Thatcherites who presented themselves as enemies of the state? Perhaps they were both right, or perhaps words such as right and wrong are misplaced in this kind of argument? The latter conclusion would be tempting, and some people remain convinced by it. However, it seems too convenient, and the question deserves more investigation.

The intense and continuing controversy over the ideological identity of Thatcherism usually focuses on the years since 1970, but a proper examination of the question necessarily involves the whole post-war period. In 1947, Quintin Hogg (the future Lord

Hailsham) published *The Case for Conservatism*, a book which has escaped criticism during the squabbles of recent years. In his book, Hogg distinguished carefully between British conservatism and a blind resistance to reform. If conservatives tend to fear change, it is because they think that human nature is, and will remain, imperfect and unpredictable. Attempts to mould society into some untried form would be to court disaster. While socialists and other radicals seek to create a perfect environment for humankind, conservatives are more concerned to combat existing evils. Hogg, a deeply religious man, traced the human propensity for evil to the Fall, but he recognised that other conservatives could share his conclusions without adopting his premises.

Hogg, like most British conservatives, tried to distinguish between his world-view and the approach of believers in 'new religions' such as socialism. For him, conservatives were different because they accepted human nature as it was, and were content to grapple with its consequences. In fact, conservatism was a philosophy of government, which had been developed over centuries by the accumulated wisdom of politicians who had readily accepted the responsibilities of power in an imperfect world. Unlike their opponents, conservatives rejected programmatic politics on the basis of their experiences; indeed, for them politics was far from being the most important aspect of life. Conservatism, in fact, was simply the exercise of common sense by practical people (Hogg, 1947).

Hogg's eloquent advocacy certainly illustrates the important differences between conservatism and other ideologies. However, he cannot establish that these differences are sufficient to outweigh the underlying similarities. *The Case for Conservatism* will be persuasive only for those who share Hogg's view of human nature. It might be true that most people presently think that 'common sense' dictates the defence of private property, for example, but this would be a poor argument against those who believe that human nature can be fulfilled only if all forms of individual ownership are destroyed. The majority might think of themselves as more 'practical', but in the end this is a matter of opinion, because what they regard as practical is itself defined by their view of what human beings really are. If there is a structural difference between the conservative and other ideologies, it concerns the political *strategies* which arise from it rather than its theoretical basis. Other ideologues can be flexible when events force them to be; conservatives are flexible by choice. In some circumstances this gives conservatives a decided political advantage, but, as we shall see, in recent years it has acted as a crippling handicap.

Post-war conservatism

When the Second World War ended in 1945, the Conservative Party ought to have been well placed for electoral victory. After all, in Winston Churchill it possessed a leader who was Britain's most popular politician. Yet when the election came the party suffered a humiliating defeat, and was out of office for the next six years.

The reasons for this unexpected reverse are crucial to an understanding of post-war conservatism. Perhaps most important was the popular memory of the 1930s, when unemployment soared and Conservative-dominated governments seemed powerless to stop it. This experience convinced many Conservatives that they should always try to prevent such a human tragedy from recurring; unfortunately for them, it convinced a majority of the electorate that they should vote Labour in 1945. A second reason was the dilemma which confronted Conservatives when they presented their case against Labour. Although Labour's programme advocated a radical departure from previous peace-time experience, including extensive nationalisation and economic planning, some of Labour's plans had been worked out while the two parties co-operated in the wartime government. Proposals to extend welfare benefits and to ensure full employment received official approval while Churchill remained Prime Minister. It was also undeniable that economic planning had made a significant contribution to Britain's war effort.

With hindsight, Churchill's reluctance to call a new general election at the end of the war seems understandable. Active opposition to Labour's programme would expose the Conservative Party to the charge that promises made in wartime would be broken as soon as peace returned. More importantly, while the *scope* of Labour's plans worried many conservatives, the principles underlying them could not be rejected out of hand. As Herbert Spencer had said, an active role for the state was fully in line with the Tory tradition. If the state could be used to help ensure social stability, conservative objectives would be satisfied. The capacity for evil might remain within people who were sure of either a job or a generous level of benefit, but such improved security might easily prevent decent people from turning to crime in desperation. It would also encourage people to feel that they were part of 'One Nation' – the goal of Disraelian conservatism in the previous century.

For Churchill himself, the dilemma was particularly acute. Early in his political career, he had helped to lay the foundations of the welfare state as a minister in Herbert Asquith's Liberal Cabinet; in short, he had been a representative of the liberal school which Spencer denounced as 'New Tories'. Since that time, as we have seen, collectivist liberals such as Beveridge and Keynes had developed this tradition further, producing ideas which demanded an even greater role for the state. It was difficult for Churchill to distinguish the welfarist policies which built on his own achievements from the socialist nationalisation programme in a fashion which would appeal to the electorate. His response was probably the most serious electoral misjudgement of his career. In a broadcast he implied that Clement Attlee, the leader of the Labour Party and, until recently, his trusted coalition partner, threatened Britain with the introduction of a 'Gestapo' regime. Even the young Margaret Hilda Roberts, listening in her Oxford college, initially thought that this was going too far. It certainly failed to win the election for Churchill. What it did do, however, was to give the Churchillian seal of approval to arguments being advanced at that time by the Austrian liberal, Friedrich von Hayek, who denounced any form of state activity beyond a bare minimum as the beginning of a 'Road to Serfdom' (Hayek, 1962). By a strange twist of historical events, the most outspoken modern advocate of Herbert Spencer's views on freedom and a leading exponent of the 'New Toryism' seemed to be united in their protestations about the dangers of socialism.

For the moment, this ideological misalliance was short-lived. While liberals like Hayek remained convinced that freedom was in danger, conservatives could appreciate that in practice Labour was far more flexible than its programme had suggested. Wartime restrictions on economic activity, such as rationing, remained in force for some years, but by March 1949 Harold Wilson, the young President of the Board of Trade, was able to announce a 'bonfire of controls'. When the Conservative Party Conference of 1947 endorsed an *Industrial Charter*, it accepted that the state needed to act in partnership with industry in order to ensure prosperity and full employment. In *The Case for Conservatism*, published the same year, Quintin Hogg outlined the reasons why conservatives should oppose nationalisation, while arguing that when his party returned to office it should do no more than call a halt to further state ownership (Hogg, 1947, 284–95). In practice only road haulage and iron and steel were denationalised by the next Conservative government.

The Conservatives held power for more than half of the period between 1945 and 1970 without finding it necessary to force a radical departure from the approach laid down by the Attlee government. Since successful politicians have to operate within the same framework of events, it often happens that people holding different ideological viewpoints can reach very similar policy decisions. This was the experience of leading Labour and Conservative policy-makers during these years. Pragmatic considerations undoubtedly played a part in the Conservative acceptance of the welfare state and a more active government involvement in the economy, but as Hogg demonstrated there were no significant reasons why conservatives should stand out against these developments on principled grounds. The Labour Party might have provided the initial legislative impetus for the broad outline of post-war British politics, but the Conservative Party's acceptance of this framework was not just the result of a tendency to acquiesce in the established facts of political life. If there was a 'consensus' after the Second World War, it was reasonable for conservatives to claim that it was just as compatible with their ideas as it was with social democracy.

True to the flexibility of their ideological tradition, Conservative governments between the end of the war and the advent of Mrs Thatcher varied their emphasis from time to time. The brief period during which Peter Thorneycroft was Chancellor (1957–58), for example, is often identified as a precursor to the monetarist experiment after 1979. According to one distinguished commentator, 'the post-war objectives of full employment and economic expansion . . . seemed for a time to have been abandoned' (Brittan, 1971, 209). Yet under the same Prime Minister, Harold Macmillan, the Conservative Party established the National Economic Development Council (NEDC), where ministers, trade unionists and employers met to discuss economic performance. This 'corporatist' framework was intended to ensure that the priorities of both workers and bosses could be considered together; indeed, it is doubtful whether the Council would have been set up in the absence of general agreement on the goals of full employment and economic growth (originally projected to be a healthy 4 per cent annually). Alan Budd has argued that this initiative 'was by no means alien to the tradition of the Conservative Party' (Budd, 1978, 80). By 1962, when the NEDC was set up, the arguments of party members like Enoch Powell who thought that state activity in the economic sphere was counter-productive truly seemed like 'a little local difficulty'. Although Powell resigned with Thorneycroft over what they saw as financial irresponsibility in 1958, both of them were back in the government by 1960. The Tory Party debate about the role of the state seemed to be settled in favour of the interventionists.

In opposition, 1964–70

Scandals such as the Profumo affair marred the early 1960s, yet the Conservative election defeat of 1964 was still a shock to the party after their thirteen years in power. Like most setbacks of this kind, returning to opposition seemed to offer a chance for reflection. This process could not be finished before Harold

Wilson called a new election in 1966, but before the next contest in 1970 the party embarked on a detailed policy review. The new Conservative leader, Edward Heath, had been elected in 1965 as an appropriate challenger to Harold Wilson. Like Wilson, Heath had risen through his own abilities, thus symbolising the 'meritocratic' mood of the times. He also resembled Wilson in presenting an efficient, business-like image. Heath certainly translated this image into action as Leader of the Opposition; according to one of his aides, he ensured that the party 'was equipped with policies more elaborate and better researched than any opposition had ever attempted' in preparation for the 1970 general election (Hurd, 1979, 7).

With Labour back in power, the Conservative Party's attitude towards state intervention in the economy changed. It was one thing for a Conservative government to provide subsidies and to run the nationalised industries, but could Labour be trusted to operate the system responsibly? During the 1960s young and ambitious Tories, such as Geoffrey Howe, began to study pamphlets produced by the Institute of Economic Affairs (IEA), which had kept alive the *laissez-faire* liberal tradition of Herbert Spencer and Friedrich Hayek. Although Enoch Powell was sacked from the Shadow Cabinet in 1968 because of his provocative views on immigration, his 'Morecambe Programme' of sweeping tax cuts and denationalisation still attracted a degree of support within the party (Powell, 1970). These ideas, which had never been wholly absent from the Conservative Party since the war, could not be ignored by Heath, who needed to keep his party united and realised the complexity of this task from his experiences as a former Chief Whip.

Heath's exact position in 1970 has been fiercely debated (Russel, 1978, 11). Thatcherites tend to argue that he was committed to a platform very similar to the one adopted in 1979: the only difference was that Heath, unlike Margaret Thatcher, lacked the courage to carry it through (Holmes, 1982). Some versions of the story are self-contradictory, but the most coherent one explains Heath's subsequent opposition to Thatcherite policies as the product of personal bitterness, rather than any serious difference of principle (Tebbit, 1989, 134–5). At the centre of the controversy is the well-publicised meeting of Heath and the Shadow Cabinet, held at the Selsdon Park Hotel in January 1970. Harold Wilson certainly thought that this meeting produced a significant shift towards economic liberalism; in response, he coined the phrase 'Selsdon Man', to emphasise what he regarded as the reactionary nature of Heath's platform.

The 1970 Conservative manifesto was forcefully worded, and provided plenty of hostages to fortune. In his foreword, Edward

Heath asserted that 'once a policy is established, the Prime Minister and his colleagues should have the courage to stick to it' (Craig, 1990, 114). The manifesto promised a reduction in direct taxation and public spending, reform of the trade unions, and more efficient use of public funds in the areas of economic intervention and welfare payments. Unlike the Wilson government, a new Conservative administration would not attempt to control prices and wages through legislative action. After the indecision and waste of the Wilson years, Britain would become strong again under tough and principled leadership. Restored to economic and social health, it could finally join the EEC and play a central role in the development of European institutions.

One suspects that if the Conservatives had won the February 1974 general election – which they very nearly did – then the controversy over Selsdon Man would not have been so loud and lasting. Defeat then, and a similar result in October, gave Heath's ideological opponents the chance to get their own version of events accepted. Yet this interpretation was seriously exaggerated. The proposals contained in the manifesto certainly represented a change from recent policies in some areas, and there would be no continuation of the interventionist momentum established by the Macmillan government. Yet the detail of the proposals represented a shift to more discriminating intervention by the state, rather than a concerted attack on the whole idea of big government (Middlemas, 1990, 319). Nicholas Ridley's subsequent claim that Heath had 'promised to stop subsidising industry' was quite untrue; it also disguised the fact that, for all his claims to ideological purity, Ridley was writing after subsidising industry himself (in a more devious fashion) as Secretary of State for Trade and Industry under Margaret Thatcher (Ridley, 1991, 13). Still, the tone of the 1970 manifesto was open to such misinterpretations. A study of the election campaign concluded that in drawing up the document, the party leadership 'compensated for rejecting the views of *laissez-faire* radicals by using their language' (Butler and Pinto-Duschinsky, 1970, 91). Possibly Margaret Thatcher's later verdict that 'our rethinking of policy had not been as fundamental as it should have been' will mark the end of the myth that Heath really intended to push through a free-market revolution (Thatcher, 1995, 160–1).

In office, 1970–74

The first few months of the Heath government suggested that election promises would be honoured. A mini-budget in October 1970 matched tax cuts with public expenditure reductions. Margaret Thatcher, in the Cabinet for the first time as Education Secretary, fought hard to maintain her large departmental budget, but had to accept the abolition of free milk for primary school children over 7, and an increase in the cost of school meals. The travel firm Thomas Cook was denationalised, and the Industrial Reorganisation Corporation, which had encouraged mergers under Labour, was abolished. John Davies, the former director-general of the Confederation of British Industry (CBI), was brought into the government to head the new Department of Trade and Industry (DTI); one of his first pronouncements was to deny that he would intervene to save any of British industry's 'lame ducks'. Heath also took up the challenge which had proved too much for Harold Wilson, and introduced an Industrial Relations Act before the end of the year. Like Labour's ill-fated *In Place of Strife* proposals, the Act mixed concessions with stricter conditions for strike action; it set up an Industrial Relations Court to deal with union non-compliance. Just after the first anniversary of the government had passed, Heath secured the aim which he considered the most important, by negotiating the UK's entry into the EEC.

Unfortunately, these steps towards fulfilment of the 1970 manifesto pledges could not disguise the impression that this was to be an unlucky government. Within a few weeks of taking the office of Chancellor, the popular and able Iain Macleod was killed by a heart attack. Macleod's value as a force for unity is ironically attested by the fact that both sides of the ideological divide within the party still claim that he agreed with their views (Tebbit, 1989, 94–5). The 'lame ducks' policy of refusing to subsidise failing companies did not survive much longer; Rolls-Royce was nationalised in February 1971 in order to avert bankruptcy. Rolls-Royce's importance in terms of both international prestige and technological research made it something more than a 'duck', but the contradiction with previous rhetoric did not pass unnoticed among the government's critics. It was not the last time that front-bench speakers would have to defend apparent reversals of policy on behalf of this government.

When the Conservatives took office, inflation was identified by the electorate as the most pressing domestic problem (Wybrow, 1989, 95). Yet the government had rejected both monetarism and prices and incomes policy as possible remedies for this, while the plan to switch some of the tax burden from income on to consumption (through the introduction of VAT) was likely to add to existing inflationary tendencies. There was clearly an expectation that sustained economic growth would help to solve the problem, but by the end of 1971 this hope had not been fulfilled. Even without the continuing headache of inflation, the government also had to contend with rising unemployment, which topped 1 million in January 1972. With no sign of an increase in industrial investment, the economy seemed to be stuck in an inevitable cycle of decline.

In response to this uninviting prospect, the Chancellor Anthony Barber introduced what has been called 'the most expansionary Budget ever' (Stewart, 1978, 142). In pursuit of a 5 per cent annual growth target, Barber reduced income tax by more than £1 billion, and restored regional grants to industry (which had been earlier victims of Heath's desire for more selective intervention). The Budget was quickly followed by the passage of an Industry Act which gave the government unprecedented scope for investment. In combination with lower interest rates which sparked off a steep rise in consumer borrowing, this was certainly a spectacular dash for growth.

Even though public spending was on the increase, the government could claim that it was broadly following its original plan; it was certainly cutting taxes, and although the Industry Act was a blunt instrument, it could still be used 'selectively' by a prudent minister. Not surprisingly, however, the Budget did nothing to stem the rise in prices, and wages soared as employees struggled to keep up. Even before the Budget, the miners had received a 30 per cent pay increase after calling their first national strike for almost fifty years. By September the government had decided on a move which really could not be squared with the rhetoric of the 1970 manifesto; it opted for a prices and incomes policy, the tactic which it had derided when Labour were in power. At least Labour entered into the spirit, and now attacked Heath for bringing in a policy which they had used themselves. Even so, this was a difficult time for Conservative back-benchers.

The severity of the blow would have been reduced if other measures had worked. This was not the case, particularly with the industrial relations legislation. It was always likely to be a hazardous operation. The trade unions had refused to accept similar proposals from Labour, despite their ties of friendship, so why should they now co-operate with the Conservative enemy? Although the Act was not repealed until Labour returned to office, it was clearly unworkable from the time that the unions hit on the idea of refusing to register under the Act. Unless unions pursued their grievances in line with the terms laid down by the Act, they would be acting illegally and would be liable to potentially ruinous fines, but the system threatened to collapse under its own weight unless at least the great majority of unions signed up. For the government, it was more embarrassing to have prosecutions brought under the Act that it was to have the legislation ignored by everyone, especially after the Court of Appeal ruled that unions should not be held responsible for the actions of its local shop stewards. This led to the creation of individual 'martyrs' such as the 'Pentonville Five', dockers who were arrested while on picket duty.

In outfacing the government over the Industrial Relations Act, the trade unions showed that they had the muscle to humiliate any party in power. However, they had not finished with Heath. Despite the Prime Minister's best efforts, the TUC refused to cooperate with the second stage of the prices and incomes policy, due to take effect in April 1973. Stage III, which was announced in October of that year, included a flexible (if complicated) formula which would allow pay rises to take account of inflation automatically. In this way it was at least hoped that unions would not put in excessive pay claims in anticipation of future increases in the cost of living, a process which itself caused prices to rise further. Unfortunately for the government, this plan coincided with the outbreak of the 'Yom Kippur' Arab–Israeli War. In order to punish Israel's western sympathisers, Middle Eastern oil producers increased prices and restricted supplies. This was disastrous enough in itself, to add to a general increase in world commodity prices over the year. What made it fatal for the Heath government was that it greatly increased the bargaining power of the miners, who had already put in a big pay claim. The government was prepared to treat the miners as a special case under Stage III but unwilling to accommodate their demands in full. As a result of the second miners' dispute, starting with an overtime ban in November, Heath called a three-day working week, with other restrictions which included a fifty mile-per-hour speed limit and a 10.30 p.m. shutdown for television broadcasts. Before Christmas Anthony Barber also cut public expenditure by more than £1 billion. The government had effectively abandoned its first economic strategy after a year in office; now a host of unfriendly events were driving it away from its revised course. Heath was advised to call a snap general election to provide the government with a mandate for further strong action, and eventually the country went to the polls on 28 February 1974 (Campbell, 1993, 585–97).

Defeats and recrimination, 1974–75

Many commentators believe that if Edward Heath had called a general election earlier, perhaps in January rather than February, the Conservatives would have won. Delay could not stop speculation, giving the opposition parties ample time to organise (Hurd, 1979, 133). Heath was reluctant to give the appearance of wanting voters to choose between the democratically-elected government and the miners. Even so, he earned himself wounding criticism only from Enoch Powell, who avenged himself for his

1968 sacking by protesting against an election called by a Prime Minister who still enjoyed a working parliamentary majority. Powell, who had been alienated further by the UK entry into the EEC in 1973, urged his supporters to vote Labour, apparently, in some areas at least, to good effect. Although the Conservatives won more votes than Labour, they could not form a government without support from elsewhere, and after negotiations the Liberals refused to offer this. Labour returned to office, and started to deliver the promises made to the trade unions under the Social Contract.

As Andrew Gamble observes, 'the Conservatives entered the election campaign with one of the least promising records any British Government has ever offered to the British electorate' (Gamble, 1974, 228). Apart from the successful EEC negotiations (which were fiercely opposed in many quarters), Conservative achievements were as limited as those of Labour in 1964–70 and 1974–79. In all these cases, it was difficult to decide whether errors or ill-luck had been deciding factors; certainly the Heath Government fell victim to both. Perhaps the confrontational message of the 1970 manifesto was the worst mistake it made, because it raised unjustified fears amongst trade unionists and corresponding hopes in the hard-line minority of the Conservative Party.

Even before the 1970 election, commentators were questioning the nature of Heath's political thinking (McKie and Cook, 1970, 148–50). He gave the impression of being more interested in action than ideas. Yet while his opponent Harold Wilson deliberately tried to avoid identification with any ideological faction within his party, Heath enjoyed personal friendship and loyalty with a distinct Cabinet grouping. The 'Heathmen' were all in broad agreement with the main themes of post-war conservatism. For them, the welfare state and the mixed economy were wholly in line with conservative principles. Once this framework was accepted, the balance of policy might differ from time to time; although free enterprise was the system most likely to produce prosperity for all, at times of crisis more significant state intervention would be necessary. Unlike the social democrats, they rejected equality as even a vague long-term goal; this anti-egalitarian stance accorded with their distinctive conservative view of human nature. If action was necessary to prevent serious poverty (and, in particular, unemployment) then it should be taken for the sake of social harmony. Differences in wealth could never truly reflect individual merit, so those who had been fortunate in life owed a moral duty to give the poor at least the opportunity of a worthwhile existence.

Heath and his supporters, then, held a distinctive ideological position which implied no significant disagreement with the post-war settlement as it worked out in practice. As such, they were opposed by a relatively small group within the party whose ideas led to different conclusions. This group was by no means uniform: true to their belief in individualism, many were prickly characters for whom co-operation did not come easily. During the 1970–74 government some of them were known as 'Powellites', indicating support for Enoch Powell's economic ideas rather than his views on race. These ideas are variously described as 'monetarist', 'neo-liberal' or *laissez-faire*; for convenience, it is best to use the term 'economic liberalism' to denote the ideology that inspires them.

Between 1970 and 1974, as the Heath government changed tack in response to the stagnation of the economy, Conservative MPs such as Nicholas Ridley, John Biffen and Powell himself regularly spoke and voted against what they regarded as an irresponsible move towards wider state intervention (Norton, 1978, 93–7, 120–4). They had little success in changing government policies, but when Heath was defeated in February 1974 their activities could serve as an inspiration to others who had swallowed their doubts while the party remained in office. The return of a Labour government was a signal to former Cabinet ministers who sympathised with economic liberalism to make their dissent public. Keith Joseph, who had been a high-spending Minister of Health in the Heath government, was the most prominent of these ministers. In June 1974 he announced that he was setting up the privately-funded Centre for Policy Studies (CPS) with another former minister, Margaret Thatcher, as a director. Although both of these ministers were well known to a long-established free-market think-tank, the IEA, forming a new body was a useful way to publicise the direction of their thinking; it also mimicked Heath's earlier decision to set up a governmental think-tank, the Central Policy Review Staff (CPRS) under Lord Rothschild. The re-education that Joseph received from the head of the CPS (the former communist Alfred Sherman) led him to deliver a speech at Preston in September 1974 which marked him as the intellectual successor to Powell, who had now left the Conservative Party. He might easily have become a candidate for the party leadership if he had not implied in a later speech that the 'human stock' of Britain was threatened because the poor bred too quickly (Halcrow, 1989, 77–87).

Joseph was probably more interested in the cause of truth than in his own leadership ambitions (although he would not have complained had the two prospered together). He later proudly announced that he had experienced a conversion: 'I had thought that I was a Conservative (before 1974) but now I see that I was not one at all.' This statement was not calculated to make life easier for the student of ideology. Even Joseph's allies were quick to assure him that he had discovered economic liberalism rather than conservatism, and a close study of his views over the years shows remarkably little change (Halcrow, 1989, 56, 64). The significance of the remark lies in the fact that Joseph *thought* that his views had changed radically; this goes some way towards illustrating the ideological gulf within the Conservative Party at that time.

'Thatcherism', the slightly indiscriminate name which now embraces British economic liberals (and others), does share some broad characteristics with conservatism. Yet where they seem to coincide, there remain significant differences of emphasis. Thatcherites reject the idea of equality, but for them inequality takes on the appearance of a desirable goal, rather than an inevitable feature of human society (Joseph and Sumption, 1979). Conservatives do not rejoice that human beings are capable of selfishness; they are surprised, but scarcely disappointed, when people act out of different motives. Thatcherites, by contrast, tend to assume that all forms of conduct can be attributed to selfishness; since altruism is impossible, those who claim to act from this motive are either fooling themselves or trying to hoodwink others. Luckily there is no reason to feel guilty about selfishness, because this driving impulse can be turned to the good of all members of society. Conservatives are sceptical of any theory which suggests that people can act 'rationally' in any meaningful sense, but the Thatcherite belief in the superiority of the free market is based on the premise that individuals can be trusted to act in accordance with their own rational self-interest in economic matters. This 'rational individualism' lies at the heart of Thatcherism, and is even less palatable to conservatives than the socialist vision, which at least recognises that society is interdependent. Thatcherites place great emphasis on freedom, defining this as the absence of deliberately fashioned constraints (such as state intervention). They do not advocate freedom without responsibility, but they are much more likely than conservatives to regard freedom as a virtue in itself. This notion of freedom leads Thatcherites to reject the idea of 'dependency', which they see as one of the great evils of a system of welfare payments. For conservatives, however, society cannot function without dependency in some form. This list of disagreements, which could be greatly expanded, includes almost all the central questions of domestic policy. More importantly, the contrast between the underlying premises of conservatism and Thatcherism is so marked that it is difficult to imagine circumstances in which they could ever be made to agree. Now that the quarrel has come into the open, it is likely to remain.

This account of Thatcherism necessarily misses the full complexity of the creed, but it suffices to prove that the split between Thatcherites and conservatives is no less serious than that between socialists and social democrats. It can be claimed that the division is as old as the Conservative Party itself, dating from the time when Sir Robert Peel decided to adopt the liberal proposal to abolish the Corn Laws in 1846, against a majority in his own party who were quite happy with interference in the free market (especially when, as in this instance, it worked to their advantage). Yet the gulf between the two ideologies has never been more apparent than since 1979. There are several reasons for this, some of which have been in operation for many decades but have exercised a decisive effect only in combination. These include the deterioration in Britain's economic performance, the apparently relentless growth in the activities of the state, and a definite change in the ethos of the party, reflecting the gradual eclipse of aristocratic dominance (Ramsden, 1978). In some respects, the 'Thatcherisation' of the party can be interpreted as a logical outcome once Britain moved towards full democracy. It must also reflect the decline of the Liberal Party as an alternative to the developing Labour Party, in both electoral and ideological terms. The party which boasted Keynes and Beveridge among its supporters could not be a comfortable home for those who wanted to roll back the frontiers of the state; their only remaining option was to practise 'entryism' within the Conservative Party.

After February 1974 Edward Heath was in an unenviable position as Conservative leader, having lost two out of the three elections he had contested. The momentum within the party passed to the economic liberals, who could now claim that the 'Selsdon' programme would have been a triumph if Heath had stuck to it. The leader responded by calling for a Government of National Unity. Opponents naturally interpreted this as a confession that Heath's conservatism had no distinctive answers; more accurately, it was an invitation for politicians of all parties to reject the very distinctive answers provided by socialism and economic liberalism, which Heath regarded as divisive. In the end, the October 1974 election was not a disaster for the Conservative Party, as it held Labour's majority to single figures. If Heath had not made powerful enemies through his strangely aloof manner, he might just have survived as party leader.

The crusade begins, 1975–79

Margaret Thatcher's election to the Conservative Party leadership in February 1975 was unexpected, and certainly did not represent a Joseph-like 'conversion' of the whole party. One authoritative study estimates support for the new leader's ideas within the parliamentary party at between 10 and 25 per cent (Crewe and Searing, 1988). Specific ideas did not decide the result, although Mrs Thatcher used a *Daily Telegraph* article to imply that the

Conservative Party had surrendered to 'socialism' (Thatcher, 1995, 274–5). William Whitelaw, the chairman of the Conservative Party and favourite to succeed Heath, refused to stand against his leader on the first ballot. Mrs Thatcher had no such scruples, and by establishing a lead over Heath enjoyed a bandwagon effect which could not be reversed when Whitelaw joined in the second ballot.

The skills which Thatcher had deployed in her leadership campaign served her equally well when deciding on her Shadow Cabinet. Although many of Heath's supporters were kept on, the post of Shadow Chancellor went to Sir Geoffrey Howe, and Peter Walker was dropped because he had been such an effective opponent of Thatcher and Joseph. Realising the importance of controlling the party machine, Thatcher appointed the veteran Lord Thorneycroft as party chairman; the sympathetic Angus Maude replaced Ian Gilmour at the Conservative Research Department (CRD) (Thatcher, 1995, 290–2). The sense of loyalty which had prevented William Whitelaw from becoming leader would now ensure that he was a compliant deputy. The overall balance of the Shadow Cabinet remained conservative, but while Thatcher's apparent generosity to her known opponents surprised and temporarily disarmed them, she ensured that key posts went to her supporters. This sure touch did not desert her until after the 1987 election, when she presumably believed herself to be beyond challenge.

In opposition, Thatcher's main purpose was to win what she saw as 'the battle of ideas' against socialism. One major development in preparation for the coming conflict with 'socialism' in all its forms was the establishment of a Conservative Philosophy Group of academics and MPs; at one of their meetings, Mrs Thatcher reportedly announced 'We must have an ideology' (Ranelagh, 1991, 187; Young, 1990, 406). Another important milestone was the publication of *The Right Approach*, a statement of the Conservative position which cleverly patched over continuing internal disputes (Conservative Central Office, 1976). Identifying the 'ethos of modern Conservatism' as 'balance and moderation', the pamphlet pointed out the decay of social democracy and attacked *Labour's Programme for Britain, 1976* as a sign of Labour's drift towards Marxism. The difference between Labour and the Conservatives, however, was that Labour's radicals were being ignored, while the Conservative radicals were in charge. The chief radicals, Joseph and Thatcher, revealed their intentions in speeches inspired mainly by the work of the economic liberal think-tanks (Thatcher, 1977; Joseph, 1976). Joseph warned that Keynesian ideas had merely paved the way for socialism; as the intervention of one government failed, its successor would intervene further in an attempt to clear up the mess. This effort would fail in its turn, and this 'ratchet' would continue until freedom had been destroyed. For economic liberals, the obvious answer was to ditch Keynes. As we have seen, Keynes had never been a socialist, and neither was the Labour government. Joseph and Thatcher had no time for what they regarded as ideological hair-splitting. They were more concerned by Callaghan's renunciation of Keynes in 1976, but the Prime Minister had opposed *In Place of Strife* back in 1969, and unlike the Thatcherites he did not intend to satisfy the growing public feeling that the trade unions needed to be reformed (Crewe and Searing, 1988, 375–6).

In 1977 the Conservatives issued *The Right Approach to the Economy*, which announced that the next Conservative government would be mainly concerned with setting a framework for economic activity by acting against inflation through control of the money supply (Maude, 1977). Lower taxation was also promised. Mrs Thatcher did not entirely approve of this document, because it mentioned 'corporatist' consultations between government, employers and unions. This was a sign that the old order was coming to an end; presumably Mrs Thatcher was concerned to keep ahead of the Labour Party, which was stealing her monetarist agenda. Conservatives within the Shadow Cabinet were now becoming restless. Ian Gilmour, whose *Inside Right* appeared in the same year as *The Right Approach to the Economy*, insisted that conservatism was not an ideology (Gilmour, 1978). The very thinly veiled implication of his book was that Mrs Thatcher was an ideologue, and as such neither a conservative nor electable unless she changed her thinking. Lord Hailsham did not seem so anxious; his 1978 book *The Dilemma of Democracy* contained a plea for limited government, and his warnings about a possible 'Elective Dictatorship' seemed to be directed only against the Labour Party (Hogg, 1978). In the pre-election dash into print, one rising star of the party who might have been expected to support Gilmour produced a similar attack on the overmighty state (Waldegrave, 1979). Other senior Conservatives who shared Gilmour's views were content to hope that the experience of office would mellow Mrs Thatcher; in fact, since her 'outsider' mentality remained with her as she fought against vested interests after 1979, the only change was that she became an oppositionist backed by the machinery of government. In this enviable position she felt strong enough to sack the increasingly vocal Gilmour from his Cabinet position of Lord Privy Seal in 1981.

The 1979 Conservative manifesto, in fact, was a relatively moderate-sounding document. It promised tax cuts, better value for public expenditure, very limited denationalisation, lower inflation, union reform and the sale of council houses. Little of this would have been out of place in any post-war Conservative manifesto. The content reflected concerns that Labour intended to portray Mrs Thatcher as a dangerous extremist, in contrast to James Callaghan, who was widely perceived as a good-natured moderate. In an effort to combat this, the very first line of Mrs Thatcher's foreword downplayed the importance of political theorising. Ironically, then, the Selsdon manifesto could be seen as a prototype for Thatcherism because its tone exaggerated its radical purpose, while the aspirations of the 1979 manifesto were misleadingly modest. Perhaps the most worrying aspect of the manifesto from the point of view of conservatives was the promise 'to work *with the grain* of human nature'; if conservatives did not know already, the following years were to show that their interpretation of human nature was very different from Mrs Thatcher's.

Conclusion

By the end of the 1970s, both the Conservative and Labour parties seemed to have fallen under the control of ideological factions which advocated a clean break with post-war politics. Obviously both the socialists and the economic liberals believed that their remedies would work, but their solutions seemed to gain added attraction from the apparent failure of alternative positions within the respective parties. The argument that unlooked-for events had beaten Wilson, Callaghan and Heath cut no ice with these factions; as they saw it, the determined implementation of their beliefs in government would transform society in such a fashion that mere events would be transcended.

Both of these internal revolutions – the 'peasants' revolt' which toppled Edward Heath, and the campaign for party democracy which seemed to place sitting Labour MPs at the mercy of their constituency activists – were essentially incomplete in 1979. Their subsequent fortunes will be traced in later chapters. Contrary to the view propagated by sections of the media, however, the supporters of Tony Benn within the Labour Party were far more vulnerable than their Thatcherite counterparts. Mrs Thatcher, after all, led her party; once Jim Callaghan had resigned from the Labour leadership, the poisoned chalice passed to Michael Foot, whose radical sympathies clashed with a consistent desire to maintain party unity which had led him to support uncongenial policies in recent years. Foot beat Denis Healey to the leadership *because* of the split in his party; Margaret Thatcher's defeat of Heath and Whitelaw largely *created* the internal problems of the Conservative Party. The fact that the national press was far more sympathetic to the Conservatives than to Labour helped to create a public perception which reversed the true state of both parties in 1979.

The social democrats were defeated within the Labour Party because they seemed to have run out of new ideas in a situation which their greatest thinkers had not foreseen. It would be a mistake to say the same of conservatism. After all, this is a world-view which prides itself on flexibility. If Enoch Powell had been leader in 1970 – not an entirely far-fetched idea – it would have been interesting to see whether he would have fared any better in the face of a buoyant Labour movement and the oil price rise.

In fact, the problems for conservatives began much earlier. Michael Oakeshott once wrote that conservatism thrives best when there is much to be enjoyed in life (Oakeshott, 1962, 169). Post-war Britain has generally failed to fit that description, contrary to the views of nostalgia-mongers. If the problems associated with Britain's decline were not grave enough, the technological advances of the post-war period mean that ministers now get to know about far more problems in much greater detail; in addition to the problems which have actually arisen, they are also bombarded with predictions about hazards to come. Media pundits encourage the electorate to demand immediate solutions to all of these difficulties, both real, distorted or imagined. After the war, conservatives agreed that big problems demanded big governmental solutions – but could big government be wholly justified in terms of a creed which is sceptical about human nature? Conservatism originally provided a solid justification for the rule of a gifted elite, but it needed to be adapted in the age of bureaucratic armies. Despite the work of Hogg and others, this problem was never tackled in sufficient depth.

Modern government seems ill-suited to the gentle scepticism of a Halifax or a Hume (or even the angrier version of Burke). The writings of Michael Oakeshott, the twentieth-century legatee of these thinkers, symbolises a general loss of confidence among conservatives who are forced to operate in an unwelcoming world. In a famous essay, Oakeshott argued that conservatism is a *disposition* rather than an ideology (Oakeshott, 1962). His account of this disposition is alluring, but it remains ambiguous; it fits the characteristics of Lenin as well as those of Churchill. In fact, although it is easy to detect the developments which Oakeshott opposed, his work offers very few positive remedies (Crick, 1973). It is tempting to attribute this reticence to a sense that things had gone irretrievably wrong, and it was now impossible to do more than 'chart the route to disaster' (Gilmour, 1978, 99). Some of Oakeshott's admirers, unable to sustain this mood of resignation, gravitated towards Thatcherism – even though it is difficult to imagine a disposition as far removed from Oakeshott's description as Mrs Thatcher's.

We saw earlier that conservatives claim to express nothing more than common sense, but that their conclusions will be shared only by those who agree with their view of human nature. Burke wrote his *Reflections* to reassert his own idea of common sense at a time when the French Revolutionaries were questioning all that he cherished. With only one or two exceptions, conservatives failed to copy Burke's example when their approach to government was being assaulted on all sides after the fall of Edward Heath. Their failure to do so shows how seriously they took their own cliché that conservatism was not an ideology – that setting out an impassioned defence of their beliefs was somehow bad form, and contrary to the conservative tradition. This self-denying ordinance, and the genteel style of politics associated with it, could not have been better suited to Mrs Thatcher's purpose if it had been dreamed up by the IEA. If William Whitelaw was an ideological opponent of Mrs Thatcher, she had no need of ideological allies.

The revival of economic liberalism after 1975 was an odd twist of ideological history. In part, its success with certain politicians can be attributed to the promising solution it offered to the problem of 'overloaded' government. It also thrived because its followers transformed the apparent intellectual weaknesses of the doctrine into practical strengths. Its greatest popularity had coincided with Britain's industrial supremacy in the nineteenth century. Even then the doctrine of free trade was an odd way of describing a system in which Britain controlled vast overseas possessions. If economic liberalism was best suited to the time when Britannia ruled the waves, its central figure, the rugged, rational entrepreneur, was an unlikely hero for a post-war world of huge monopolistic concerns. In order to overlook the real reasons for the growing economic involvement of the state, Thatcherites had to engage in a historical rewriting campaign, using Hayek's *Road to Serfdom* in much the same way that the unsophisticated might use Marx. Yet this systematic programme of simplification provided Thatcherism with a potent weapon. Mass democracy is the enemy of complex messages, and Mrs Thatcher's opponents in all parties found it difficult to translate their thoughts into an idiom which could convince the electorate. Even if Mrs Thatcher's speech writers proved unable to do this, elements of the popular press such as the *Sun* newspaper were very happy to supply the deficiency.

Within the Conservative Party as in Labour, the 1970s were not easy years for those who were unprotected by firm ideological principles. Those who had not defended their beliefs with enough passion now found themselves either applauding views they detested or seeking employment elsewhere. The failure of social democrats and conservatives to rise to the challenge presented the prize of North Sea oil to others. This development was another ironic twist; politicians who believed in the post-war settlement thought that the possession of oil might provide Britain with an economic miracle, but its full benefits arrived under a Prime Minister who thought she could perform a miracle whether there was oil or not. Whatever the fate of the Thatcherite crusade, the zeal of both the leader and her supporters meant that someone would always be willing to proclaim that she had really made the miracle happen.

List of works cited

Beattie, Alan (1979), 'Macmillan's Mantle: The Conservative Party in the 1970s', *Political Quarterly*, volume 50, number 4

Brittan, Samuel (1971), *Steering the Economy: The Role of the Treasury*, Pelican.

Budd, Alan (1978), *The Politics of Economic Planning*, Fontana.

Butler, David, and Pinto-Duschinsky, Michael (1970), *The British General Election of 1970*, Macmillan.

Campbell, John (1993), *Edward Heath: A Biography*, Jonathan Cape.

Conservative Central Office (1976), *The Right Approach: A Statement of Conservative Aims*, Conservative Central Office.

Craig, F. W. S. (ed.) (1990), *British General Election Manifestos 1959–1987*, Dartmouth.

Crewe, Ivor, and Searing, Donald (1988), 'Ideological Change in the British Conservative Party', *American Political Science Review*, volume 82, number 2.

Crick, Bernard (1973), 'The World of Michael Oakeshott', in *Political Theory and Practice*, Allen Lane.

Gamble, Andrew (1974), *The Conservative Nation*, Routledge and Kegan Paul.

Gilmour, Ian (1978), *Inside Right: A Study of Conservatism*, Quartet.

Halcrow, Morrison (1989), *Keith Joseph: A Single Mind*, Macmillan.

Hayek, Friedrich A. (1962 ed), *The Road to Serfdom*, Routledge.

Hogg, Quintin (1947), *The Case for Conservatism*, Penguin.

Hogg, Quintin (Lord Hailsham) (1978), *The Dilemma of Democracy: Diagnosis and Prescription*, Collins.

Holmes, Martin (1982), *Political Pressure and Economic Policy: British Government 1970–74*, Butterworth.

Hurd, Douglas (1979), *An End to Promises: Sketch of a Government 1970–1974*, Collins.

Joseph, Keith (1976), *Stranded in the Middle Ground? Reflections on Circumstances and Politics*, Centre for Policy Studies.

Joseph, Keith, and Sumption, Jonathan (1979), *Equality*, John Murray.

Maude, Angus (1977), *The Right Approach to the Economy: Outline of an Economic Strategy for the Next Conservative Government*, Conservative Central Office.

McKie, David, and Cook, Chris (1970), *Election '70*, Panther.

Middlemas, Keith (1990), *Power, Competition and the State, Volume II: Threats to the Post-War Settlement: Britain, 1961–74*, Macmillan.

Norton, Philip (1978), Conservative Dissidents: Dissent within the Parliamentary Conservative Party 1970–74, Temple Smith.

Norton, Philip (1990), ' "The Lady's Not for Turning", But What About the Rest?', *Parliamentary Affairs*, volume 43, number 1.

Oakeshott, Michael (1962), 'On Being Conservative', in *Rationalism in Politics and Other Essays*, Methuen.

Powell, Enoch (1970), *Income Tax at 4/3 in the £*, Tom Stacey.

Ramsden, John (1978), 'The Changing Base of British Conservatism', in Chris Cook and John Ramsden (eds) *Trends in British Politics since 1945*, St Martin's.

Ranelagh, John (1991), *Thatcher's People*, HarperCollins.

Ridley, Nicholas (1991), *My Style of Government: The Thatcher Years*, Hutchinson.

Russel, Trevor (1978), *The Tory Party: Its Policies, Divisions and Future*, Penguin.

Spencer, Herbert (1969 edn), *The Man Versus the State*, Pelican.

Stewart, Michael (1978), *Politics and Economic Policy in the UK since 1964: The Jekyll and Hyde Years*, Pergamon.

Tebbit, Norman (1989), *Upwardly Mobile*, Futura.

Thatcher, Margaret (1977), *Let Our Children Grow Tall: Selected Speeches 1975–1977*, Centre for Policy Studies.

Thatcher, Margaret (1995), *The Path to Power*, HarperCollins.

Waldegrave, William (1979), *The Binding of Leviathan: Conservatism and the Future*, Hamish Hamilton.

Wybrow, Robert (1989), *Britain Speaks Out, 1937–87: A Social History as Seen through the Gallup Data*, Macmillan.

Young, Hugo (1990), *One of Us: A Biography of Margaret Thatcher*, Pan.

Questions for discussion

- Would it be fair to say that between 1966 and 1974 there was little difference between either the ideologies or policies of Harold Wilson and Edward Heath?
- What differences of principle (if any) divided Margaret Thatcher from her Conservative opponents in 1975?

Selected further reading (see also Chapter 4)

Addison, Paul (1975), *The Road to 1945: British Politics and the Second World War*, Jonathan Cape.

Bacon, Robert, and Eltis, Walter (1976), *Britain's Economic Problem: Too Few Producers*, Macmillan.

Behrens, Robert (1980), *The Conservative Party from Heath to Thatcher: Policies and Politics 1974–79*, Saxon House.

Blackstone, Tessa, and Plowden, William (1990), *Inside the Think Tank: Advising the Cabinet 1971–1983*, Mandarin.

Blake, Robert (1985), *The Conservative Party from Peel to Thatcher*, Fontana.

Blake, Robert, and Patten, John (1976), *The Conservative Opportunity*, Macmillan.

Bogdanor, Vernon, and Skidelsky, Robert (eds) (1970), *The Age of Affluence, 1951–1964*, Macmillan.

Boyson, Rhodes (ed.) (1970), *Right Turn*, Churchill.

Butler, R. A. (1971), *The Art of the Possible*, Hamish Hamilton.

Clutterbuck, Richard (1978), *Britain in Agony: The Growth of Political Violence*, Faber and Faber.

Conservative Political Centre (1965), *The Conservative Opportunity: Fifteen Bow Group Essays on Tomorrow's Toryism*, Batsford.

Cowling, Maurice (1990), 'The Sources of the New Right', preface to *Mill and Liberalism*, Cambridge University Press, 2nd edition.

Gamble, Andrew (1981), *Britain in Decline: Economic Policy, Political Strategy and the British State*, Macmillan.

Greenleaf, W (1973), 'The Character of Modern British Conservatism', in Robert Benewick, Robert Berki and Bhiku Parekh (eds) *Knowledge and Belief in Politics: The Problems of Ideology*, Allen and Unwin.

Hornby, Richard (1961), 'Conservative Principles', *Political Quarterly*, volume 32, number 3.

Hutber, Patrick (1977), *The Decline and Fall of the Middle Class*, Penguin.

Kavanagh, Dennis (1987), 'The Heath Government, 1970–1974', in Peter Hennessy and Anthony Seldon (eds) *Ruling Performance: British Governments from Attlee to Thatcher*, Blackwell.

Layton-Henry, Zig (1980), *Conservative Party Politics*, Macmillan.

Norton, Philip (1980), *Dissension in the House of Commons 1974–79*, Clarendon Press.

Ramsden, John (1980), *The Making of Conservative Party Policy: The Conservative Research Department since 1929*, Longman.

Rhodes James, Robert (1972), *Ambitions and Realities: British Politics 1964–70*, Weidenfeld and Nicolson.

Roth, Andrew (1972), *Heath and the Heathmen*, Routledge.

Seldon, Arthur (ed.) (1978), *The Coming Confrontation: Will the Open Society Survive to 1989?*, Institute of Economic Affairs.

Watkins, K. W. (ed.) (1978), In Defence of Freedom, Cassell.

CHAPTER 3

The Liberals and their allies, 1970–92

Background

The British general election of 1906 produced an overall majority of eighty-eight seats for the Liberal Party. After years of internal arguments, notably over Irish Home Rule and the Boer War, the Liberals now seemed far more stable than the Conservatives, who were bitterly divided over Tariff Reform. Apparently the Liberal Party could look forward to a bright future. It formed a talented government, which in time would produce some of the century's most important legislation. In addition to its own MPs it could normally count on the support of eighty-eight Irish Nationalists, along with fifty-one representatives of the newly-formed Labour Party. Many of the latter group owed their seats to the Liberals, who had agreed not to oppose thirty-one Labour candidates in a bargain struck three years earlier. Perhaps in future the Labour Party might be a helpful junior partner in an anti-Conservative coalition; for now the scale of the Liberal landslide meant that no assistance was required.

Sixteen years later the last Liberal Prime Minister was hounded out of office by very different coalition partners. Instead of a handful of friendly Labour MPs, a suspicious and resurgent Conservative Party sustained David Lloyd George in power from December 1918 until they voted to discard him in October 1922. Since that time, only coalition governments have provided the party with Cabinet ministers. On occasion (notably during the Lib-Lab Pact of 1977–78) they have exercised some power, but this has depended on the position of the two main parties rather than Liberal strength in the House of Commons.

The reasons for the decline of the Liberal Party have been thoroughly investigated (Wilson, T., 1966). Whether or not Labour was predestined to replace the Liberals as the main electoral opponent of the Conservatives, the personal rift between Lloyd George and his predecessor as Liberal Prime Minister, Herbert Asquith, was fatal to the party's electoral prospects. Six years after Lloyd George's death in 1945 the Liberals were able to field only 109 candidates in a general election; of these, more than half lost their deposits. The party which had once nurtured the Labour Party now depended upon Conservative charity to keep up its parliamentary numbers. It seemed only a matter of time before it disappeared altogether (Wallace, 1983, 43). When Robert McKenzie wrote *British Political Parties* in 1955, he apologised for the apparent cruelty of simply relegating the Liberal Party to an appendix – but then, the Liberals had received less than 3 per cent of the vote at the preceding general election (McKenzie, 1964, v).

The poor electoral performance of the party did not mean that individual Liberals were wholly without influence. It is difficult to exaggerate the contribution to post-war economic and social policy made by John Maynard Keynes and Sir William Beveridge. Keynes' commitment to the party lasted for most of his life, although his interest fluctuated; when he was awarded a peerage in 1942 he agreed to sit as a Liberal (Harrod, 1972, 636). Beveridge became a Liberal MP at the end of the Second World War. The work of Keynes and Beveridge built on the reforms of the Asquith government, which had laid the foundations for the British welfare state in the years before the First World War. Between the wars, the Liberal Party seemed to produce all the promising ideas while the Conservatives and Labour shared political power; it was almost as if the future Liberal role would be to act as a voluntary think-tank for political opponents.

While individual Liberals have exerted more influence over twentieth-century Britain (and beyond) than their party as a whole, the ideology of liberalism has also prospered. It survived a crisis at the end of the nineteenth century, when liberal thinkers such as T. H. Green and L. T. Hobhouse recognised that the philosophy of *laissez-faire* which had flourished during Britain's industrial supremacy would not suffice now that the economy had begun to stagnate and most workers could express their grievances in elections. Retaining the liberal focus on the individual, these revisionist or 'New' liberals argued that the state must intervene to ensure that at least a minimum level of income was available for unemployed, elderly and sick people. Provided that the necessary increase in taxation fell mainly on the well-off, the balance of meaningful freedom in society would increase. Previous liberals had defined 'freedom' as the absence of restraints; in arguing that such freedom was pointless for those who lacked resources, the New liberals caused offence among advocates of *laissez-faire* such as Herbert Spencer. Yet their ideas represented no significant breach of the central elements of liberalism; the quarrel was bitter (and remains unresolved), but this is typical of disagreements within any ideological family.

Despite the activities of New liberals such as Keynes and Beveridge, *laissez-faire* ideas still had a foothold within the

Liberal Party after the Second World War. A prominent advocate of 'rolling back the state' was Major Oliver Smedley, a founder of the Institute of Economic Affairs, which later provided intellectual support for economic liberalism within the Conservative Party. In 1956 some of Smedley's allies left the Liberal Party to form the People's League for the Defence of Freedom, while Smedley himself set up a Free Trade Liberal Party in 1962 (Cockett, 1994, 127). These defections marked the gradual victory within the Liberal Party of the Radical Reform group, which accepted the post-war mixed economy on New Liberal grounds. In 1956 Jo Grimond, whose sympathies lay with the Radical Reformers, was elected as leader of the party. It was a doubtful inheritance, but Grimond was a popular figure who promised to restore Liberal fortunes at last.

Under Grimond's leadership, the Liberals lived up to their bold-thinking reputation. They responded positively to the formation of the EEC while the other major parties hesitated, and advocated withdrawal of British forces from bases East of Suez (with the exception of Singapore). Parliamentary reform was also a distinctive Liberal policy; it was argued that the UK's 'winner-takes-all' electoral system was grossly unfair because it devalued the votes of those who opposed the Labour and Conservative parties. This argument was obviously convenient for Liberals, but it was also quite compatible with their belief that the opinions of all individuals should carry equal weight. The Liberals also accepted nationalisation, but rejected the bureaucratic form in which it had been carried out by the Attlee government. Their preference for worker participation would become a consistent theme.

At a time when official policy differences between the Labour and Conservative parties seemed to be diminishing, the Liberals could present a distinctive alternative. The main Liberal dis-advantage was that unlike their main party rivals they did not enjoy the backing of a significant social group. The support which workers gave to the Labour Party and industrialists provided for the Conservatives brought them both votes and money; like the electoral system, this link between parties and interests could be denounced by Liberals as anti-democratic. During the 1950s, however, there were hopeful signs of change. The social democratic ideas of Anthony Crosland and the Conservative acceptance of nationalisation could both be interpreted as signs that the major parties were less inclined to pay undue attention to their client interests. Crosland's ideas in particular pointed to a decline in the importance of class divisions. Grimond believed that values, rather than interests, would be the key to winning elections in a classless society. In these circumstances the Liberal Party would thrive, and there was likely to be a radical realignment of political forces in Britain. Policies which reduced class divisions were therefore in the Liberal interest; by contrast, *laissez-faire* ideas were seen as both a threat to social cohesion and to the prospects of the party.

On occasions between 1956 and 1967, when Jo Grimond resigned as Liberal leader, the party seemed to be on the verge of a conclusive breakthrough. It enjoyed some notable by-election successes, the most sensational of which was the victory at Orpington in March 1962. Membership boomed, and was estimated to have risen from 150,000 in 1959 to 350,000 in 1963 (Wallace, 1983, 52). New members meant extra revenue, and a research department was set up to look at future policy developments. The party's success promised to be self-perpetuating, as innovative ideas enticed still more recruits, which would have a further beneficial effect on finance. As the Labour Party argued over nationalisation and membership of the EEC, and the Conservative government suffered from scandals and a feeling that it had been in power too long, the Liberals looked poised to draw support from both sources, as well as from young idealists who had no sympathy with either of the main parties.

These hopes went unrealised. The succession of Harold Wilson to the Labour leadership after the death of Hugh Gaitskell in 1963 was probably the main reason for this. Wilson presented a dynamic, classless image; having once been Beveridge's research assistant (and, briefly, a member of the Liberal Party) there could not have been a more appropriate choice to see off the Liberal threat. According to William Wallace, the 1964 general election brought 'the worst possible outcome for the Liberals' (Wallace, 1983, 57). The Labour Party had a tiny majority, but still did not need Liberal support. Under Wilson's ambiguous leadership, it had every reason to bury internal differences. When a new general election was called in 1966 Liberal representation increased, but only to twelve. With the momentum of the early 1960s running out and a major party realignment now unlikely, Grimond resigned from the Liberal leadership in January 1967.

The electoral prospects of the party might have seemed gloomy when Jeremy Thorpe replaced Jo Grimond as leader, but the Liberals were impossible to ignore in the late 1960s. The membership now included a high proportion of young (predominantly middle-class) activists, who found inspiration in the student activism and civil rights movements of these years. Parliamentary Liberals reflected this new impetus in their support for social reforms affecting abortion, race relations and homosexuality, and the increasingly vocal Young Liberal section of the party was particularly prominent in the attack on racism at home and abroad. Activists such as Peter Hain opposed the

South African cricket tour of 1970, and the energetic Young Liberals began to advocate 'Community Politics', which raised the profile of the party by focusing on specific grievances within different constituencies. For many senior Liberals, this was the unacceptable face of individualism; without encouragement from the top, many of these enthusiastic recruits drifted away in later years. When Peter Hain was eventually elected to Parliament in 1990 it was as a member of the Labour Party.

Looking for allies, 1970–81

By 1970 the Liberals had relatively settled principles, which formed the basis of a distinctive programme. True to the core liberal belief in the rational individual, they opposed the growth of a paternalistic state bureaucracy, and concentrated on the establishment of equal civil rights rather than espousing economic equality. Their acceptance of the welfare state followed the principles of Keynes and Beveridge; for them, it was nonsensical to speak of freedom in the context of crippling poverty. The state should provide a framework of benefits to enable individuals to plan their lives with a reasonable degree of security, and a free education system was necessary to give young people something like an equal chance of leading a productive and fulfilling life. The sacrifices necessary to fund these state activities were necessary evils; used properly, the receipts from taxation would result in greater benefits for all.

The problem for the Liberal Party was not the lack of ideas, but communicating them to the electorate. Even when the Young Liberals were the most controversial political activists in the country, it remained difficult to convince voters that the party stood for anything more than a middle course between Conservative and Labour. This perception was fostered by the unhelpful view of politics as essentially a clash between 'left' and 'right', a one-dimensional map which left Liberals with only unpalatable positional choices. Regular poll findings that the majority of voters thought of themselves as standing close to this elusive 'middle ground' only made things more maddening for the party; the failure to capitalise on this potential support meant that the Liberals could not even reap the advantages of being misrepresented as incurably moderate. They were ideally placed to pick up the support of protesters against the two major parties, but the British electoral system seemed to ensure that even when governments were unpopular the main opposition party automatically looked irresistible.

Of course there is no political law which dictates that third parties can never prosper; for Liberals, the Labour Party was an all-too-real example of a party which had succeeded in 'breaking the mould'. The greatest problem for the Liberals in the post-war period has been the distribution of their support rather than the number of people who vote for them. Over time the typical general election outcome, which would show a relatively high percentage of Liberal votes but very few seats, understandably promoted a tendency for Liberal leaders to pay excessive attention to tactics. Their realistic hopes lay in either a close election which would enable them to secure electoral reform as the price of their support, or the disintegration of the Labour Party, which would bring about the long-desired realignment. For members of a third party, however, political realism is not always conducive to success. When such a party spends too much time stressing the novelty of its views, it can leave the impression that it is trying to create differences for their own sake. This is just another example of the kind of Catch-22 situation faced by a third party under the British electoral system.

The Liberal manifesto for the 1970 general election reflected the developments of the 1960s, with particular emphasis on civil liberties. Superficially, the result of the election looked bad for the party, which was left with only six Members of Parliament. However, the aftermath proved more hopeful; Labour's internal division began to re-emerge, and the Conservative Party soon ran into trouble with what many perceived to be a divisive programme. Between 1970 and 1974 the Liberals gained five seats in spectacular by-elections, and Dick Taverne's defection from Labour over Europe could be interpreted as the beginning of major political changes. The February 1974 general election brought over 6 million votes for the Liberals; even though this produced only fourteen seats the injustice of the outcome could hardly have been a better illustration of the case for proportional representation. Unfortunately for the party, the overall national picture was even worse than it had been in 1964. With no single party able to form a majority government, Jeremy Thorpe was called to Downing Street for negotiations with Edward Heath. These talks failed to produce an offer of electoral reform, and in any case Liberal activists were outraged at the prospect of sustaining the Conservatives in office. The Labour Party might have disintegrated in the face of another defeat; Christopher Mayhew gave a tantalising glimpse of what could have happened when he joined the Liberals from Labour between the two 1974 elections. Instead, Wilson was back in office, and his minority administration pushed through policies which were popular enough to help him win a second contest in October. The Liberal vote declined by 1 million compared with February, and the parliamentary party was reduced to thirteen MPs.

Events seemed to be conspiring against Thorpe, particularly since the new government's fragile majority gave its leadership the perfect excuse to turn its back on the kind of full-blooded socialism which might have worked to Liberal advantage. Thorpe himself was soon in worse personal trouble, as a former male model produced allegations against him which eventually forced his resignation as party leader in May 1976. Additional revelations about financial improprieties within the party did nothing to improve matters. Despite the attempts of Liberals to offer the electorate distinctive ideas, which now included a guarantee of minimum income levels through radical reforms of the taxation and benefit systems, they were still widely seen as little more than a receptacle for the disillusioned supporters of other parties. Now it was the turn of Liberal Party members to register their own dissatisfaction.

Amidst these difficulties, however, there was one significant positive development. The 1975 referendum over UK membership of the EEC was fought on cross-party lines, and was unusual in the extent to which it gave politicians from different backgrounds the opportunity to emphasise areas of agreement. In particular, it brought the consistently pro-European Liberal leadership into contact with Labour politicians who had been angered by Harold Wilson's tactical gymnastics over the European issue. Foremost among this group was the former Chancellor and current Home Secretary, Roy Jenkins. Jenkins had co-operated with David Steel, the Liberal Chief Whip, over social legislation during the 1960s. This association would develop further.

In the summer of 1976 Steel succeeded Jeremy Thorpe as Liberal leader. Almost immediately he was presented with the situation which so many of his predecessors had dreamed of. The Labour government lost its parliamentary majority when two MPs left to form the Scottish Labour Party; faced with imminent defeat in a confidence vote, it turned to the Liberals for help in March 1977. The Prime Minister James Callaghan offered Steel a consultative committee, which would give the Liberals a chance to influence the government's proposals before they reached the House of Commons. There would also be ministerial meetings, which would involve not only Steel and Callaghan but also the Chancellor, Denis Healey, and the Liberal economic spokesman John Pardoe. Short of actual membership of the Cabinet, it seemed that Steel had secured some important concessions; in particular, Callaghan promised to introduce a Bill to hold elections to the European Parliament on the basis of proportional representation (Cook, 1993, 163–4). If this Bill could be passed, the habit of electoral reform might spread.

The long-sought opportunity to exercise real political power turned out to be another headache for the Liberals. In part, this was evident before the deal was struck, because the last thing the Liberal Party needed was another general election with the Thorpe affair still rumbling on. Steel, in fact, was as much the prisoner of events as Callaghan. Without this weakness in his position, Steel might have satisfied demands from inside his party for a tougher bargain. As it was, Callaghan decided not to upset his back-benchers by forcing them to vote for proportional representation in European elections: many of them did not want to see elections to a European Parliament under any system. Thus the European legislation failed. Another ironic problem for the Liberals was that at this time Labour was following the deflationary policies imposed by the IMF – measures which normally both parties would have vigorously opposed. While most Liberals grumbled about this, the irony was increased by the fact that Jo Grimond, who was moving towards the *laissez-faire* politics he had once denounced, disagreed with the pact because he opposed the way Labour had run the economy *before* the IMF loan (Grimond, 1979, 249–51). The Liberals did win some victories while the pact lasted (notably over taxation), but co-operation was unpopular in the constituency parties and relations between Healey and Pardoe soon deteriorated. The situation became farcical at the time of the 1978 Budget, when the Liberals joined the Conservatives in forcing the Chancellor to cut income tax by a penny in the pound; one of the party's most significant post-war parliamentary victories was thus achieved at the cost of a government strategy which they were supposed to be assisting (Healey, 1990, 403). Meanwhile the Liberal vote in by-elections was dropping sharply. When the pact ended in May 1978 there was little lamentation from either of the partners.

The May 1979 general election was never likely to be easy for the Liberals, and in the circumstances their retention of eleven seats represented a creditable performance. As usual, the party fought the election on a distinctive platform, which mixed demands for a Bill of Rights and government decentralisation with a call for a long-term prices and incomes policy and proposals for energy conservation. It was natural for the Liberals to show concern for the environment, an issue which fitted well with their established Community Politics approach. Yet in the 1979 election it brought few rewards, and served mainly to fuel the division between activists who saw the party as a vehicle for local campaigning and the party leadership which was increasingly preoccupied with the tactical manoeuvres necessary to achieve realignment (Behrens, 1989, 85–6).

David Steel had good reason to hope for dramatic changes among opponents of the new Conservative government. On 22 November 1979 Roy Jenkins delivered the BBC's Dimbleby Lecture, and made it 'an unashamed plea for the strengthening of the political centre' (Jenkins, 1982, 21). It looked as if a major political realignment was really taking place at last. Jenkins and Steel met in January 1980, and reached an understanding that, although Jenkins would not be joining the Liberals himself, the new party he intended to set up would first work closely with Steel, then 'consider an amalgamation after a general election' (Jenkins, 1989, 553).

While the 1970s had been another decade of dashed Liberal hopes, the 1980s began with almost unmixed good news for the party. The Conservative government of Margaret Thatcher had quickly run through its honeymoon with the electorate; Mrs Thatcher's refusal to contemplate a U-turn despite soaring unemployment might have been popular with her hard-line supporters, but it was almost an open invitation for moderates to look for alternatives. Normally Labour might have been expected to exploit this opportunity by ditching any policy which could be portrayed as 'extreme', but the experience of the previous twenty years had left the socialists as the only faction within the party which retained a healthy sense of political mission. To those who rejected both socialism and Mrs Thatcher's economic liberalism, it looked as though the Liberals were on the verge of a significant breakthrough; if they could work in tandem with a new party which excited the public, then the road to Downing Street might be opened. The reaction of some Liberals was less than enthusiastic; Cyril Smith, for example, thought that the SDP should be 'strangled at birth' (Steel, 1989, 223). Steel's negotiating skills proved sufficient to quell the doubters, at least temporarily. Amid the ensuing euphoria, he told delegates at the 1981 Liberal Party Assembly to 'Go back to your constituencies and prepare for government'. Subsequently the statement was ridiculed, but at the time it did not seem to be an unwarranted precaution for a party which were so unused to the thought of power.

Realignment, 1981

The Dimbleby Lecture was a crucial catalyst for the development of a new political party, but it can also be seen as the logical result of a much earlier incident. In October 1971 seventy Labour MPs voted against a three-line whip on the principle of UK entry into the EEC. For social democrats like Roy Jenkins, membership of the Community was essential if Britain was to remain prosperous, and to exercise significant influence over world events (Jenkins, 1972, 74–80). Harold Wilson had attempted to negotiate for entry in 1967; by choosing to oppose Edward Heath's resumption of talks, Jenkins believed that he was exploiting the European question for purely party-political reasons. When Wilson allowed Tony Benn to convince him that the next Labour government should hold a referendum on membership, Jenkins resigned from his position as deputy leader of the party.

Jenkins and his supporters had other reasons for unhappiness. In opposition, Labour had drifted towards more socialist policies, including a renewed programme of nationalisation. The social democrats saw nationalisation as an irrelevance at best. Harold Wilson (and the state of the economy) ensured that socialist hopes were eventually disappointed, and social democrats did serve in the 1974–79 governments. After the IMF agreement of December 1976, however, these ministers were left in positions of responsibility without exercising significant power. The usual reward for people in this predicament is to be blamed by everyone; apart from the predictable socialist criticisms, social democrats were pilloried in *The Future that Doesn't Work*, a collection of essays by Anglo-American commentators including the future Ambassador to the USA, Peter Jay (Tyrrell, 1977). Jenkins' departure to take up the post of President of the European Commission was quite consistent with his views, but it also implied a deepening and understandable disillusionment with domestic politics.

From his post in Brussels, Jenkins kept in touch with the British political scene, but his perspective was bound to be more detached than that of the social democrats who still held senior posts within the Labour Party. The response to his appeal was therefore crucial. His concern was focused mainly on two close friends and former ministers, William Rodgers and Shirley Williams; another potential recruit was an ally from the early 1970s, Dr David Owen, who had succeeded Anthony Crosland as Foreign Secretary in the Callaghan government. Rodgers, Williams and Owen all opposed Labour's European policy, and were worried by moves to increase trade union and constituency power within the party at the expense of MPs. Unlike Jenkins, all three had good reasons to stay in the Labour Party provided that its present course could be changed. There were hopes, for example, that the grass-roots Campaign for Labour Victory (set up in 1977) could reverse the trend towards socialism in the constituency parties. Much also depended upon the party's choice of a successor to Callaghan, whose retirement was seen as inevitable. For the moment, the reaction of Jenkins' friends was lukewarm; David Owen, whose personal relations with Jenkins were not so close, actually denounced what he called 'siren voices from outside, from those who have given up the fight from within' (Owen, 1992, 426). Jenkins would remain in Brussels for a further year, so for now he could be happy that at least press reaction to the speech was favourable, and a public debate had begun.

In some parties this public threat of a split would have effectively prevented one; both sides to the dispute would have thrashed out a compromise. For the Labour Party, however, any hint of 'treachery' could only make matters worse. At a special conference in May 1980 David Owen was heckled when he opposed unilateral nuclear disarmament; in the following month he met Rodgers and Williams to issue a joint statement on Europe. Roy Jenkins chose this moment to remind the public of his support for a new party. Owen, Rodgers and Williams, now popularly known as 'The Gang of Three', were pushed further towards Jenkins in September when Labour's annual conference voted for unconditional withdrawal from the EEC and the abandonment of nuclear weapons. Michael Foot's defeat of Denis Healey in the November leadership election was a further blow, and when another special conference decided that in future the party leader would be elected jointly by MPs, constituencies and trade unions (with the unions enjoying the greatest influence), the Gang of Three were ready to abandon their struggle. On Sunday 25 January 1981, soon after Jenkins' return from Brussels, the membership of the Gang increased to four. The group issued the 'Limehouse Declaration' setting up a Council for Social Democracy which was the basis for a new Social Democratic Party (SDP). The formation of the party was announced on 26 March.

A partnership of principle or a marriage of convenience, 1981–92?

The Limehouse Declaration explicitly rejected the notion that the new party would follow 'the politics of an inert centre merely representing the lowest common denominator between two extremes' (Stephenson, 1982, 186). Despite this disavowal, the two main parties knew that the best way of attacking the SDP was to deny that it had any principled basis (Owen, 1992, 504). Whatever its future relationship with the Liberal Party turned out to be, the SDP already shared the Liberal problem of establishing an identity as more than just a colourless alternative for disgruntled voters. The media attention which the Limehouse Declaration sparked off might have helped to generate initial public interest, but it also increased the necessity of establishing firm principles for sale to a mass audience. By June a working party of Liberals and Social Democrats had established a statement of principles entitled 'A Fresh Start for Britain', yet this took on the appearance of a generalised wish-list rather than a detailed programme (Stephenson, 1982, 187–9).

The immediate fulfilment of the agreement between Steel and Jenkins about inter-party co-operation led to difficulties within the Gang of Four. The most reluctant member, David Owen, thought that too close an association with the Liberals would prevent the SDP from establishing itself as a principled party. Even if the SDP's new members had previously voted Liberal, they had not felt motivated enough to actually join the party. Why disappoint these recruits by allowing the SDP to get bogged down with the Liberals in the political middle ground? Owen was particularly worried about the division of seats to be fought by each party in a future election. By contrast, Roy Jenkins appreciated the value of alliance with the experienced grass-roots activists which the Liberals could provide; in addition, he denied that the ideas of social democrats and liberals were very different. In short, while Owen wanted to build a distinct, radical party, which could even compete with the Liberals in future if circumstances changed, Jenkins saw no reason why there should not be a merger at the appropriate time – perhaps after the two parties had governed in coalition.

The disagreement between Jenkins and Owen covered both tactics and principles, and provides an interesting case-study in the interplay of ideas with other political considerations. The task of isolating one factor from the other would be fascinating but ultimately fruitless; it can be concluded only by producing an inaccurately simplistic interpretation of political action. For example, in his memoirs David Owen portrays Roy Jenkins as an elderly politician 'in a hurry', who intended to use the SDP as 'a disposable vehicle for his ambition to be Prime Minister' (Owen, 1992, 531). As the most experienced leader in either party, Jenkins would be the likely Prime Minister of any coalition government, provided that victory was achieved quickly. In the mean time, any radical thinking which might scare off both the Liberals and the electorate should be avoided. In other words, Jenkins was driven almost exclusively by his desperation to become Prime Minister. On the other hand, it is equally possible to interpret Owen's opposition to eventual merger as the product of his own ambition. There was every chance that David Steel would succeed Jenkins as leader of a merged party, and this would probably put an end to Owen's chances, since he was only three months younger than Steel.

It would be naive to suppose that these calculations were wholly absent on either side, but they should not obscure the underlying divisions of principle which helped to destroy the dreams of 1981. By this time Jenkins had long ceased to call himself a socialist; true to the ideas of his old friend and rival Anthony Crosland, he believed that the mixed economy could provide the basis for greater social and economic equality, and acknowledged that this was not socialism as understood within the Labour Party. By contrast, when Owen published *Face the Future* in 1981, the word 'socialism' featured prominently (at least in the first edition). Unlike Jenkins, Owen was unhappy with post-war thinking and constantly sought fresh solutions. This attitude produced some sympathy for Mrs Thatcher's crusading style of politics, which was matched by agreement with at least some of her reforms. Neither William Rodgers nor Shirley Williams, who also published books before the 1983 election, felt this ambivalence about Thatcherism (Williams, 1981; Rodgers, 1982). They agreed with Jenkins (and Steel) in finding little to applaud in Conservative Party policies.

Before establishing an agreement with the Liberals, the SDP leaders needed to sort out their own differences. Yet the divisions were too deep, and could never be resolved. When the SDP's membership (which then stood at 68,000) voted for the party's new leader, Jenkins narrowly defeated Owen, despite the fact that the latter seemed to be more popular with the electorate as a whole. By this time (June 1982), the party had twenty-nine MPs, and both Jenkins and Williams had achieved spectacular by-election victories (at Glasgow Hillhead and Crosby respectively). For the first year of the SDP's existence, the allied parties achieved a steady 40 per cent in most opinion polls; in December 1981 their support was recorded at 50.5 per cent (Wybrow, 1989, 126). The success of the party was not an unmixed blessing, however; as Ivor Crewe and Anthony King have shown, the differences within the SDP were not confined to the leadership (Crewe and King, 1995, 61–83). A more obvious blow was the Argentine invasion of the Falkland Islands in April 1982, and their subsequent recapture by British forces. These developments removed the attention of the media from the new party, which depended heavily on consistent publicity. Only one Conservative MP (Christopher Brocklebank-Fowler) had defected to the SDP, and after the Falklands campaign the government received a boost in opinion polls which were already registering a recovery as economic problems eased.

Despite underlying disagreements, the SDP and the Liberals fought the 1983 elections as allies, with Roy Jenkins as 'Prime Minister Designate'. Joint policy committees produced a manifesto, *Working Together for Britain*, which reaffirmed the liberal and social democrat commitment to the mixed economy in the face of attacks from Thatcherites and socialists. The European Convention on Human Rights would be incorporated into British law, and Britain would remain a member of the North Atlantic Treaty Organisation (NATO) and the EC. Electoral reform, democracy in the workplace and environmental protection were other survivals from previous Liberal manifestos; indeed, the programme would have looked very similar had the SDP never existed. For Roy Jenkins, broad agreement was only to be expected, but David Owen and his supporters took this as further evidence of the Liberals' ability to get their own way.

In the words of the Prime Minister Designate, the 1983 Alliance campaign was 'a brilliant success', but the result did not tally with this judgement (Jenkins, 1994, 574). Although the Alliance achieved over a quarter of the vote, narrowly failing to overtake Labour, Liberal activists found that their preparations for government had been premature. The outcome of the election disappointed Jenkins, but the fact that he could take some comfort from a contest which saw the SDP's representation in the House of Commons reduced to six is perhaps a measure of the extent to which his expectations had been guided by the record of the Liberals. In Parliament, the original Gang had been reduced to two – both Shirley Williams and William Rodgers lost their seats.

After the general election Owen telephoned Jenkins to say that unless he resigned from the SDP leadership immediately there would be a contest between them. Jenkins regarded this behaviour as 'somewhat incontinent', but acquiesced (Jenkins, 1994, 578). Owen was elected unopposed, and continued his theoretical musings with greater urgency. In 1984 he published *A Future that Will Work: Competitiveness and Compassion*. This book revealed the effect of Thatcherism on Owen's thinking. He introduced the concept of a Social Market, a phrase which had been used by Keith Joseph in the 1970s. Denouncing an over-extended and bureaucratic state, Owen argued that market forces should be introduced within the public sector, and that welfare benefits ought to be targeted more narrowly on the worst-off in society (Owen, 1984, 1–29, 104–31). The need to reduce class divisions in society was forcefully reiterated, but critics saw this as a rhetorical gloss on a programme which embraced too many Thatcherite premises. By mid-1985 Owen was being warned by David Steel and William Rodgers that his flirtation with Thatcherism was going too far; Roy Jenkins made a barely-coded allusion to Owen's 'sub-Thatcherism'.

Economic and social policies were not the only source of disagreement. In the following year the latent subject of nuclear weapons added to the tension. A joint commission of the parties agreed that in view of current moves towards superpower disarmament, no immediate decision about a replacement for Britain's existing Polaris missile system was necessary. Owen, whose opposition to unilateral disarmament had not diminished, saw this as a compromise to appease the opponents of nuclear weapons within the Liberal Party. As both Shirley Williams and William Rodgers pointed out, the commission's findings were carefully worded to avoid fomenting any differences of principle (Steel, 1989, 265). Owen could not agree, declaring that 'Conviction politics must not become a monopoly of Mrs Thatcher' (Wilson, D., 1987, 28). The situation was not helped when the 1986 Liberal Party Assembly passed a resolution in support of non-nuclear European defence co-operation (Steel, 1989, 270–1). This was a major setback to chances of co-operation between the parties after an election victory. Owen felt so strongly about defence that during the 1987 campaign he announced that Labour would not be fit to govern until it changed its unilateralist position (Owen, 1992, 693). At this time, the Conservatives were benefiting from Labour's defence policy, but Owen's repeated outbursts only publicised an internal difficulty which the Liberal leadership was anxious to smooth over.

For the election, the Alliance produced a manifesto based on a book published under the joint names of Owen and Steel, *The Time has Come: Partnership for Progress* (Owen and Steel, 1987). The attempt to disguise differences led to what Owen regarded as a 'rather bland' manifesto, but skilful presentation on paper could not prevent the splits from re-emerging when the two leaders were subjected to the interrogations of an election campaign (Owen, 1992, 679). The confusion caused by the divided leadership meant that the 'Two Davids' could not capitalise on poll findings which suggested that whatever their voting intentions most people felt that the Alliance best represented their views (Heath et al., 1991, 217). The result reduced SDP strength in the House of Commons to five; it was easy for the Liberals, with seventeen seats, to see themselves as the senior partner in the Alliance. In the aftermath of defeat, Steel announced plans for a merger. Owen had opposed this from the outset; his opinion of the typical Liberal Party member had never been high, and it was not improved by the controversy over nuclear weapons. Despite his opposition, the SDP membership voted for merger talks on 6 August 1987, and the party finally agreed to the terms on 2 March 1988. David Owen resigned from the SDP leadership after the vote of 6 August. He took no part in the negotiations, and decided to lead those who opposed the merger in a new, much reduced, SDP. Only two MPs, John Cartwright and Rosie Barnes, decided to follow him, and after some disastrous by-election results the national party was wound up in June 1990.

For a while, it looked as though the merged party would suffer the same fate. Not all Liberals had approved the merger, and a faction led by Michael Meadowcroft subsequently set up a new party, retaining the name of Liberal. Finding that 'Social and Liberal Democrats' only produced the nickname of 'The Salads', their former colleagues finally settled on 'Liberal Democrats' for themselves in October 1989. Paddy Ashdown took over the leadership as the party hovered close to bankruptcy. In the May 1989 elections to the European Parliament it lost third place in the popular vote to the Green Party; support had dropped to only 6 per cent. Ashdown, who had once annoyed the Liberal leadership (and David Owen) by advocating the withdrawal of US cruise missiles from Britain, gradually emerged as a popular figure, and in the run up to the 1992 general election the party enjoyed a revival. The Liberal Democrats scored a notable by-election victory at Eastbourne in 1990, and two further gains followed in 1991. Their 1992 manifesto was acclaimed by the *Guardian* as 'the best show in town'; apart from the familiar proposals for electoral reform, decentralisation and state intervention to secure economic recovery, it included a promise to raise income tax by a penny to improve education (Cook, 1993, 208–9). The party polled just under 6 million votes, although the tally of MPs dropped from twenty-two to twenty. As usual, mid-term by-election gains were wiped out. Given the difficulties of 1987–89, however, the Liberal Democrats could be reasonably satisfied with their performance. They were back in the habitual post-war position of hoping for a hung Parliament after the next election, which might bring them a promise of electoral reform in return for their support. However, with Labour apparently looking more sympathetically at proportional representation, there was still a reasonable hope that this long-cherished measure would soon be realised, even without a close result at the next election.

Conclusion

For Liberal Democrats, the frustration of the period since 1970 has been aggravated by the occasional signs of imminent breakthrough. By 1988 many must have felt that they had spent a decade running very hard to stand still; all the Alliance seemed to have done was to show how difficult it was for a third party to win seats, and Liberal Democrats did not need any more lessons in the injustices of the winner-takes-all electoral system. At a time when the two major parties were widely perceived as too extreme, the party's percentage of the vote might have risen steeply without all the heartaches of the Alliance years.

Outwardly the period was one of dramatic changes for the Liberals, perhaps more so than for any other party. Yet while the two main parties rethought their principles the Liberals remained relatively consistent. The legacy of New liberals such as Keynes and Beveridge might be denounced by Labour's socialists and Thatcherites within the Conservative Party, but the Liberal Party stayed loyal. They regarded the state as too bureaucratic and centralised, but denied that there was an acceptable alternative to economic intervention and a well-funded welfare system.

Members of the Liberal Party could share these conclusions with social democrats. After all, New liberalism had also provided the basis for post-war social democratic thought. Differences did exist, but they concerned emphases rather than fundamentals. In practice both Liberals and social democrats wanted greater economic equality, but the extent to which that should go was not spelled out precisely by either group. In the past social democrats might have been less critical of state bureaucracy than the Liberals, but compromise on this issue was not difficult to contemplate. A genuine 'partnership of principle' was quite conceivable; the problem remained one of convincing the electorate that these principles amounted to more than splitting the difference between Conservative and Labour.

For David Owen, this dilemma was about more than principles. The failure of centre parties to break the political mould could also be traced to personalities; indeed, the two factors were inseparable. He came to believe that 'Moderates make bad militants' (Owen, 1992, 482). This view implied that unless the Alliance changed its principles it would never discover a successful electoral idiom; in turn, a philosophical rethink might produce the dynamism which had previously been absent from third party politics. Previous third parties had lacked a social basis, but the goal of Owen's rethink was to wrest the middle classes and skilled workers away from the Conservative Party. *A Future that Will Work* presented the most promising means to this end – the Social Market, or Thatcherism with a conscience. In order to make social democracy popular, Owen ceased to be a social democrat; he had become a 'militant', but was no longer a 'moderate'. It was his misfortune that neither his SDP colleagues nor their Liberal Party allies were interested in the prospect of winning power at that price; ironically, the only prominent Liberal who could broadly agree with Owen's new principles was Jo Grimond, who had helped to destroy the power of similar ideas within his party during the 1950s.

Owen's abandonment of Croslandite social democracy was based on a faulty analysis. Jenkins, Rodgers and Williams were determined not to attribute the failures of recent Labour governments to the undoubted weaknesses of social democratic thought. For them, the real cause of Labour's plight was its connection with an irresponsible trade union movement. The SDP, liberated from this distasteful partnership, would set the record straight. Crosland's 'revisionism' was itself capable of being revised and updated, as David Marquand proved later in the decade with his *The Unprincipled Society* (1988). By the time that this book had appeared, however, something had gone wrong. Perhaps Jenkins and his allies thought that they would win elections just by not being either the Labour Party or Mrs Thatcher. Whatever the reason, in the early days of the SDP no one came forward with the necessary rethink.

A Future that Will Work could have changed all this. Instead, it showed that Owen actually agreed with the opponents of social democracy. Like Mrs Thatcher and the socialists, he thought that the poor record of the 1960s and 1970s was the result of woolly 'consensual' thinking. Social democracy had seemed to be a romantic fighting creed during the Labour Party's battles; now that the social democrats had a party to themselves, their ideas just looked dull in comparison to Thatcherism. 'Conviction politics' were back in fashion, and Owen wanted a piece of the action. He did not notice that the convictions of the Liberal Party had inspired its membership to survive against the odds throughout the post-war period, and that the ideas of New liberalism had once inspired the oratory of Lloyd George; in fact, he despised the modern Liberals for the manner in which they fought, particularly during by-elections. In combination with this fighting force, Owen's charisma might have brought him the power he craved. Instead he decided to translate his impatience with Roy Jenkins into an issue of principle. This was the kind of clever manoeuvre that rarely succeeds in British politics.

Owen claims that he does not regret his time with the SDP; if this is true, it shows him in a charitable light. Some believe that he might have become leader of the Labour Party if he had not left before 1983. Alternatively, instead of letting his market value fall as a result of his association with the SDP, he might have been making his way within the Conservative Party (after a token period of fighting within the Labour Party to bolster his dynamic image). In time, he would have made an ideal successor to Margaret Thatcher as leader of the party. When negotiations were finally opened to bring him into a Conservative Cabinet, it was far too late. It might be unfair to accuse the Conservatives of pulling off a cynical publicity stunt, but in 1991 John Major offered a deal from which only he could truly benefit. Even if the old SDP vote was not substantial enough to ensure a Conservative victory in the forthcoming election, Major was unlikely to experience a sudden conversion to the principle of proportional representation which Owen could not renounce. The offer of a place in Major's Cabinet came to nothing, but Owen's willingness to negotiate presents a stark contrast to his attitude when the Liberal–SDP merger was being discussed. It signalled his belief that the two-party mould had triumphed after all. After all the excitements of the 1980s, the potency of the New liberal legacy in an era of conviction politics had still to be properly tested.

List of works cited

Behrens, Robert (1989), 'The Centre: Social Democracy and Liberalism', in Leonard Tivey and Anthony Wright (eds) *Party Ideology in Britain*, Routledge.

Cockett, Richard (1994), *Thinking the Unthinkable: Think-Tanks and the Economic Counter-Revolution 1931–1983*, HarperCollins.

Cook, Chris (1993), *A Short History of the Liberal Party 1900–92*, Macmillan, 4th edition.

Crewe, Ivor, and King, Anthony (1995), 'Loyalists and Defectors: the SDP Breakaway from the Parliamentary Labour Party 1981–2', in Peter Jones (ed.) *Party, Parliament and Personality: Essays Presented to Hugh Berrington*, Routledge.

Grimond, Jo (1979), *Memoirs*, Heinemann.

Harrod, Roy (1972) *The Life of John Maynard Keynes*, Penguin.

Healey, Denis (1990), *The Time of My Life*, Penguin.

Heath, Anthony, Evans, Geoff, Field, Julia, and Witherspoon, Sharon (1991), *Understanding Political Change: The British Voter 1964–1987*, Pergamon.

Jenkins, Roy (1972), *What Matters Now*, Fontana.

Jenkins, Roy (1982), 'Home Thoughts from Abroad', in Wayland Kennet (ed.) *The Rebirth of Britain*, Weidenfeld and Nicolson.

Jenkins, Roy (1989) *European Diary 1977–1981*, Collins.

Jenkins, Roy (1994), *A Life at the Centre*, Macmillan.

McKenzie, Robert (1964), *British Political Parties*, Heinemann, reprint of 2nd edition.

Marquand, David (1988), *The Unprincipled Society: New Demands and Old Politics*, Fontana.

Owen, David (1981), *Face the Future*, Oxford University Press.

Owen, David (1984), *A Future that Will Work: Competitiveness and Compassion*, Penguin.

Owen, David (1992), *Time to Declare*, Penguin.

Owen, David, and Steel, David (1987), *The Time has Come: Partnership for Progress*, Weidenfeld and Nicolson.

Rodgers, William (1982), *The Politics of Change*, Secker and Warburg.

Steel, David (1989), *Against Goliath: David Steel's Story*, Weidenfeld and Nicolson.

Stephenson, Hugh (1982), *Claret and Chips: The Rise of the SDP*, Michael Joseph.

Tyrrell, R. Emmett (ed.) (1977), *The Future that Doesn't Work: Social Democracy's Failures in Britain*, Doubleday.

Wallace, William (1983), 'Survival and Revival', in Vernon Bogdanor (ed.) *Liberal Party Politics*, Oxford University Press.

Williams, Shirley (1981), *Politics is for People*, Penguin.

Wilson, Des (1987), *Battle for Power*, Sphere.

Wilson, Trevor (1966), *The Downfall of the Liberal Party*, Collins.

Wybrow, Robert (1989), *Britain Speaks Out, 1937–87: A Social History as Seen through the Gallop Data*, Macmillan.

Questions for discussion

- Is it meaningful to talk of a 'middle ground' of British politics?
- Examine the differences between the policies of the Liberal Party and the liberalism of Margaret Thatcher.

Selected further reading (see also Chapters 1 and 5)

Bellamy, Richard (1992), *Liberalism and Modern Society*, Polity.

Bradley, Ian (1981), *Breaking the Mould? The Birth and Prospects of the Social Democratic Party*, Martin Robertson.

Churchill, Winston S. (1909), *The People's Rights*, Hodder and Stoughton.

Coates, Ken (1983), *The Social Democrats: Those Who Went and Those Who Stayed*, Spokesman.

Eccleshall, Robert (1986), *British Liberalism: Liberal Thought from the 1640s to the 1980s*, Longman.

Freeden, Michael (1978), *The New Liberalism: An Ideology of Social Reform*, Clarendon Press.

Gilmour, Ian (1983), 'Tories, Social Democracy and the Centre', *Political Quarterly*, volume 54, number 3.

Green, Thomas Hill (1941), *Lectures on the Principles of Political Obligation*, Longmans.

Grimond, Jo (1963), *The Liberal Challenge*, Hollis and Carter.

Jenkins, Roy (1985), *Partnership of Principle: Writings and Speeches on the Making of the Alliance*, Secker and Warburg.

Luard, Evan (1979), *Socialism without the State*, Macmillan.

Meadowcroft, James (ed.) (1994), *L. T. Hobhouse: Liberalism and Other Writings*, Cambridge University Press.

Mitchie, Alastair, and Hoggart, Simon (1978), *The Pact: The Inside Story of the Lib–Lab Government 1977–78*, Quartet.

Paterson, W. and Thomas, A. (1986), *The Future of Social Democracy: Problems and Prospects of Social Democratic Parties in Western Europe*, Clarendon Press.

Rawls, John (1971), *A Theory of Justice*, Oxford University Press.

Steel, David, and Holme, Richard (eds) (1985), *Partners in One Nation: A New Vision of Britain 2000*, Bodley Head.

CHAPTER 4

Thatcherism and its legacy, 1979–90

Opening shots, 1979–83

On 4 May 1979, Margaret Thatcher became Britain's first woman Prime Minister, as the Conservatives won a majority of forty-three over all other parties. The feeling that this had been an unusually significant general election was marked by the fact that the Conservatives achieved the biggest swing since 1945. Even before the election, James Callaghan had detected 'a sea-change in politics' (Whitehead, 1985, 366). Evidence from opinion polls did not clarify whether the electorate had voted for this change because of a positive response to Mrs Thatcher's vigorous leadership, or as a reaction against the Labour government. Since 1975, Thatcher had been on trial as Conservative leader; despite apparently passing this first test, it was recognised that she remained to some extent on probation.

The uncertainty of Thatcher's position stemmed largely from the fact that her admirers still constituted a minority of senior Conservatives. Possibly in deference to her opponents, before entering 10 Downing Street she quoted a prayer (attributed to St Francis of Assisi) which promised to replace discord with harmony. St Francis's genuine teaching about giving up worldly goods went unmentioned. Following up her conciliatory Shadow Cabinet appointments, Thatcher's first administration was a fair reflection of the balance of forces within the party. Of Edward Heath's adherents, Lord Carrington went to the Foreign Office, the recalled Peter Walker was given Agriculture, and James Prior was entrusted with trade union reform at Employment. Francis Pym, another known opponent of *laissez-faire* policies, became Secretary of State for Defence, and even Ian Gilmour, the most vocal opponent of Mrs Thatcher's ideas, took Cabinet rank as Lord Privy Seal. The precise views of Michael Heseltine (Environment) were less certain, and at least Thatcher already knew that she could depend upon William Whitelaw (Home Secretary). According to one very sympathetic observer, Thatcher had been 'fair to the point of being generous to her potential opponents' (Holmes, 1985a, 20).

These appointments were important concessions: they might even have been taken as a sign that Mrs Thatcher would prove to be a consensual Prime Minister after all. Yet this impression was misleading. Economic policy was by far Mrs Thatcher's highest priority, and she ensured that fellow-believers were installed in the key offices. Sir Geoffrey Howe became Chancellor of the Exchequer, with the economic Powellite John Biffen also entering the Cabinet as Chief Secretary to the Treasury. Sir Keith Joseph, Thatcher's first choice for the Treasury, took a post of almost equal importance at Industry. With John Nott at Trade and David Howell at Energy, economic liberals could feel that they had a very fair representation in the departments that mattered. The new junior-ranking ministers showed an even greater tilt towards the Thatcherite tendency, with such figures as Nicholas Ridley, Norman Tebbit, Nigel Lawson and Cecil Parkinson winning preferment. For these rising stars, radical economic reform could not proceed quickly enough; none of them had any patience with conservative arguments for caution. Before long, the opponents of Thatcherism within the Conservative Party had been dubbed 'the wets' by enemies of compromise.

The economic situation left behind by Labour looked unpromising on paper, but in three respects at least it was helpful to the Thatcherite project. First, North Sea oil was about to make Britain a net exporter of this valuable commodity, which had done so much to destroy Mrs Thatcher's Conservative predecessor. Secondly, the trade unions had incurred a loss of public goodwill after the Winter of Discontent, which promised to make reforms more easy to implement. Finally, in the last years of the Callaghan government unemployment had fallen, but inflation stood at over 10 per cent in June 1979. The Thatcherite programme, which would have chosen the control of inflation as its primary aim in any case, was thus given added credibility.

By the end of this Parliament in 1983, the government could boast of important achievements in the fight against inflation. Although the rate increased to 21.9 per cent by April 1980, the figure stood at around 5 per cent in January 1983. While this result was highly satisfactory for the government, it had certainly not been secured in the intended fashion. True to the monetarist approach forced on Labour after 1976, Howe published targets for future growth of the money supply. According to the theory, once the quantity of money was under control the rate of inflation would start to fall. Unfortunately for the theory, the quantity of money proved difficult to define, and when the government chose sterling M3 (notes and coins in circulation plus current and deposit accounts) as its measuring-rod, this proved to have little predictive value. Inflation fell, even though the government's targets for growth of M3 were massively exceeded. Although the government was reluctant to admit anything which smacked of a U-turn, the monetarist experiment was effectively dead by January 1985 (Smith, 1987, 123).

Another success which could not have entirely satisfied Mrs Thatcher's supporters was trade union legislation. Overcoming criticism and a back-bench revolt, James Prior embarked on a gradualist strategy with the Employment Act 1980, which outlawed secondary picketing and laid down that union 'closed shops' would be legal only if a ballot gave overwhelming support. Prior's success was rewarded in a reshuffle which sent him into harm's way at the Northern Ireland Office, but his successor at Employment, Norman Tebbit, continued his cautious approach in 1982 with an Act which clamped down further on closed shops and made unions liable for damages incurred during unlawful strikes. Supplementary benefits were reduced for the families of strikers to concentrate the minds of anyone contemplating industrial action. Although industrial disruption continued, and the government actually settled with the miners to avert a strike in 1981, the number of working days lost sharply declined, as did union membership.

The manifesto pledge on income tax was also adequately fulfilled. The top rates of tax on both 'earned' and 'unearned' incomes were slashed by more than 20 per cent, and the basic rate was reduced from 33 to 30 per cent. Personal allowances were also raised by more than the rate of inflation. However, these tax reforms were controversial; even in 1979 Gallup polls were already finding that most people thought of this as a rich person's government, and the overall balance of the tax cuts could only reinforce this view (Wybrow, 1989, 121). The government were unabashed, claiming that high earners needed incentives, although the psychological theory behind this view was problematic. According to later survey evidence, high earners were not gracious enough to support it by working any harder after they had pocketed their tax cuts (Riddell, 1991, 226). Meanwhile the poor were certainly given a powerful disincentive against the purchase of VAT-rated goods when the level of this tax on consumption was raised from 8 to 15 per cent in Geoffrey Howe's first Budget. Prescription charges were also increased, to set against a rise in pensions.

The Thatcher government was intent on reducing public spending, which would provide scope for further tax cuts as well as limiting the size of the state. Sir Derek Rayner was seconded from Marks and Spencer (a favourite firm of Mrs Thatcher's) to look for savings within the civil service, while the radical John Hoskyns went to the Downing Street Policy Unit to provide ideas for other cut-backs. Unfortunately, the record on spending was not as good as the government had hoped. As an electoral gambit Mrs Thatcher had accepted the Clegg Commission recommendations on public sector pay, which caused the government's wage bill to rise by a quarter (Young, 1990, 151). Mrs Thatcher's tough line did not deter the usual clamour from spending ministers; an unlikely offender was Keith Joseph, who implicitly reconverted to his sinful ways by pouring money into nationalised industries such as British Steel and British Leyland. Admittedly, these concerns needed cash injections to finance redundancy payments; in December 1979 the chairman of British Steel announced that 53,000 jobs were to go over nine months (Holmes, 1985a, 43).

The financial burden of redundancy pay and unemployment benefits probably surprised the government's policy-makers. Even their guru, the economist Professor Milton Friedman, claimed to be a little taken aback by the rate of job-destruction. Having made the most of Labour's poor record on employment (notably through the notorious 'Labour Isn't Working' poster campaign), Mrs Thatcher watched the dole queues grow from 1.2 million in May 1979 to over 3 million by late 1982. The Conservatives could claim that much of the increase simply showed how inefficient British industry had been during the 1970s: these jobs had not been economically justified in the first place. Yet as Geoffrey Howe's high interest rate policy acted to deter investment (which had been too low in the first place), manufacturing output fell by 17.5 per cent between 1979 and 1982, and many otherwise healthy businesses collapsed. While Keith Joseph agonised over propping up nationalised 'lame ducks' such as British Leyland, the private sector which the government had promised to boost was still struggling to regain lost markets when the next recession arrived in 1989.

Apart from the practical difficulties associated with the rising social security budget, unemployment proved to be a serious theoretical blind spot for Thatcherites. It called into question the individualist premise which crucially underpinned their theories. In 1981, as if to show his contempt for Edward Heath's example, Geoffrey Howe introduced a Budget which reduced demand further during a recession. In the words of a former Cabinet minister, this was 'inverted Keynesianism', which inevitably delayed economic recovery and increased unemployment (Gilmour, 1992, 33). How could such measures be explained to those who had accepted Thatcherite rhetoric about the need for hard work and thrift, but now found themselves out of work or bankrupt? Perhaps it was fortunate for the government that an outbreak of inner-city rioting during the summer of 1981 allowed ministers to deflect attention from those who were suffering more silently. Yet the problem remained, and since a policy U-turn was ruled out the only alternative was to blame unemployed people for their own problems. The most notable example of this was Norman Tebbit's 1981 party conference speech, when he remarked that his father had 'got on his bike and looked for work' during the 1930s (Tebbit, 1989, 236). Once unemployed people became reliant on social security benefits, of course, they were open to further attack as products of a 'dependency culture'. The worst effects of the recession were geographically localised, in areas such as the north-east of England and the midlands, and electoral arithmetic meant that the government saw no good reason for resolving its theoretical dilemma. Instead of capturing idealistic majority support, however, Thatcherism could hardly do more than provoke grudging acceptance or resignation from most people in the light of this record. Even this brought dividends for the Prime Minister; a culture of apathy was a perfect background for her radical programme, and reduced the chances of an enthusiastic following for alternative ideas.

Mrs Thatcher's decisive election victory of June 1983 is often attributed to the 'Falklands Factor'. The recapture of the Falkland Islands after the Argentine invasion of April 1982 certainly helped to raise Mrs Thatcher's approval rating above her record-breaking low of 23 per cent – if only for a while. Her inflexibility, which had received a mixed public reception when applied to domestic matters, now seemed to be a national asset. The performance of the 'Iron Lady' effectively obscured the fact that government defence cuts had played a vital role in encouraging the invasion in the first place. It also switched media attention from the SDP, for whom Roy Jenkins had just won the Glasgow Hillhead by-election. Even without the war, however, the Conservatives might easily have secured a second term. The opposition was divided, and the inevitable economic upturn had begun (although unemployment remained stubbornly high). The Falklands undoubtedly did have an impact on the scale of the Conservative victory, which gave them a majority of 144 seats. Even then, the party attracted fewer votes than in 1979. This was short of being a ringing endorsement for the far-reaching changes Mrs Thatcher had already introduced.

Up to 1983, the verdict of an IEA pamphlet entitled *Could do Better* seems, if anything, to be an understatement (Beenstock et al., 1982). The UK was coming out of recession, but government policy had made this a more painful process than it ought to have been. The government's greatest successes, in fact, had come with trade union reform and the sale of council houses; one of these policies had been followed with un-Thatcherite caution, while the other had been a Conservative Party aspiration at least since the 1950s. Another policy which could be described as a success was denationalisation (or privatisation, as it was now usually called), but this had hardly featured in the 1979 manifesto. Instead of securing the commanding heights of the economy for the state, the National Enterprise Board was now acting as the government's sales showroom; British Aerospace, Britoil and the National Freight Company were all disposed of during this Parliament. Ironically, the government was also in danger of demonstrating that nationalised industries such as British Leyland (BL) could be made to yield a profit to the taxpayer – albeit at a cost, in BL's case, of over 100,000 jobs since 1978. To demonstrate the changed attitude from the days when Edward Heath and his Cabinet agonised over a possible return to the conditions of the 1930s, the Conservative Research Department's 1983 summary of the government's activities turned the decimation of jobs in the public sector into a boast that 'State monopolies have been exposed to the disciplines of competition' (Conservative Research Department, 1983). This was a refreshing outbreak of honesty, because the abandonment of the post-war goal of full employment was the key factor in achieving the government's major goals of lower inflation and trade union reform.

Second innings, 1983–87

During the 1983 general election campaign, the new Foreign Secretary Francis Pym suggested that a landslide victory would not be helpful to the Conservatives. As a speculative remark this was impeccable; the example of the last Labour government had shown that a precarious majority is a good way to ensure parliamentary discipline. Under the circumstances, though, Pym would have been wiser to keep his thoughts private. Mrs Thatcher saw him as the most dangerous of the wets, and could interpret his views only as an invitation for the electorate to give the Prime Minister something less than a vote of confidence. Thatcher's response was to withdraw her confidence from Pym. After his sacking he launched the 'Centre Forward' group to argue for conservative policies; this body attracted some publicity, especially after the publication of Pym's book *The Politics of Consent*. Yet if Pym had raised the flag of rebellion, he was still disinclined to wave it with much enthusiasm: his book was an attack on extremism, but he exempted the government and the Prime Minister from that charge (Pym, 1985, 211–12). In the mean time, the vacancy at the Foreign Office allowed Mrs Thatcher to move Geoffrey Howe from the Treasury. His replacement, Nigel Lawson, seemed to be even closer to the Prime Minister's thinking than Howe had been. The Prime Minister no doubt calculated that the latter's growing ability to irritate her would be less of a problem if he went to the Foreign Office, which she already hated on principle.

With the wets now largely smoked out of their threatening outposts, and the opposition parties regrouping after their defeat, the Thatcher revolution moved on to fresh territory. Room for manoeuvre was increased by the revival in the economy, helped by the world upturn associated with the US budget deficit. Since 1980 Ronald Reagan had acted as a powerful ideological ally for Mrs Thatcher, although the emphasis of his policies had been on tax cuts rather than sound money. This personal version of the 'special relationship' certainly helped Britain during the Falklands War, and Reagan's presence gave Thatcher reassurance that she was not alone in her battle against 'socialism'. As relations with the exhausted Soviet Union thawed, the Prime Minister was in need of new enemies.

Fortunately for Mrs Thatcher, fresh challengers were soon forthcoming. The 1983 manifesto had promised to abolish the Greater London Council (GLC), along with other metropolitan councils. This was part of the campaign to reduce public spending, which also included proposals to cap the amount of money which local councils could raise through their rates. In the case of the GLC, at least, a potent motive was a desire to destroy a symbol of opposition to the government; Ken Livingstone, the charismatic leader of the ruling Labour Group, had described the Council as 'a bastion of power for the Labour movement', which could carry through socialist policies while the nation as a whole awaited the final Tory defeat (Baker, 1993, 99).

Despite Mrs Thatcher's claim that the government's policy enjoyed 'the generalised approval of the silent majority', the issue provoked serious party revolts in both the House of Commons and the Lords (Thatcher, 1993, 305). Heath, Gilmour and Pym, citing the importance of preserving local democracy, were prominent in these campaigns. This was not an issue for a government U-turn, however, and the GLC was replaced at the end of March 1986 by centrally-appointed quangos. By that time Mrs Thatcher had fought and defeated a more serious threat – the National Union of Mineworkers (NUM), led by the communist Arthur Scargill. The miners' strike, which lasted a year from March 1984, was called over planned pit closures. Whereas the 1981 miners' dispute had found the government unprepared, this time, in accordance with a plan laid down by Nicholas Ridley in opposition, coal stocks were plentiful and Scargill mistakenly called the strike in the spring, when demand was low (Young, 1990, 358–9, 368). The government had also created the framework for a nationally co-ordinated police force – a move which might have risked its popularity in other times. Scargill's fatal error, however, was to proceed without holding a ballot, giving the government a propaganda triumph and leaving the NUM open to prosecution. The NUM leader hoped that the dispute would lead to a repeat of 1974, and the fall of another Conservative government; for Mrs Thatcher, revenge for that humiliation was particularly sweet. Ironically, the Energy Secretary directly responsible for handling the strike was Edward Heath's old ally, Peter Walker.

These events might have left Mrs Thatcher safe from external foes for the moment, but there were still some 'enemies within' ready to challenge her authority. In the last months of 1985 her new Chancellor, Nigel Lawson, urged her to join the Exchange Rate Mechanism (ERM) of the European Monetary System (EMS). Having tacitly abandoned the attempt to find an appropriate measurement of money, Lawson had concluded that the exchange rate stability promised by membership of the ERM would have the same virtuous effect on inflation; it also tied the UK to the successful low-inflation West German economy. While this issue remained unresolved, Thatcher agreed to the Single European Act (SEA), which was to set up a European Single Market by January 1993, but at a cost of extending the use of qualified majority voting.

These developments would have significant long-term consequences for the Thatcher premiership. A more immediate problem, also connected to Europe, arrived when Michael Heseltine, now Secretary of State for Defence, resigned from the Cabinet on 9 January 1986. Through 1985 Heseltine had conducted an argument with the Secretary of State for Trade and Industry, Leon Brittan, about the fate of the ailing Westland company, Britain's only manufacturer of helicopters. Heseltine, a strong supporter of the Community, wanted a European consortium to take over the firm, while Brittan favoured a bid from the USA. At first the public bickering between the ministers gave the impression that Thatcher could not control her Cabinet; after Heseltine resigned, he claimed that Thatcher's control was too strong. Ideology played a part in the dispute, since Brittan was in broad sympathy with the Prime Minister while Heseltine had been regarded as a critic (though not exactly a wet) since advocating extra state help to depressed areas in the aftermath of the 1981 riots. The affair nearly brought about the downfall of Mrs Thatcher, who was widely suspected of having conspired against Heseltine. Instead, it was Leon Brittan who followed Heseltine out of the cabinet (Linklater and Leigh, 1986).

The European issue was an additional complication to the ideological debates in the UK during these years. Both major parties were divided, between determined advocates of closer union, people generally in favour but wary of developments, and the so-called 'Euro-sceptics', who were rarely very sceptical in practice and sought to take the UK out of the EC. The impression left by the 1975 referendum campaign might suggest that opposition to Europe was shared by Labour's socialists and the economic liberals associated with the Conservative Party; the most prominent advocates of withdrawal were Tony Benn and Enoch Powell (now, of course, the Ulster Unionist MP for South Down). The 'Yes' campaign, by contrast, was led by Edward Heath and Roy Jenkins. At that time Margaret Thatcher favoured continued membership, but over the years her position hardened. In office, she adopted a tough negotiating stance to reduce the UK's budgetary contributions, and her hostility to 'Brussels bureaucrats' became more apparent. On the basis of her speeches, notably the one delivered at Bruges on 20 September 1988, the Euro-sceptics who shared Thatcher's economic liberalism were certain that she also agreed with their view that the Community should never be more than a free-trade area (Thatcher, 1988).

The straightforward equation of socialist and Thatcherite = Euro-sceptic is an oversimplification, however. While economic liberals such as Sir Geoffrey Howe and Nigel Lawson could both see the virtue of greater European co-operation in some areas, Mrs Thatcher was suspicious of anything which implied that the Community was destined to become a federal union. Not only did European institutions develop over the years, but also as politicians took on different roles their views often changed. For example, after the Thatcherite Lord Cockfield was appointed to the European Commission in 1985 he became an enthusiast for deeper European economic integration, and Leon Brittan, who took a Commission post as compensation for acting as the Westland scapegoat, underwent a similar transformation. By contrast, the social democrat David Owen grew more sceptical during his tenure of the Foreign Office (Owen, 1992, 245–6). Attitudes to Europe often reflect ideological beliefs, but as in other policy areas ideology and personal experiences interact.

Mrs Thatcher's suspicion of Europe grew as she came to think that the UK's partners wished to impose 'socialist' laws on the British people. During the 1980s this was an eccentric fear; the only notable attempt to pursue a socialist policy in western Europe was made by the French President Mitterrand, but was abandoned in 1982 after only one year. However, Mrs Thatcher's definition of socialism could embrace a wide variety of ideas. Even so, it was strange that the Prime Minister denounced the intentions of European figures such as the President of the European Commission Jacques Delors, while simultaneously boasting that she had won the battle of ideas throughout the developed world. One of the most telling pieces of evidence for this claim was the extent to which other nations had adopted her most characteristic policy – privatisation.

From being a subsidiary element of the 1979 manifesto, the privatisation programme attained the status of a Thatcherite flagship after the 1983 election. The sales of British Gas and British Telecom were probably the most important, since they combined many attractive features for the party. Privatisation satisfied the ideological requirement that the government should withdraw from direct economic management. The revenue raised from the flotations provided useful funds, and by creating the opportunity for small investors to buy a stake in the companies the Conservatives could pose as the advocates of 'popular capitalism'. This chimed in with their existing successful policy of council house sales. The policy also brought the danger of simply replacing public with private monopolies, and the supply of suitable candidates for privatisation was limited. Yet the programme, nurtured by John Redwood in the Downing Street Policy Unit, undoubtedly helped to create the impression that the Conservative Party, rather than Labour, was the source of new thinking in the 1980s.

Mrs Thatcher's decision to call a general election for 11 June 1987 was not regarded as a great risk. The Conservative manifesto was designed to show that the party had not run out of ideas; it promised a cut in the basic rate of income tax to 25 per cent, further reforms of the trade unions, the introduction of a National Curriculum to raise education standards, and the replacement of rates with a 'fairer' Community Charge. As in 1983, the state of the opposition was a crucial factor in ensuring a third victory. Neil Kinnock's efforts to exert control over the Labour Party served only to redistribute the opposition vote; cracks were appearing in the SDP–Liberal Alliance, and Labour recovered sufficiently to secure a comfortable second place. There were some strange last-minute panics within the Conservative campaign, but the party's vote was almost unchanged, and their majority was 102 seats. This was more than adequate to carry the revolution even further.

Hubris, 1987–90

Mrs Thatcher was now the first twentieth-century Prime Minister to win three general elections in a row. All of her opponents, both domestic and foreign, were apparently humiliated. This even applied to the BBC, which wrongly forecast a Parliament with no overall majority. The Prime Minister seemed uncomfortable in the absence of foes, and on the day after the election she sacked her ideological soul-mate John Biffen, who had made the mistake of speculating on television about the virtues of a 'balanced ticket'. To outsiders, at least, Norman Tebbit's decision to leave the government was even more surprising, despite the serious injuries he had suffered in the IRA bomb attack on the Grand Hotel in Brighton during the 1984 Conservative Party Conference. As Andrew Gamble has remarked, Thatcher 'appeared to exhaust and then alienate even some of the colleagues closest to her' (Gamble, 1994, 129). In fact, although the careers of both Biffen and Tebbit had been advanced by Mrs Thatcher, they were suspect because they now enjoyed independent reputations. The Prime Minister did not want her own creations to become rivals. The fate of Tebbit in particular was a worrying precedent for future dealings with Nigel Lawson and Geoffrey Howe, who were proud men of independent stature, despite their devotion to Thatcherism.

After the 1987 election, the absence of dangerous enemies outside the Conservative Party meant that the government was able to focus on consolidating its revolution by re-designing the institutions of the welfare state. However, it was agreed that this could not be carried beyond certain limits. In 1981 the government's think-tank (the CPRS) had proposed the privatisation of the NHS; the outcry caused by the leak of this idea showed that it would lead to electoral disaster. Mrs Thatcher responded by abolishing the CPRS, although she had mixed feelings about its findings (Blackstone and Plowden, 1990, 179–90; Young, 1990, 300–1). The fate of this advisory body did not deter private free-market groups (including Mrs Thatcher's own joint creation, the CPS), from offering their thoughts on the subject of state-funded provision in all areas. Ministers hoping to impress the Prime Minister with their passion for reform had a full stock of ideas to sift through.

The process had begun during the previous Parliament, when Norman Fowler (assisted by John Major) pushed through some ambitious (and ill-fated) reforms of the pension system (Marr, 1995, 143–8). Privatisation was an important element of the overall strategy, and after the 1987 election this notably embraced the electricity and water industries, with the promise of more to come. As usual, critics claimed that these national assets were undervalued for sale to the private sector, but ministers ignored such allegations. Meanwhile, radical reforms of education and the NHS were being devised with some help from the think-tanks. The advertised theme of these reforms was the widening of choice, although they actually involved a strange mix of democracy and central dictation. In education, for example, Kenneth Baker allowed parents to vote on whether or not schools should remain under local authority control. Whatever the decision, however, individual schools were forced to take responsibility for their own budgets. A uniform national curriculum would be decided by the government's experts. The main targets of these reforms were clearly those favourite ogres of Conservative conferences – non-Thatcherite councils and 'trendy' teachers.

The NHS presented different challenges. While a fluctuating birth-rate meant that necessary education spending would vary in future, potential costs in the health service seemed to be unlimited. The new techniques available to prolong life cost more in themselves, and they would also produce an imbalance within the population. Elderly people were more likely to need medical care, and now there would be more of them. The government tried to meet this challenge by encouraging private health insurance, but this obviously was unavailable to low-paid and unemployed people. Its immediate solution was to retain the state-funded system, but to introduce changes which created an 'internal market'; hospitals would now compete against each other for patients, and, as in the case of schools, spending was decentralised. These measures were intended to increase efficiency, and it was hoped that bureaucracy would be reduced. However, the complexities of the system meant that the latter goal was always unrealistic; in addition, the government was criticised for appointing its own supporters to the boards of the new administrative trusts (thus adding to the scandal of quangos). The government's obsession with setting targets for services which could not be quantified did nothing to reduce bureaucracy, and doctors (like teachers) found themselves increasingly diverted from their main work by the need to fill in forms. Critics who claimed that these reforms were inspired by ideology rather than the needs of the health service had their task made much easier by the government's inadequate attempts to consult those affected. Even the presentational skills of Kenneth Clarke could not reassure the public on this matter; between 1983 and 1990, the percentage of those who were dissatisfied with the NHS almost doubled (Taylor-Gooby, 1991, 37).

The need for good presentation was a key theme of the third Thatcher government, particularly after Kenneth Baker was appointed chairman of the party in July 1989. Thatcherite assumptions about human nature decrees that votes are decided by economic factors; on this (mistaken) view, provided that a significant minority of people were content with their bank accounts and the opposition parties were divided, the government could afford to be careless in other respects. It would be helpful, nevertheless, if mishaps could be explained by a skilful communicator. In the USA, Ronald Reagan had shown that an affable public image could make voters overlook even dangerous economic indicators, like his record state budget deficit. This was just one respect in which UK politics (like the rest of life) was 'Americanised' during the Thatcher years. The Prime Minister herself seemed to act like a presidential head of state (although she was well advised not to copy Reagan's 'fireside chats' to the nation). Almost fifty years earlier the electoral successes of

Franklin D. Roosevelt had led desperate Republicans to limit the number of terms any individual could serve in the White House; if the economy stayed healthy, it looked as if Thatcher's opponents would have to start pressing for similar legislation in Britain.

In the 1987 election the Conservatives had benefited from a general feeling of economic well-being, at least among those who were in well-paid jobs. Despite the insecurity of a large section of the community, consumers took advantage of the deregulated credit markets to indulge in unprecedented borrowing. The most spectacular example of this took place in the housing sector; in spite of the additional supply created by council house sales, prices rose steeply, particularly in the south-east of England. The stock market crash of October 1987 did nothing to shake this 'feel-good factor'. Having allowed the money supply to rise prior to the 1987 election, the government now refused to tighten it. With inflation still low and unemployment finally beginning to fall, it seemed as if the austerity of the early 1980s could now be treated as just a bad memory. The Thatcherite 'economic miracle' might not have restored full health to manufacturing industry – and, ominously, North Sea oil would not last forever – but underlying economic realities were easily ignored by consumers at this time.

The buoyant mood reached its height with Nigel Lawson's 1988 Budget. The manifesto pledge to slash the basic rate of income tax to 25 per cent was honoured, and in the general euphoria it was scarcely noticed that, once again, the rich did far better with a top rate reduction to just 40 per cent. Inheritance and corporation taxes were also cut. The yearly effect of the Budget was to reduce taxation by over £6 billion. This Budget was the mirror image of Geoffrey Howe's measures in 1981. Despite having once been an enthusiastic Keynesian, Lawson took delight in contradicting his old master's theory by acting to increase demand when Britain already enjoyed boom conditions. With hindsight, Lawson claimed that 'it was a tight budget in overall terms', but this protestation was not widely believed (Lawson, 1993, 808). The 1988 Budget certainly cheered the government's supporters, but when the good times came to their inevitable end in a new recession the Chancellor had 'retired' to a lucrative City post. Those who had once welcomed his proposals now found him a convenient target for their frustrations, but he could still hit back with a remarkable 1,000-page volume of memoirs.

In response to the excessive demand, inflation began to rise again through 1989, to peak at over 10 per cent in 1990. The consumer boom also sucked in additional imports (UK manufacturing was scarcely in a position to respond), and as the balance of payments deteriorated the Chancellor raised interest rates to 15 per cent by October 1989 in order to protect sterling.

By this time Lawson had lost the confidence of the Prime Minister, who preferred to listen to her economic adviser Sir Alan Walters (a veteran free-market propagandist). In March 1989 Lawson and Thatcher had fallen out publicly over the Chancellor's policy of 'shadowing the Deutschmark'; by pegging the value of sterling to the German currency, Lawson hoped to gain the advantages of ERM membership without having to persuade Thatcher to actually join it. Thatcher, bolstered by Walters, thought that the pound should find its own level on the exchange markets. In late October Lawson decided that he would no longer tolerate the role of Walters; he told the Prime Minister that unless she sacked her economic adviser he would resign. In the end, both of them went (Lawson, 1993, 960–8; Thatcher, 1993, 715–17).

This incident marked the beginning of the end for Mrs Thatcher. Lawson was not the most clubbable of politicians, but his intellectual strength was widely recognised, even among those who disagreed with his philosophy and loathed the 1988 Budget. Furthermore, his departure occurred soon after another major Cabinet upheaval, when Geoffrey Howe was moved from the Foreign Office to the post of Deputy Prime Minister, recently vacated by Lord Whitelaw. Briefings from the Prime Minister's Press Secretary, Bernard Ingham, indicated that this was a meaningless title (Harris, 1990, 174–5). In combination, the joint resentment of Howe and Lawson would be irresistible, but for the moment Howe stayed in his new office.

With Lawson's resignation, the inexperienced John Major found himself shuffled from the Foreign Office, where he had replaced Howe, to the Treasury. In turn, Douglas Hurd moved from the Home Office to become Foreign Secretary, a job which eminently suited his skills. By September 1990 Hurd and Major had convinced Thatcher that the UK must join the ERM; by this time, Britain's economy was weak, and Lawson's high interest rate policy meant that sterling was over-priced when it entered the mechanism. This humiliation for the Prime Minister closely followed the loss of her loyal follower Nicholas Ridley, who was forced to resign as Secretary of State for Trade and Industry because of some injudicious remarks about Germany. Despite three election victories, Mrs Thatcher was now becoming isolated within the Cabinet; those who sympathised enough to give constructive advice now tended to owe the Prime Minister too much to tell her distasteful truths. William Waldegrave and Kenneth Baker, once seen as allies of the wets, played significant roles in promoting that most Thatcherite of policies, the Community Charge; later the tax was defended by Christopher Patten. In 1983 Patten had risked his career prospects by writing an elegant attack on Thatcherism, *The Tory Case*; the Prime Minister might have calculated that his dissenting days were over, but his promotion still shows that she was running out of die-hard ideological supporters who were fit for promotion (Patten, 1983).

Towards the end of Mrs Thatcher's regime events quickly gathered momentum. Once sixty MPs had refused to support Mrs Thatcher in a leadership challenge from the pro-European Sir Anthony Meyer in November 1989, the Prime Minister looked vulnerable to attack from a more prominent opponent; Michael Heseltine was well prepared for the right moment. Norman Fowler, the Employment Secretary, decided that he would like to spend more time with his family and resigned in January 1990. Peter Walker chose to end his high-spending stint as Welsh Secretary two months later. On the surface, this seemed like delicious timing by someone who had never become even a 'career Thatcherite', but Walker had made his decision some time earlier, and unlike Fowler he stuck to it.

The furore over the Community Charge, or Poll Tax, was a further weakening blow to the Prime Minister. The replacement of domestic rates with a flat-rate charge was prepared in haste and implemented without proper consideration (Butler et al., 1994). Just after the Conservatives lost the mid-Staffordshire by-election at the end of March, 1990, a demonstration against the tax in Trafalgar Square turned into a riot. Attempts to explain the violence as an example of 'hooliganism' had less effect than usual, since the tax was clearly regressive and marked a further redistribution of wealth away from the poor. In the wake of the 1988 Budget another bonanza for the rich proved impossible to justify. On 21 October 1990 the Conservatives lost another by-election at Eastbourne; this was particularly telling, because a government victory might have been expected in a contest which occurred only because the IRA had murdered Ian Gow, formerly Mrs Thatcher's Parliamentary Private Secretary.

Economic troubles and the Poll Tax formed the essential background to Mrs Thatcher's fall, although this was ultimately precipitated by the European issue. Senior figures within the party were dismayed when Mrs Thatcher returned from the Rome Inter-Governmental Conference of October 1990 with a message of defiance against Jacques Delors and other supporters of 'Ever Closer Union' (Thatcher, 1990). The argument that closer economic co-operation with Europe would actually secure the triumph of economic liberalism – an argument believed by both socialist Euro-sceptics and Thatcherites like Howe and Lawson – could not convince Mrs Thatcher. If there was a choice between national sovereignty and full integration within a free-trade, monetarist Europe, Thatcher would side with the nation; at least that way she could be sure of being able to control politics at home. Realising this after the meeting in Rome,

Howe finally lost patience. His ensuing speech in the House of Commons, when he spoke of his agonising 'conflict of loyalties', provided Michael Heseltine with the necessary justification for contesting the leadership of the party (Howe, 1990). Among many ironies, Thatcher's fall took place just one year after she had felt able to tell the Lord Mayor's Banquet that the recent collapse of communism represented conclusive victory in the battle of ideas to which she had dedicated herself since 1975 (Young, 1990, 561).

The legacy of the Thatcher project will take years to work out. From the outset, commentators were divided. Some regarded Mrs Thatcher as perhaps the only wholehearted ideologue ever to become Prime Minister, yet there were some who denied that her policies were inspired by ideology at all (Riddell, 1983, 1–20; Holmes, 1985a, 51). Often (but not always) this view was held by admirers who felt that she had not gone far enough. In some cases the argument depended upon the notion that Thatcher's ideas arose from 'instincts', as if this somehow prevented them from being classified as ideological. Mrs Thatcher herself was not a great student of political theory; in the words of one personal admirer, 'her feminine mind is seldom diverted by profitless essays into abstract thought' (Wyatt, 1985, 343). However, she had read her Hayek and she continued to listen to liberal think-tanks (the IEA and CPS had been joined by the Adam Smith Institute (ASI) in 1978) (Denham, 1996). Contrary to Wyatt's account, Thatcher's homespun metaphors barely disguised a very abstract mind; unlike political intellectuals, however, she was eager to grasp solutions instead of wrestling with difficulties. Others, more fruitfully, have concentrated upon Thatcher's 'statecraft', but in the end this is difficult to separate from her ideas (Bulpitt, 1986, 19–39). Critiques which play down the importance of ideas to Mrs Thatcher are based on a misinterpretation of British politics – or indeed of most political systems. Political survival is rarely possible without an element of compromise, or an acknowledgement of the power of circumstance and existing institutions. Lenin was hardly a believer in consensus, but he was forced to tolerate capitalism in the short term. The fact that Mrs Thatcher had to curb her 'instincts' at times tells us more about the British system of government than it does about her.

Commentators also disagree about the extent to which Mrs Thatcher was able to reshape ideas of what was politically possible in Britain. Socialists are quite ready to emphasise her success in this respect, possibly because they share her impatience with the framework of post-war politics. In fact, Thatcherite ideas thrived in the vacuum left by the decline of the best-known alternatives. The apparent failure of other approaches was exaggerated because the feeling that Britain was a formidable world power lingered long after it had become outdated. When the performance of the economy was compared with what people assumed that it should be, post-war politics fell into disrepute. In particular, the relative prosperity of Germany was a source of disquiet. Mrs Thatcher's greatest achievement was to talk as if Britain could be made great again while her policies were undermining the basis of that greatness – manufacturing industry. This rhetoric could be regarded as the indulgence of a harmless dream if the human cost had been smaller. Throughout the post-war period policy-makers knew that certain crucial economic indicators could be improved if unemployment were allowed to rise; sometimes this alternative might have been resisted for electoral reasons, but the ethos of the Beveridge report demanded that it should be rejected on principle. The possibility of re-election amidst mass unemployment had already dawned on the Labour Party in the years up to 1979 – Joel Barnett, for instance, could not recall 'a single letter' on the subject – but unlike Mrs Thatcher ministers had mixed feelings about the discovery (Holmes, 1985b, 114). Mrs Thatcher provided conclusive proof that unemployment could be survived – at least by governments. Yet even this would be a short-lived triumph unless the Prime Minister could make voters believe that it was morally tolerable.

For all Mrs Thatcher's talk of a battle of ideas, the record of her government in this respect is doubtful. Among elite opinion, it is significant that most prominent 'conversions' to Thatcherism took place before the 1979 election (Cormack, 1978). The born-again enthusiasm of former Labour supporters such as Woodrow Wyatt and Paul Johnson could not entirely compensate for their lack of numbers. The general failure of Thatcherism to impress the academic community was demonstrated by Oxford University's refusal to award her an honorary degree; in the 1987 general election, the Conservatives won a greater degree of support from unemployed people than they did from academics (Willetts, 1992, 21). Outside the opinion-formers the record looks no better. In November 1987, 87 per cent of respondents refused to accept that unemployed people were responsible for their own plight. Ivor Crewe has also shown that while tax cuts and better public services were equally desired in 1979, within months of exposure to Thatcherite rule the majority for better public services was 22 per cent; by October 1987 it stood at 55 per cent (Crewe, 1989, 244–6). This impression of increasing discontent with Thatcherite priorities might be discounted as the product of 'bourgeois guilt', and the evidence of actual voting can be cited against it, but it is significant that so many people felt ashamed to agree with the Prime Minister.

The nature of Thatcherism

Mrs Thatcher's ideas might not have convinced people in the way she would have hoped, but they were certainly discussed very widely. Some of her supporters were very happy to see her as a representative of the liberal tradition of Herbert Spencer. For others, however, it was important to argue that she was a sound conservative who simply had to make radical changes because of Britain's critical position; as Thatcher had said, there really was 'no alternative' (Willetts, 1992; Lawson, 1993, 1039–54; Tebbit, 1985). On this argument, conservatism had been betrayed by post-war governments, not by Mrs Thatcher. A more subtle analysis, based mainly on the work of Professor Andrew Gamble, could portray Thatcherism as a strange hybrid of economic liberalism ('The Free Economy') and social conservatism ('The Strong State') (Gamble, 1994). This approach had been heralded at the start of her first premiership in a *Daily Telegraph* leading article, which applauded her mix of 'old-fashioned' liberalism with 'conservatism, patriotism, thrift and hard work'.

An essential element of the first argument is the often-repeated claim that Thatcherites, like conservatives, 'work with the grain of human nature', while their collectivist opponents try to make people different. Yet this interpretation of human nature turns out to be the nineteenth-century liberal one – competitive, impatient of restraint, motivated primarily by self-interest. Above all, it is an *individualistic* vision (Kingdom, 1992). According to Mrs Thatcher, British people were different from their European neighbours because of their 'great sense of individuality and initiative' (Thatcher, 1992). Her remark in a famous *Woman's Own* interview that 'There's no such thing as society' is often quoted out of context, but this form of words would never have occurred to a conservative (Rentoul, 1989, 17–20). For conservatives, society is a complex web of interactions without which civilised existence is impossible. Angus Maude's claim that 'Man is a rational being, capable of making and acting upon rational decisions' is also anathema to conservatives; as a political guide, it points towards anarchy rather than the strong state which conservatives see as a permanent (if unfortunate) necessity (Maude, 1969, 98). Indeed, some of the most enthusiastic 'libertarian' supporters of the government (notably those within the ill-fated Federation of Conservative Students) urged that the state should disappear completely.

Did Mrs Thatcher act on this guidance? Clearly not, if one considers the extra resources allotted to the forces of law and order, and the regular passage of legislation to restrict civil liberties. Stuart Hall and Andrew Gamble have branded Mrs Thatcher as an 'Authoritarian Populist', who exploited common fears of a moral and social breakdown in order to enhance the authority of the state (Hall, 1980; Gamble, 1994, 178–84). The writers associated with the *Salisbury Review*, who believed that morality was more important than economics, allowed their distaste for economic liberalism to be overcome by Mrs Thatcher's moral stance. Roger Scruton, editor of the *Salisbury Review*, joined the Conservative Philosophy Group even though he later correctly identified liberalism 'as the principal enemy of conservatism' (Scruton, 1980, 16). Other social conservatives reacted in a similar fashion (Cowling, 1978). The moral campaigner Mary Whitehouse, for example, related how her 'heart rejoiced' when the Conservative Party won in 1979 (Durham, 1989, 185). Mrs Thatcher could draw on the advice of experts in family policy, such as Ferdinand Mount and David Willetts. Yet all the developments which worried social conservatives continued during the 1980s, and some trends actually accelerated. Between 1979 and 1987, the percentage of births inside marriage declined from 87 to 75 per cent (Letwin, 1992, 94). Divorce and crime rates also rose sharply, and remained a concern mid-way through the second decade of Conservative rule (Riddell, 1991, 169; Greaves and Crosbie, 1995).

In fact, it can be argued that for all her talk of 'Victorian Values', Mrs Thatcher pleased social conservatives only in so far as she provided them with more to complain about. For all their initial hopes, campaigners such as Whitehouse found that the government was much happier meeting their demands with rhetoric than with legislative assistance. Much of the 1980s legislation with a moral content arose from back-bench action, and on issues such as Sunday trading and divorce laws the government actually seemed to be working against the priorities of the social conservatives (Durham, 1991). In part, the government's attitude stemmed from the Thatcherite view of human nature; Rhodes Boyson, for example, thought that 'possibly 80 or 90 per cent of my fellow countrymen and women' already shared the party's moral outlook, the implication being that this 'silent majority' would reassert themselves once the nightmare of collectivist politics was ended (Boyson, 1978, 8). This view was later echoed by Shirley Letwin, who acknowledged that direct government action would not have been an appropriate means of stimulating a moral revival (Letwin, 1992, 41). Yet the urgency of the problem diagnosed by Thatcherites implied that the talking needed to be backed up by concerted action; after all, Edmund Burke had warned that 'Manners are of more importance than laws. Upon them, in a great measure, the laws depend' (Himmelfarb, 1987, 15).

Supporters of Thatcherism will hotly deny that government policies actually increased the problems of social order, but many commentators thought that they did. Notably, the Church of England issued a report in late 1985 (*Faith in the City*), which advocated measures to tackle unemployment and to increase welfare payments. These views were promptly denounced by government spokespersons, who argued that social malaise was the product of evil (and the 1960s) rather than the effects of Thatcherite policies. Norman Tebbit, for example, blamed 'the valueless values of the Permissive Society'; the rise in crime could have nothing to do with unemployment, because there had been no similar trend in the 1930s (Tebbit, 1985, 15, 14). This response neatly illustrates the difference between Thatcherism and conservatism; conservatives agree that evil is inherent in everyone, but the conclusion they draw is that, as far as possible, social conditions should be improved to reduce the temptation for crime. While Thatcherites claim that poverty is absolute, not relative, conservatives accept that when the majority of the population enjoy unprecedented living standards, those who are excluded from these benefits will suffer from feelings of deprivation even if they have enough to scrape a bare existence. In answer to Tebbit, observers could point out that the governments of the 1930s did not celebrate greed – at least in public. Some mischievious commentators thought that Thatcherism itself was a product of the individualism of the 1960s – a fertile suggestion which has not been adequately investigated (Jenkins, 1988, 66–77).

In the absence of legislation based on distinctive conservative social philosophy, it is only possible to conclude that the strong Thatcherite state was designed to protect those who benefited from the liberal revolution. The strong state was an *essential feature* of Mrs Thatcher's liberalism, not an addition to it. After all, the government believed that it had to combat the attitudes which had prevailed since the war; prosperity for all would not happen immediately, and in the intervening years they could expect a high level of protest only from those who had been indoctrinated by the dependency culture. Eventually, as the good sense of the British people revived, the emphasis on law and order could be toned down. In the mean time, hard-line rhetoric at the party conference would serve a useful electoral purpose. This picture is quite different from the genuine idealism which fuelled Thatcherism before 1979. Instead of resorting to a conspiracy theory, in which this idealism is seen as a camouflage for purely material interests, one must remember that Thatcherism was adopted as an 'oppositional' creed; its aims were always self-contradictory, and in some ways it was unfortunate for economic liberals that these weaknesses were exposed through the cruel test of practice.

Another aspect of Mrs Thatcher's creed which demands explanation is her nationalism. In at least one respect this was in keeping with the rest of her thinking, because it was unusually abstract. Thatcherites could claim that it merely followed the conservative tradition of Disraeli, but this was a mistake; Disraeli, after all, had coupled his patriotic rhetoric with a belief that Britain was 'One Nation', in which the state should act to ensure something like equal consideration for rich and poor. Even in the geographical sense, Thatcherism was not a One Nation movement. Little was done to correct the imbalance of prosperity between north and south, and the gap between the rich and the poorest widened considerably. 'Britain', for Mrs Thatcher, was synonymous with those individuals who shared her priorities. As such, her loyalty to what she conceived to be its interests was not very surprising.

Towards the end of her premiership Mrs Thatcher's nationalism was often associated with her opposition to closer European unity. Her assertion that British people did not want to be ruled from Brussels coincided with a popular feeling, even if it did rest on a gross distortion of EC decision-making. Behind this lurked concern that the developing EC threatened at least to modify Thatcherite policies. As the Prime Minister declared in her Bruges speech, 'We have not successfully rolled back the frontiers of the state in Britain, only to see them reimposed at a European level' (Thatcher, 1988, 48). Mrs Thatcher might disagree with senior colleagues about the potency of this threat, but in this instance at least it would be wrong to say that her nationalism overrode her belief in the free market. Instead, the two concerns suggested identical policies to her, while other economic liberals who looked more deeply into the issues faced agonising choices.

Conclusion

The immediate legacy of the Thatcher years was deeply ambiguous. Events in Eastern Europe in 1989 and 1990 suggested that the battle of ideas had been won on an international scale. The economic liberalism of Reagan and Thatcher, together with the military technology which supported it, had apparently exposed the economic and intellectual bankruptcy of the Soviet Union. In the rest of Europe the signals were similar; any socialist aspirations of François Mitterrand in France and Spain's Felipe Gonzalez had been abandoned, and these governments were now accepting Thatcherite policies such as privatisation. At home, the Labour Party was looking to Scandinavian social democratic models in its search for an election-winning formula. Mrs Thatcher's fall almost coincided with the disbandment of the British Communist Party, and the closure of the magazine *Marxism Today* (which had correctly predicted her fate in 1989)

(Hobsbawm, 1989). The dangers of 'loony left' councils still had to be exaggerated for electoral reasons, but a sober assessment showed that the movement associated with Tony Benn was unlikely to recover, at least for many years.

In some respects, however, this deluge of good news for Thatcherites was dangerous for them. The feeling that there really was 'no alternative' was bound to induce complacency, and the tendency for leading ministers to indulge in damaging quarrels increased after the 1987 general election. Also, Thatcherism thrived best when it was confronted by enemies, and Mrs Thatcher's style was particularly suited to situations when she was apparently battling against the odds (Denham and Garnett, 1994). After the collapse of communism potent enemies were suddenly scarce. This allowed attention to focus on the actual achievements of Thatcherism, especially around the tenth anniversary of her first electoral victory. Here the record was open to serious question. Reforms in the welfare state were unpopular, and even their sponsoring ministers were forced to tinker with them. If a real economic miracle had occurred, the hardships of the early 1980s would now seem insignificant. Yet the approach of a new recession just at this time revealed that Thatcherite success in this sphere had been superficial at best. Even the much-trumpeted tax cuts were a mirage; the share of national product taken by the state remained relatively constant, and even the richest 5 per cent of the population paid more of their income to the Inland Revenue in 1991 than they had done in 1979 (Norton, 1994). Statistics told only half of the relevant story; with the collapse of communism in Europe attention began to focus on the conduct of governing parties, and scandals broke throughout the capitalist world, in France, Italy and also in Japan. Margaret Thatcher left office before this mood struck the UK, but when it did commentators could reflect that corruption had been encouraged partly by the longeivity of the government, but also by the philosophy of Thatcherism itself.

When all the evidence is examined in context, it is possible to explain Thatcherism only as a reassertion of nineteenth-century liberalism. This was a radical change from post-war politics; although the advocates of economic liberalism were never silent, their impact on policy-making at any time until 1976 had been limited. Mrs Thatcher's commitment to these ideas cannot be disputed. She was capable of being pragmatic (particularly in foreign affairs), but her failure to enact a thorough-going liberal programme proves only how resistant the British system is to revolutionary change. Even so, her impact was enormous and lasting. The contrast between Thatcherism and earlier policies has seduced commentators into thinking that it was different because it was ideological; in fact, it was just a different ideology, upheld with unusual determination. Part of its power came from the fact that it took opponents by surprise; these ideas, after all, had seemed to be politically dead for almost a century. Even though Mrs Thatcher was drummed out of office amid signs that her ideology was vulnerable to criticism both in theory and practice, her critics would still be hard-pressed to convince the electorate that their principles were more likely to succeed.

List of works cited

Baker, Kenneth (1993), *The Turbulent Years: My Life in Politics*, Faber and Faber

Beenstock, Michael, et al. (1982), *Could do Better: Contrasting Assessments of the Economic Progress and Prospects of the Thatcher Government at Mid-Term*, Institute of Economic Affairs

Blackstone, Tessa, and Plowden, William (1990) *Inside the Think Tank: Advising the Cabinet 1971–1983*, Mandarin

Boyson, Rhodes (1978), *Centre Forward: A Radical Conservative Programme*, Temple Smith

Bulpitt, Jim (1986), 'The Discipline of the New Democracy: Mrs Thatcher's Domestic Statecraft', *Political Studies*, volume 34, 19–39

Butler, David, Adams, Andrew, and Travers, Tony (1994) *Failure in British Government: The Politics of the Poll Tax*, Oxford University Press

Conservative Research Department (1983), *Four Years Work: A Summary of the Achievements of the Conservative Government since May 1979*, Conservative Central Office

Cormack, Peter (1978), *Right Turn: Eight Men who Changed their Minds*, Leo Cooper

Cowling, Maurice (ed.) (1978), *Conservative Essays*, Cassell

Crewe, Ivor (1989), 'Values: The Crusade that Failed', in Dennis Kavanagh and Anthony Seldon (eds) *The Thatcher Effect: A Decade of Change*, Oxford University Press

Denham, Andrew (1996), *Enthusiastic Amateurs: Think-Tanks in Britain*, University College London Press

Denham, Andrew, and Garnett, Mark (1994), ' "Conflicts of Loyalty": Cohesion and Division in Conservatism, 1975–1990', in Patrick Dunleavy and Jeffrey Stanyer (eds) *Contemporary Political Studies 1994*, volume I, Political Studies Association

Durham, Martin (1989), 'The Thatcher Government and the Moral Right', *Parliamentary Affairs*, volume 42, number 1

Durham, Martin (1991), *Moral Crusades: Family and Morality in the Thatcher Years*, New York University Press

Gamble, Andrew (1994), *The Free Economy and the Strong State*, Macmillan, 2nd edition

Gilmour, Ian (1992), *Dancing with Dogma; Britiain under Thatcherism*, Simon and Schuster

Greaves, Gerard, and Crosbie, Paul (1995), 'End of Family Life in Britain', *Daily Express*, 23 August

Hall, Stuart (1980), 'Popular Democratic versus Authoritarian Populism', in A. Hunt (ed.), *Marxism and Democracy*, Lawrence and Wishart

Harris, Robert (1990), *Good and Faithful Servant: The Unauthorized Biography of Bernard Ingham*, Faber and Faber

Himmelfarb, Gertrude (1987), *Victorian Values and Twentieth-Century Conservatism*, Centre for Policy Studies

Hobsbawm, Eric (1989), 'Another Forward March Halted', *Marxism Today*, October.

Holmes, Martin (1985a), *The First Thatcher Government 1979–1983: Contemporary Conservatism and Economic Change*, Wheatsheaf

Holmes, Martin (1985b), *The Labour Government, 1974–79: Political Aims and Economic Reality*, Macmillan

Howe, Geoffrey (1990), Resignation Statement, 13 November 1990, *Parliamentary Debates*, volume 180, 461–5

Jenkins, Peter (1988), *Mrs Thatcher's Revolution: The Ending of the Socialist Era*, Pan

Kingdom, John (1992), *No Such Thing As Society? Individualism and Community*, Open University Press

Lawson, Nigel (1993), *The View from No. 11: Memoirs of a Tory Radical*, Corgi

Letwin, Shirley (1992), *The Anatomy of Thatcherism*, Fontana

Linklater, Magnus, and Leigh, David (1986), *Not with Honour: The Inside Story of the Westland Scandal*, Sphere

Marr, Andrew (1995), *Ruling Britannia: The Failure and Future of British Democracy*, Michael Joseph

Maude, Angus (1969), *The Common Problem: A Policy for the Future*, Constable

Norton, Philip (1994), *The British Polity*, Longman, 3rd edition

Owen, David (1992), *Time to Declare*, Penguin

Patten, Chris (1983), *The Tory Case*, Longman

Pym, Francis (1985), *The Politics of Consent*, Sphere, 2nd edition

Rentoul, John (1989), *Me and Mine: The Triumph of the New Individualism?*, Unwin Hyman

Riddell, Peter (1983), *The Thatcher Government*, Martin Robertson

Riddell, Peter (1991), *The Thatcher Era and its Legacy*, Blackwell

Scruton, Roger (1980), *The Meaning of Conservatism*, Penguin

Smith, David (1987), *The Rise and Fall of Monetarism: The Theory and Politics of an Economic Experiment*, Penguin

Taylor-Gooby, Peter (1991), 'Attachment to the Welfare State', in Roger Jowell, Lindsay Brook and Bridget Taylor (eds) *British Social Attitudes: The 8th Report*, Dartmouth

Tebbit, Norman (1985), Disraeli Lecture, 13 November, Conservative Party News Service

Tebbit, Norman (1989) *Upwardly Mobile*, Futura

Thatcher, Margaret (1988), 'A Family of Nations' (speech at Bruges), in Brent Nelson and Alexander Stubb (eds) (1994) *The European Union: Readings on the Theory and Practice of European Integration*, Macmillan

Thatcher, Margaret (1990), Statement on Rome European Council, 30 October 1990, *Parliamentary Debates*, volume 178, 869–88

Thatcher, Margaret (1992), 'Don't Undo What I Have Done', *Guardian*, 22 April
Thatcher, Margaret (1993), *The Downing Street Years*, HarperCollins.
Whitehead, Philip (1985), *The Writing on the Wall: Britain in the Seventies*, Michael Joseph
Willetts, David (1992), *Modern Conservatism*, Penguin
Wyatt, Woodrow (1985), *Confessions of an Optimist*, Collins
Wybrow, Robert (1989), *Britain Speaks Out, 1937–87: A Social History as Seen through the Gallup Data*, Macmillan
Young, Hugo (1990), One of Us: A Biography of Margaret Thatcher, Pan, 2nd edition

Questions for discussion

- Was Thatcherism anything more than a return to nineteenth-century liberalism?
- Explain the record of the Thatcher governments on moral issues.

Selected further reading

Adonis, Andrew, and Hames, Tim (eds) (1994), *A Conservative Revolution? The Thatcher–Reagan Decade in Perspective*, Manchester University Press.
Brittan, Samuel (1982), 'The Politics and Economics of Privatization', *Political Quarterly*, volume 55, number 2.
Bruce-Gardyne, Jock (1984), *Mrs Thatcher's First Administration: The Prophets Confounded*, Macmillan.
Bull, David, and Wilding, Paul (1983), *Thatcherism and the Poor*, Child Poverty Action Group.
Burke, Edmund (1968), *Reflections on the Revolution in France*, Penguin.
Crick, Michael, and Van Klaveren, Adrian (1991), 'Mrs Thatcher's Greatest Blunder', *Contemporary Record*, volume 5, number 3.
Durham, Martin (1989), 'The Right: The Conservative Party and Conservatism', in Leonard Tivey and Anthony Wright (eds) *Party Ideology in Britain*, Routledge.
Gilmour, Ian (1983), *Britain Can Work*, Martin Robertson.
Gilmour, Ian (1994), 'The Thatcher Memoirs', *Twentieth Century British History*, volume 5 number 2.
Griffiths, Brian (1983), *The Moral Basis of the Market Economy*, Conservative Political Centre.
Hall, Stuart, and Jacques, Martin (ed.) (1983), *The Politics of Thatcherism*, Lawrence and Wishart.
Hennessy, Peter (1990), *Whitehall*, Fontana.
Heseltine, Michael (1987), *Where There's A Will*, Hutchinson.
Holliday, Ian (1992), *The NHS Transformed: A Guide to the Health Reforms*, Baseline.

Hoover, Kenneth, and Plant, Raymond (1988), *Conservative Capitalism in Britain and the United States*, Routledge.

Johnson, Christopher (1991), *The Economy under Mrs Thatcher 1979–1990*, Penguin.

Kavanagh, Dennis (1987), *Thatcherism and British Politics: The End of Consensus?*, Oxford University Press.

Keegan, William (1984), *Mrs Thatcher's Economic Experiment*, Allen Lane.

Levitas, Ruth (ed.) (1986), *The Ideology of the New Right*, Polity.

Minogue, Kenneth, and Biddis, Michael (eds) (1987), *Thatcherism: Personality and Politics*, Macmillan.

Prior, James (1986), *A Balance of Power*, Hamish Hamilton.

Skidelsky, Robert (ed.) (1988), *Thatcherism*, Chatto and Windus.

Stephenson, Hugh (1980), *Mrs Thatcher's First Year*, Jill Norman.

Stockman, David (1986), *The Triumph of Politics*, Bodley Head.

Utley, T. E. (1980), *Capitalism: The Moral Case*, Conservative Research Department.

Walters, Alan (1986), *Britain's Economic Renaissance: Mrs Thatcher's Reforms 1979–84*, Oxford University Press.

CHAPTER 5

Socialism or social democracy? The Labour Party, 1979–92

Settling scores, 1979–83

The responsibilities of office normally act as a powerful force for unity in British political parties. Dissent within the Conservative Party was not stifled completely by Margaret Thatcher's general election victory of 1979, but it would have been much louder if the Conservatives had lost. After the election Labour did not enjoy this protection. It had the additional handicap of a generally hostile press, ready to publicise any signs of internal bickering. If there had been no rows to exaggerate, they would have been invented. As it turned out, the Conservatives' friends in Fleet Street had no need to be creative, at least until Neil Kinnock began to assert his authority over the Labour Party between 1983 and 1987.

Labour's position after the 1979 election could hardly have been worse. The record of the 1974–79 governments acted as a stimulant to existing ideological difficulties. A major reason for Labour's wins in 1974 had been the perception that the party could deal with the unions better than their opponents. Yet in 1979 trade union members split their votes almost equally between Labour and the Conservatives. According to moderates within the party, the unions were blamed even by their own members for the disruptions of the Winter of Discontent; on this reading, the buck was passed to Labour in the election because of its close links with the unions (Healey, 1990, 467–8). By contrast, socialists were convinced that Labour had lost because it had let its supporters down. In office it had betrayed the socialist programme of 1974, and the 1979 manifesto had dumped the radical pledges demanded by Labour Party conferences. These diagnoses of defeat pointed to rival remedies which could not be reconciled by even the most skilful party managers.

Labour's performance in government did nothing to reverse the additional problem of declining party membership. Against a published figure of 675,000, it has been estimated that the real number of individual members in 1978 was about 250,000 (Whiteley, 1983, 55). Even Labour was prepared to admit that it was losing members at the rate of 11,000 per year. Ominously for the future, the swing from Labour to Conservative in 1979 was greater among first-time voters than for the electorate as a whole. A diminishing membership would affect finance and morale; it was also likely that those who continued to persevere with the party would be unrepresentative of the average voter. As Labour's factions prepared for a conclusive struggle, the prize for victory was becoming increasingly undesirable.

Since the socialists within the Labour Party had effectively been in opposition during the government's last years, they were well organised for battle by 1979. At the conference held at Brighton in the wake of defeat the CLPD gained the first of its constitutional goals, the mandatory reselection of MPs. Constituency parties already had the right to deselect sitting MPs, but the procedure was now greatly simplified. Outwardly this move could be justified as a measure to promote democracy within the party, but it still meant that even popular MPs could lose their seats if they displeased the most active members of their constituency parties. At a time of low morale and dwindling membership, a relatively small number of determined people throughout the country might now be able to control the votes of the entire Parliamentary Labour Party (PLP). The decision on reselection was referred to a Commission of Enquiry which met in June 1980. In the mean time, Tony Benn's ally Chris Mullin published a pamphlet entitled 'How to Select or Re-select your MP' to help the hesitant.

The Commission agreed to reselection, but it had other constitutional matters to consider. The 1979 conference had decided that in future the manifesto should be under the control of the party's National Executive Committee (NEC); although a proposal to change the method of electing the party leader had been defeated at the conference, the question was revived by the Commission. It suggested that an electoral college should be set up, which should also have the final say over the content of the manifesto. Half of the votes in this college would go to the PLP, 25 per cent to the trade unions, 20 per cent to the constituency parties and 5 per cent to affiliated groups such as the Fabian Society. The 1980 party conference agreed with the idea of an electoral college in principle, although it left the details undecided; the proposal to give the college control over the manifesto was defeated.

By this time the various organisations pressing for change had entered into an alliance, known as the Rank and File Mobilising Committee (RFMC). This embraced ten groups including the CLPD, the LCC, the Socialist Campaign for Labour Victory (SCLV) and the 'Tendency' associated with the Trotskyite newspaper *Militant*. These groups had a wide variety of aims, and some hated each other more than the Conservatives. The Militant

Tendency, for example, thought of most fellow-Trotskyites as 'human rubbish' (Crick, 1986, 91). Despite these unfraternal sentiments, the groups established a temporary tactical unity for this battle. They were strong in many constituencies, and enjoyed prominent support within the PLP from Tony Benn, Eric Heffer and others. In his book *Arguments for Socialism*, Benn added another element to the consitutional debate by suggesting that the PLP should decide the membership of Cabinet when Labour was in power, thus further reducing the patronage of a future Labour Prime Minister (Benn, 1980, 172).

Despite Benn's opposition to the personalisation of politics, his prominence in the debate made the media focus on individuals inevitable. On the first day of the 1980 conference he advocated the immediate abolition of the House of Lords, a significant extension of public ownership and withdrawal from the EC without a referendum (Jefferys, 1993, 109). It seemed inevitable that when James Callaghan decided to give up the party leadership Benn would be his successor. This prospect caused great alarm among social democrats and even some Tribunites. Benn's personal commitment to democracy (and the traditions of Parliament in particular) cannot be questioned; if anything, over the years his libertarian beliefs had strengthened. However, in his dispute with what he regarded as an authoritarian leadership he had aligned himself with less fervent democrats. The Militant Tendency, in particular, was an unusual recruit to the cause; according to one very hostile observer, this revolutionary body threatened 'parliamentary democracy and society' (Baker, 1981, 31). Even a more scholarly study claimed that Militant 'is completely intolerant of those who dare to disagree' with its aims (Callaghan, 1987, 199). This was not the only issue that divided Benn from Militant. In the 1970s Benn had advocated the nationalisation of twenty-five major companies, but Militant demanded two hundred (with token compensation for previous owners).

With a special conference to finally settle the question of an electoral college due in January 1981, Callaghan resigned in order to ensure that the next leader would be elected under the old rules, which gave the choice to the PLP alone. Benn consulted his advisers, who thought that he should not stand under a system which had no moral authority in their eyes (Adams, 1993, 407–8). The former Chancellor Denis Healey was Callaghan's own choice for the succession, but his abrasive manner alienated some of the party's social democrats, who believed that he was taking their support for granted. In the end, Michael Foot emerged as the candidate who could best unite the party, and Healey was narrowly defeated on the second ballot. This result brought closer the defection of the social democratic 'Gang of Three'

(David Owen, William Rodgers and Shirley Williams); although Foot was regarded with personal affection by almost all of the party, the Gang believed that his socialist sympathies would make him unlikely to oppose the mood of radical change. In fact, the circumstances of 1980 meant that Foot's ideas were closer to the social democrats than to Benn; he was wholly committed to the ideals of socialism, but warned against any 'new rigidities of doctrine' which might prove even more destructive than capitalism (Foot, 1983, 14). This position, often labelled as 'soft left', represented the closest thing to a viable compromise within the party; unhappily for Foot, Labour was so polarised that even he was forced to take sides against Benn and his supporters. This did not mean that he was prepared to strike a bargain with those who were preparing to leave the party.

The special conference, held at Wembley in January 1981, confirmed the Gang members in their decision to leave. Those who were already uneasy at the direction the party was taking must have despaired after this meeting. Four main proposals were offered to solve the problem of electing the party leader. The social democrats attempted to outflank their opponents by arguing that every party member ought to have a vote, but this alternative was heavily defeated. The Commission of Enquiry's 50:25:20:5 proposal was also rejected, because it still gave too much say to the PLP. The CLPD preferred that the votes should be divided equally between the PLP, the unions and the constituencies, but this idea also failed. Ultimately, in bizarre circumstances, the conference plumped for a 40:30:30 division between unions, PLP and constituencies. This plan would also have been defeated, but the Engineers' Union, which had been mandated to cast its block vote only in support of motions which gave the bulk of the electoral college to the PLP, took its instructions too literally and abstained, thus ensuring the success of a system it opposed. This farce was a marvellous christening-present to the newly-reinforced Gang of Four, who could now argue that the conference block vote produced strange decisions even when the delegates were mandated to support sensible ones. It was a very unhappy beginning for Michael Foot, whose status as a radical hero was already waning. After the crucial votes, a leading member of the RFMC included Foot in a list of 'establishment figures' who had been defeated – a rather odd way of describing a veteran Bevanite who had once been deprived of the party whip (Kogan and Kogan, 1983, 105).

This internal wrangling took place against a background of rising unemployment and economic crisis. Even before the 1979 election the communist academic Eric Hobsbawm had voiced concern that Labour's 'Forward March' had stalled, and urged greater unity among those who upheld working-class interests, but the party's feuding factions made Margaret Thatcher and Edward Heath seem like a married couple (Hobsbawm, 1989, 9–41). Advocates of reform argued that Labour's self-absorption was quite justified, because in its old corrupt state the party could not be trusted to put up effective opposition to Conservative policies. Much still remained to be done. A necessary first step would be Tony Benn's election as deputy leader, particularly since Denis Healey was contesting the position. As Chancellor, Healey's deflationary policies had made him a particular target for socialist hatred, and his uncompromising style represented a danger to their hopes. More seriously, 150 MPs had issued a statement opposing the Wembley decision on the electoral college; significantly, they included Frank Field, who was a member of CLPD and a contributor to the Institute for Workers' Control volume *What Went Wrong?* This sign of defiance signalled the formation of a Labour Solidarity Campaign (LSC), which attempted to mobilise opposition to the RFMC in the constituencies and the trade unions (Kogan and Kogan, 1983, 107).

The campaign went badly for Benn from an early stage; he contracted a debilitating illness, and John Silkin announced his decision to stand, thus splitting the anti-Healey vote. Silkin's candidature gave soft left opponents of Benn (such as Neil Kinnock) someone to vote for on the first ballot without seeming to betray their radical views. At the Brighton conference of October 1981 the ritual of the new electoral college was played out in full publicity. The impression conveyed to the electorate, however, was not one of a healthy democratic process, but of private deals and intimidation. The result was a victory for Healey on the second ballot, but only by less than 1 per cent. Had some MPs not delayed their decision to defect to the SDP until after the vote, Benn would have won. Benn rightly saw that in a close election his interests were best served by defeat: whoever won a narrow victory would seem to lack true authority (Benn, 1994, 155). The arithmetic of the outcome was not a promising basis for a re-union of the party's numerous factions.

While the Labour Party's wounds were being exposed to the public, far-reaching policy decisions were also being taken. Having agreed with Tony Benn that the UK should withdraw unconditionally from the EC, the party gradually established unilateral abandonment of nuclear weapons by the UK as official policy. These votes coincided with the resurgence of the Campaign for Nuclear Disarmament (CND), inspired by the siting of US cruise missiles in British bases. On this issue Foot agreed with the RFMC rather than the moderates who had joined him in opposing Benn. On domestic policy the trend continued with *Labour's Programme 1982*, which one critic dubbed 'a guide book to Bennite Britain' (Mitchell, 1983, 61). This was a reassertion of the AES, featuring a promise to extend common ownership (in various forms), with the disarming proviso that this would not 'reach down into every aspect of economic activity' (Labour Party, 1982, 9). Less publicity was granted to the emphasis laid on the protection of individual rights and open government; Benn's claim that the real threat to liberty came from his opponents was not widely believed, although subsequent events showed that the Labour Party had little to learn from the Militant Tendency on the subject of internal discipline.

By 1982, in fact, the possibility of a thorough socialist take-over of the Labour Party was receding. Michael Foot was now supported by a majority on the NEC, in particular by moderate socialists such as Neil Kinnock. In December 1981 this body set up an enquiry into the activities of the Militant Tendency. The newspaper *Militant* had been established in 1964, although the movement evolved from older groupings. During the 1960s such factions operating within the Labour Party aroused little concern; one study which appeared in 1966 merely poured scorn on Trotskyite groups which remained outside the party, such as the Socialist Workers' Party (SWP) (Gardner, 1966, 115–40). When the movement associated with the newspaper grew in the 1970s the party leadership began to take notice. In 1975 the NEC commissioned a report into Militant's activities; when Reg Underhill, the national agent, presented his findings it was decided not to publish them. After Underhill's retirement in 1979, however, he leaked his report to an eager press, just as the inquest into Labour's defeat was beginning.

Foot's decision to start a new enquiry went against his instincts; as a former victim of 'witch-hunts', he had opposed the publication of the Underhill report on principle. The new powers of constituency parties, however, forced him to act. Inner-city areas (where the nation-wide problem of Labour Party recruitment was accentuated by apathy and unemployment) were particularly vulnerable to 'entryism', the process whereby moribund constituency parties were taken over by revolutionary activists. When the report was finished, Foot agreed that only groups which accepted Labour's full constitution would be eligible for inclusion on a new register. In September 1982 Militant held a conference at Wembley to protest; the meeting attracted 2,600 members from around the country, thus demonstrating the size and wealth of the movement (Crick, 1986, 199). Inevitably the process dragged on, but in February 1983 the five members of the *Militant* editorial board were expelled (Jones, M, 1994, 491–7). At the same time, Foot was faced with a problem over the endorsement of Peter Tatchell as parliamentary candidate for Bermondsey. Tatchell was not a supporter of Militant, but had attacked Labour's 'obsessive legalism and parliamentarianism' in the journal *London Labour Briefing* (Jones, M, 1994, 480). Eventually Tatchell stood in a by-election called in February 1983, and his heavy defeat inspired talk about replacing Foot as Labour leader before the next general election; this subsided only when Labour won a hard struggle at Darlington in the following month.

The result of all the ferocious infighting during the 1979–83 Parliament was unsatisfactory for all of the warring factions. Even within the Labour Party, the 1983 manifesto *The New Hope for Britain* became known as 'the longest suicide note ever written'; more predictably, Margaret Thatcher claimed that it was 'the most extreme ever'. In fact, the distance between key manifesto policies and the views of the electorate has been exaggerated; for example, there was a high level of public support for import controls (Young, 1985, 20–1). However, the manifesto was based on *Labour's Programme 1982*, and thus reflected decisions taken before the mood of the party turned against Benn and his supporters. Since Bennism had been in decline within the party since the time of the deputy leadership election, members of the RFMC were able to claim subsequently that the leadership had endorsed the manifesto without real conviction. Once again, real socialism had not been given a fair electoral test. Remaining social democrats inevitably saw things differently; by ensuring that the party was both divided and tied to an unpalatable programme, Benn had ruined any chance Labour might have had. At the level of ideas, at least, this dispute was as far from a settlement as ever. Caught in the middle of the feud, Foot had contributed a passionate rallying-call against Thatcherism in his foreword to the manifesto, but his order of priorities was clearly different from that of many Labour activists. Foot's allies realised that if the Bennite factions were to be defeated it could be done only by force, yet the leader himself did not relish the task. When the election was held the Conservatives won an overall majority of 161 seats; Labour's vote had slumped to 28.3 per cent, its worst performance since 1918. The party's lead over the SDP–Liberal Alliance was only 2 per cent. Within days of this crushing defeat, Foot submitted his resignation as Labour leader.

Confrontation, 1983–87

Despite all his efforts, Michael Foot's record only proves the accuracy of Denis Healey's remark that there is 'no more difficult job in British politics' than leading Labour in opposition (Healey, 1990, 466). According to an early biographer, Neil Kinnock, who was convincingly elected as Foot's successor, was 'born lucky';

ten years later, Kinnock himself was probably only half joking when he claimed that the balance of his mind had been affected when he made the decision to stand for the leadership (Harris, 1984, 223; Kinnock, 1994, 535). At least Kinnock was spared a potentially bruising contest with Tony Benn, who was ineligible to stand having lost his seat in the election. The prospects for at least partial unity seemed to be further improved by the election of Roy Hattersley, from the social democratic wing of the party, as Kinnock's deputy. Hattersley's unsuccessful opponent was Michael Meacher, who had worked closely with Tony Benn in the early 1980s; after his defeat, Meacher was detached from this alliance.

Kinnock had been elected as MP for Bedwellty in 1970. This meant that his political career began with a general election defeat for Labour, which inspired the party to adopt more socialist policies under the Heath government. Kinnock was still relatively unknown when Harold Wilson returned to office in 1974. Having spent his first Westminster years in opposition, it was natural for Kinnock to anticipate a new Labour government with hopes that were quickly disappointed. His stirring oratory won him a reputation among Labour supporters who were impatient at the government's deviation from the promises of 1974; when circumstances changed, some of these allies were able to turn the accusation of treachery against him. Kinnock was a determined opponent of nuclear weapons, and rejected entry into the EEC on Edward Heath's terms. These views also made life difficult for him later.

As a Welshman, a member of the Tribune group and a friend of Michael Foot, it was natural that Kinnock should write a foreword for a new edition of Aneurin Bevan's *In Place of Fear* in 1978. Here Kinnock denounced the competitive view of human nature propagated by capitalists, and asserted that the idea of co-operation went 'with the grain of history'. Like the advocates of the AES, Kinnock called for 'the collective organisation of economic resources under the collective control of democracy'. He summed up his political creed as demanding 'hot ideas with . . . a cool head' (Kinnock, 1978). This was written when the Labour leadership were following cold ideas with heads of a similar temperature. By contrast, as Tudor Jones has written, Kinnock matched a 'reformist' commitment to parliamentary methods with a 'fundamentalist' mission to tranform society (Jones, T, 1994, 570).

As Labour embarked on its civil war after the 1979 defeat, Kinnock began to worry that some who agreed with his fundamentalism were willing to ally themselves to factions within the party who despised his reformism. In the *Political Quarterly* he announced that he would always choose a gradual approach to his goals if the only alternative was revolution (Kinnock, 1980, 411–12). In the polarised Labour Party, this meant that Kinnock had taken sides with the leadership against Tony Benn, who was tainted in Kinnock's eyes by his alliance with the opponents of parliamentary action. At the same time, Kinnock's views were clearly distinct from those of the defecting Gang of Three, who rejected even a long-term commitment to nationalisation and were determined to keep the UK within the EC. In combination with his passionate oratory, these views made Kinnock the perfect successor to Foot, and he gained 71 per cent of the electoral college in the 1983 leadership election.

Unfortunately for Kinnock, he took over Foot's problems as well as his position. Foot had made only preliminary moves against the Militant Tendency, and the Conservative press was glad to publicise the deeds of so-called 'loony left' councils such as Militant-controlled Liverpool. After wooing former allies of Tony Benn such as Tom Sawyer and Michael Meacher, Kinnock was able to use the machinery set up by Foot to continue the expulsions. His campaign was capped by a tough speech at the 1985 party conference, which Labour's image-makers used in a political broadcast for the 1987 election. Perhaps this was a mistake, because it encouraged Kinnock's opponents to think that the whole exercise was mainly intended to give the leader good publicity; after all the scare-stories, hardly any MPs had been deselected, and the leader already controlled policy-making. With local authorities also under attack from the government, it seemed as if Kinnock and Thatcher were working together against valid results of democracy which were inconvenient for both of them.

Kinnock's other major headache during these years was the prolonged miners' strike of 1984–85, which ended in a rout for the union movement. Normally this would have been expected to win his sympathy; the government's pit closure programme threatened to destroy traditional communities, particularly in Kinnock's Wales. Yet the role of Arthur Scargill prevented the Labour leadership from providing overt support to the strike. Kinnock's rejection of revolutionary activity meant that he was opposed in principle to any attempt to replace a government by extra-parliamentary means, yet this was precisely Scargill's intention. Understandably, Conservative newspapers were not sympathetic to Kinnock's plight. Given his radical past, they could either jeer at him for deserting his old principles or imply that he secretly agreed with Scargill; often they did both.

With the economy now recovering and unemployment figures falling, the majority of voters had no reason to scrutinise the Conservative case against Kinnock very closely. Under the circumstances, Labour's slight recovery in the 1987 general election was a reasonable achievement. A new publicity chief,

Peter Mandelson, made presentational changes in an attempt to jettison the party's extremist image. The red flag was replaced by a red rose, and broadcasts concentrated on Kinnock's personality rather than the detail of policy. The manifesto, *Britain Can Win*, represented a change of emphasis from previous ideas rather than a fundamental rethink. There was a promise to reduce unemployment by a million in two years, with a detailed breakdown of how this would be achieved. In a clear echo of the Wilsonian approach, Labour proposed to set up a National Economic Summit, which would bring together government, unions and employers. The ambitious AES programme of nationalisation was watered down, and the emphasis shifted to introducing more flexible forms of social ownership (heralded in a 1986 policy document). The manifesto gave more prominence to the idea of a British Industrial Investment bank, to provide the investment which capitalists still refused to make despite the Thatcherite stress on the virtues of free enterprise. Increasingly the Labour leadership was looking to European practices to provide ideas for industrial strategy, in line with Kinnock's agreement that 'Britain's future, like our past and present, lies with Europe' (Kinnock, 1984, 231; Held and Keane, 1984, 170–81; Hattersley, 1987a, 159–74).

Some of these proposals were open to detailed criticism, but Labour's main vote-loser in this election was clearly its defence policy. Despite encouraging world developments after the rise of Mikhail Gorbachev, Kinnock's unilateralism was bitterly attacked. The potency over the issue was increased by the problems experienced by the Alliance during the campaign (see Chapter 3). Conservative posters suggested that Labour would simply surrender to any attack from the Soviet Union; the manifesto pledge to increase spending on conventional forces could not protect the party from its critics. A humiliating meeting with President Reagan (where the US President managed to confuse Denis Healey with the British Ambassador) served only to underline Kinnock's inexperience as a world leader. Meanwhile, Mrs Thatcher embarked on a triumphal visit to Moscow; the irony of this trip to a country which Conservatives used as a potential threat in order to discredit Labour's defence policy did not register with the voters.

Consolidation, 1987–92

The 1987 election result was double-edged for Labour. The party could be satisfied with its clear defeat of the Alliance for second place – there was now an 8 per cent gap between them. However, the economic boom in the south of England meant that Labour was still confined to its old 'heartlands' of the north, midlands, Wales and Scotland. The impression that Labour was finished as a national force was not dispelled by an election which suggested that their message was still outdated, despite the new professionalism of the campaign. Kinnock seemed to have exchanged insecurity at the head of restless factions only for a more comfortable life of permanent impotence.

A more detached analysis could provide more consolation. Mrs Thatcher had benefited from an inevitable economic recovery which seemed more exciting by contrast with the previous deep recession. If this trend proved temporary, Labour was now well placed to win in future, particularly if the next recession also hit the south. The issue of defence looked likely to fade as Gorbachev negotiated for deep cuts in nuclear weapons, and at least Labour had now abandoned the idea of leaving the EC without a referendum. Finally, the Conservative proposal of a Community Charge to replace the rating system could prove to be a gift to the opposition, although they made little use of it during the election. These factors meant that Labour's frustration after a third consecutive defeat need not be lasting.

The 1987 election was also bad for Tony Benn and his supporters. The traditional explanation that Labour had not been socialist enough could still be rehearsed, but it had begun to seem a shade repetitive by now and Kinnock's tactics had deprived Benn of many allies. Benn himself was back in the House of Commons as MP for Chesterfield; although he failed to win election to the Shadow Cabinet in 1987 he still received sixty-nine votes. Within the PLP his support was centred on the Campaign Group, which had been set up in 1981 with the support of around twenty MPs; Benn also established an informal think-tank in 1985 to keep up socialist momentum. In March 1988 the Campaign Group agreed that Benn should stand against Kinnock for the leadership; Benn's insistence on democracy in all things exposed divisions even within the group, and Margaret Beckett, Clare Short and two other women members resigned as a result of the vote (Adams, 1993, 454). After six months of exhaustive campaigning, Benn was able to secure only 11.3 per cent of an electoral college which exaggerated his support within the Labour movement. His running-mate for the deputy leadership, Eric Heffer, attracted even less support. Benn would always enjoy the allegiance of socialist MPs such as Dennis Skinner, but standing against Kinnock at this time only gave the leader (and the public) a more precise indication of his impregnable status.

This was particularly welcome to Kinnock, who had decided to set up a wide-ranging policy review exercise after the 1987 election. It was already clear which direction this would take. In the year of the election Roy Hattersley published *Choose*

Freedom, which attacked the Thatcherite definition of liberty as simply the absence of external restraint. For Hattersley, 'the extension of freedom is an essential element within the philosophy of socialism'; for example, the concept of liberty is meaningless in the presence of wide economic inequalities. Governments should therefore act towards the goal of equality, even if this should prove impossible in practice (Hattersley, 1987b, 92). Hattersley cited approvingly the American liberal philosopher John Rawls, who had also inspired some of David Owen's work in the early 1980s. He described his position as 'democratic socialist' rather than social democratic, but this minor verbal difference was a good indication that there was little to separate Hattersley's thinking from that of former allies such as Shirley Williams. Now that the identity of the SDP had become blurred through Owen's ideological migrations, Hattersley could work to bring Labour back to the legacy of Anthony Crosland.

The first product of Labour's Policy Review, *A Statement of Democratic Socialist Aims and Values* (1988), was mostly written by Hattersley. Like *Choose Freedom*, this document showed a willingness to accept a central role for private enterprise. At the 1988 party conference Kinnock acknowledged that the new position was an adjustment of socialist principles in the light of Thatcherism's electoral success. This sense of a tactical shift was enhanced when the findings of the completed Policy Review were published under the title *Meet the Challenge, Make the Change* (1989). For many voters, the actual content of the new programme was overshadowed by the impression that it did not represent Kinnock's real thinking. The fact that Kinnock was now prepared to give up his life-long commitment to unilateral nuclear disarmament was particularly difficult for Labour's new image-makers to present, either to the party conference or to the electorate.

Meet the Challenge, Make the Change argued (as Anthony Crosland had done thirty years before) that the question of industrial ownership was barely relevant to the achievement of socialist goals. Even the renationalisation of industries returned to the private sector by the Conservatives would now depend upon the circumstances after Labour's re-election. The proposals envisaged greater regulation of private enterprise, rather than other forms of ownership; as the Major government later found, this compromise solution left everyone dissatisfied. There would be some changes to existing trade union law, but the status quo of 1979 would not be restored. This issue had led to friction between Kinnock and Michael Meacher; the latter had served his purpose by supporting Kinnock on the NEC, and could now be discarded. Meacher's replacement as Employment spokesman by Tony Blair in 1989 removed this difficulty. While the 1987 manifesto had promised to reverse the government's tax cuts, the Policy Review concluded that the rate on higher earners would rise to a maximum of 50 per cent – lower than it had been after Geoffrey Howe's first Budget in 1979. To tackle poverty, a national minimum wage would be introduced, but Labour was now echoing Thatcherites in its opposition to any 'dependency culture'; the state would act as an 'enabler' rather than a nanny (Garner, 1990, 31–6).

The reaction of many commentators was that the Gang of Four had won the battle for the Labour Party in their absence (Marquand, 1992, 201; Gamble, 1994, 36). Some felt that the Policy Review lacked any imaginative ideas, and failed to bring Labour's principles up-to-date (Hughes and Wintour, 1990, 205). *Meet the Challenge, Make the Change* had been publicised through a song of the same name; Tony Benn wrote his own version of the lyrics, which now ended 'Pink and harmless we must be/If we want a victory' (Adams, 1993, 458). More seriously, Benn recorded that the Policy Review represented 'the Thatcherisation of the Labour Party. We have moved now into the penumbra of her policy area, and our main argument is that we will administer it better than she will' (Benn, 1994, 546). Whatever the Policy Review had done to Labour's principles, the voters seemed to be impressed. In 1987 67 per cent had considered that the party was too extreme; by September 1989 this figure was down to 29 per cent (Sanders, 1993, 219). In the latter year the party took the Vale of Glamorgan and Mid-Staffordshire from the government in by-elections, and in June it inflicted Mrs Thatcher's first nation-wide election defeat in the vote for a new European Parliament. Perhaps Britain was now ready to 'Make the Change' at last.

Events had not been kind to the Labour Party since October 1974; now the gods decided to do Kinnock a temporary favour in order to be more cruel later on. The government was well behind in national opinion polls, as inflation and interest rates climbed together. The housing boom which had done so much to help Mrs Thatcher win the 1987 election now turned sour, with mortgage-holders under pressure from the high cost of borrowing. Just as the boom had been greatest in the south of England, now the pain was felt there most. The merged Alliance parties were struggling to find a name, let alone an identity; for a while it looked as though the Green Party would replace them as a remote challenger to the main parties. At the same time, the revolt against the Community Charge was beginning; this brought Labour some problems, as several MPs joined a campaign to break the law, but the effect on Conservative popularity was far worse. The Prime Minister now began to look like an electoral asset for Labour, and after the resignation of Nigel Lawson the divisions inside the party could no longer be disguised.

Despite the obvious temptations, Kinnock did not wait for the government to present him with victory. With party membership still only around 250,000, the leader called for a recruitment drive in January 1989. The party was in debt by over £2 million (Butler and Kavanagh, 1992, 59). Initial results were disappointing, but Kinnock's campaign drew attention to a problem which the party had not taken seriously enough. There was always likely to be a transitional phase before the reputation of Labour's constituency parties as the exclusive preserve of revolutionary activists changed sufficiently to attract new members. In contrast to Foot's problems with Peter Tatchell, the Kinnock-controlled NEC began to impose its preferred candidates in certain areas, and two Militant sympathisers in the PLP were expelled in 1991. Meanwhile, after a false start in 1984, Kinnock began to move towards the principle of 'One Member One Vote' (OMOV) to reduce the power of constituency cliques over the selection of parliamentary candidates. Just as Benn's drive to devolve power to the constituencies helped his campaign against the leadership, so OMOV was calculated to serve Kinnock's interests. In the face of opposition from some unions who felt that OMOV was ultimately designed as an attack on their influence, Kinnock was forced to compromise, although individuals members were given more say in the selection process. By 1991 a ballot of all constituency members had also become mandatory for NEC elections (Shaw, 1994, 117–18). In 1992 and 1993 this reform resulted in defeat for Dennis Skinner and Tony Benn. Kinnock's allies claimed that these measures would 'modernise' the party as an institution, to complement the changes in its policies.

If Mrs Thatcher had remained as Prime Minister, Kinnock's reforms might have produced the elusive victory in 1992. Instead, the Conservative Party acted to 'shoot Labour's fox'. After Thatcher's fall in November 1990 John Major was able to replace the Community Charge with a tax that was slightly less regressive. Perhaps more importantly in the light of subsequent events, the Gulf War offered Major the opportunity to look as though he combined a more caring approach to domestic policy with Mrs Thatcher's toughness on the world stage. Ironically, the recession also hit Labour's chances. The party's spending promises were now more restrained, but there was still a difficulty about finding the money to pay for them.

Labour's 1992 manifesto, *It's Time to Get Britain Working Again*, began by reaffirming the party's new 'core' principle of individual liberty based on effective community provision. The NHS and education were seen as special priorities. At the same time, a Labour government would 'make families better off' by reforming the tax and national insurance systems. The new top rate of income tax of 50 per cent would apply only to 'individuals with an income of at least £40,000 a year'. The Shadow Chancellor, John Smith, produced an alternative budget to explain the impact of these measures. Revenue would be raised in other ways; instead of Labour's original opposition to council house sales, the party was now demanding that the receipts should be used productively. By contrast to these detailed proposals, promises to cut unemployment were left vague. In place of nationalisation, Labour was now fully committed to partnership between government and industry, complete with generous investment grants, 'Technology Trusts' and a Minister for Science to promote innovation. Rather than directly intervening in the economy, Labour would cajole industrialists into investing themselves. This shift from Labour's traditional reliance on the state was also reflected in plans for the decentralisation of power; an elected Scottish Parliament was promised, together with a Welsh Assembly and devolution to the English regions. A charter of rights would entrench civil liberties for all. In a tantalising hint to supporters of the Liberal Democrats, Labour also promised that the findings of its working party on electoral reform (under Professor Raymond Plant) would be taken very seriously.

During the 1987–92 Parliament, Labour was consistently ahead in national opinion polls, and was widely expected to win the April 1992 general election. In the event, the Conservatives scrambled home with a majority of twenty-one. Labour's share of the vote had risen to 35 per cent, but its appeal in the south was still too limited. In part, this could be accounted for by tactical errors, such as the party rally at Sheffield in the last week of the campaign (which the press portrayed as a premature celebration of victory), and the 'War of Jennifer's Ear', which was fought over an emotive election broadcast on the state of the NHS. Since this was already a strong Labour issue, a much more low-key presentation would have been a better idea. Similarly, Kinnock's indecision over the question of proportional representation gave the impression that Labour thought it would lose without Liberal Democratic support; this was unlikely to enthuse doubtful converts. Finally, the Conservatives were able to attack the details of Smith's shadow budget, frightening middle-income householders already under pressure from high interest rates.

Apologists for recent Labour governments commonly argue that the party has always been prevented from governing properly because of the mess left behind by the Conservatives. After 1992, this theory could be elaborated further; on this occasion the Conservatives had mismanaged the economy so badly that Labour never stood a chance of winning. On this view, the electorate refused to believe that the brighter future offered by Labour was attainable. In fact, despite the efforts of Kinnock and

Smith, voters still did not trust Labour to run the economy better than the Conservatives (Sanders, 1993, 171–213). Instead of the government, trends in the world economy and Margaret Thatcher were blamed for this recession. Labour's message had failed to get through – or, perhaps, the opposing message of the Conservative press had got through too well.

The result was a personal disaster for Kinnock, who resigned shortly afterwards. Party leaders rarely survive two election defeats in a row, and some attributed the defeat to Kinnock's personality. British Prime Ministers seem to fall into two categories: they can be brilliant departmental ministers whose talents take them to the top, or conciliatory figures who have the tact to defuse tensions within their parties. Kinnock apparently failed to satisfy either of these criteria. While the long years of opposition had denied him an opportunity to demonstrate administrative skills, the need to fight his internal opponents (and a well-publicised hot temper) created a divisive image. Not even the skills of Peter Mandelson could make the public regard Kinnock as a Prime Minister in waiting. Perhaps this demonstrated the remarkable impact of Conservative propaganda rather than any important weaknesses in the Labour leader, but by March 1992 only 39 per cent of the public thought that he was doing a good job. The corresponding figure for John Major was 51 per cent; almost three-quarters of the electorate approved of Paddy Ashdown's leadership (Sanders, 1993, 193). After the 1992 defeat, Kinnock's popularity increased; even the editor of the *Sunday Times* was prepared to acknowledge that he had been 'Labour's Gorbachev'. These token compliments were safe after the event. For whatever reason, Kinnock was not sufficiently respected by the electorate when it mattered, and this must have contributed to Labour's defeat.

Conclusion: the betrayal of socialism?

As Labour's process of modernisation continues, the parallel between Kinnock and Gorbachev becomes even more interesting. It is possible to see Kinnock as a politician who fought to drag his party into the modern world, at the cost of his own future prospects. By personalising the battle for Labour Party reform he acted as a shield for his reforming ideas; when he was gone critics were prepared to tolerate from his successors what they would never have accepted from him. Like Gorbachev, he was the creation of the system which he attacked. This made him the ideal assailant, but it also ensured that he would be destroyed with the system (Fielding, 1994, 599).

This striking analysis is suggestive in some respects, although it underestimates the drive for power shared by both Gorbachev and Kinnock. Its major failure, however, is the suggestion that Kinnock made a dramatic change in the Labour Party's thinking. His main achievement here was to re-establish an approach which temporarily broke down in the unusual circumstances of 1979–83. Under this system the enthusiasm of activists would be rewarded by the passage of occasional conference resolutions; even when socialist ideas sneaked into the manifesto (as in 1974), the 'realism' of the PLP would always water these proposals down (or dissolve them altogether). By 1992 Kinnock had saved time and heart-burnings by ensuring that the manifesto contained no important socialist promises to be broken in office. This situation was not new – until 1974 it had been well established under Harold Wilson – and even after the institutional changes there was no guarantee that it would be a permanent arrangement. On this subject, commentators have tended to confuse the undoubted difficulty of Kinnock's task with the scale of the changes he actually pushed through.

Kinnock's control over the party in 1992 meant that he had no need for internal compromise over the manifesto. This does not mean that the manifesto contained no compromises of any kind; indeed, Kinnock has been criticised for making far too many concessions to Thatcherism. Having been told in 1983 not to vote Labour because it was too extreme, the electorate was invited to oppose the party in 1992 because it had no principles at all. This charge certainly was a handicap to Labour during the 1992 campaign. However, it rests upon a serious mistake which has bedevilled British politics since 1979 at least. It has even affected Kinnock himself, who admits that 'there was no central philosophical theme' behind the policy review (Kinnock, 1994, 545). This mistake is to assume that only those ideas which involve far-reaching changes can qualify as ideologies, and that if a body of ideas is not ideological it cannot arouse great enthusiasm in either its advocates or an electorate.

In fact, there was a clear social democratic theme underlying the policy review. Thanks to Roy Hattersley, this was not simply a reheating of old Croslandite recipes; even if it had been, it would still have represented one of the most powerful traditions in modern western political thought – New liberalism. It must be remembered that social democratic principles had not been followed consistently by either the Wilson or Callaghan governments. Now that the Labour Party had become what the SDP would have been without David Owen, it actually promised to provide the most radical progressive government since 1951 – provided, that is, that it kept to its philosophical viewpoint. In this respect the manifesto contained some worrying hints that Labour's strategists were over-impressed by the dubious popularity of Thatcherism. Committed social democrats would certainly have been less anxious to allay the fears of high earners, for example. Translating Labour's tax plans into Thatcherite language only made them more vulnerable to Conservative criticism. This suggests that the failure of the Policy Review was due to Labour's inability to express its findings in a suitable idiom, rather than its lack of philosophy.

In part, this might have been Kinnock's fault. His slightly disparaging attitude towards the philosophy of the Policy Review actually underlines the consistency of his private outlook. He had always opposed the goals of social democracy as ends in themselves, regarding them as desirable milestones on the journey to a socialist Britain. For Kinnock as for Foot, this journey would not be possible if socialists planned an inflexible route. Detours would be unavoidable. There was nothing in Kinnock's background which prevented him from embracing social democracy as a tactical alternative to Thatcherism, so long as it became nothing more than that. This lukewarm acceptance was not a promising platform for an orator like Kinnock. He may also have sensed future dangers to his own position. With the SDP experiment ending in failure, there would be many people returning to the party who saw social democratic goals as being quite enough – perhaps even a little too much. Kinnock might be accused of playing into their hands, but this could hardly amount to a 'betrayal' of the Labour Party, which for most of its history has been influenced at least as much by New liberalism as any other creed. Like Mikhail Gorbachev, however, Kinnock might now be discovering that his reforming efforts have only made life easier for people within his party who, in the long run, are his ideological opponents.

List of works cited

Adams, Jad (1993), *Tony Benn: A Biography*, Pan
Baker, Blake (1981), *The Far Left: An Exposé of the Extreme Left in Britain*, Weidenfeld and Nicolson
Benn, Tony (1980), *Arguments for Socialism*, Penguin
Benn, Tony (1994), *The End of an Era: Diaries 1980–90*, Arrow
Butler, David, and Kavanagh, Dennis (1992), *The British General Election of 1992*, Macmillan
Callaghan, John (1987), *The Far Left in British Politics*, Blackwell
Crick, Michael (1986), *The March of Militant*, Faber and Faber
Fielding, Steven (1994), 'Neil Kinnock: An Overview of the Labour Party', *Contemporary Record*, volume 8, number 3
Foot, Michael (1983), 'Labour's Britain in the 1980s', in Gerald Kaufman (ed.) *Renewal: Labour's Britain in the 1980s*, Penguin

Gamble, Andrew (1994), 'Love's Labours Lost', in Mark Perryman (ed.) *Altered States: Postmodernism, Politics, Culture*, Lawrence and Wishart

Gardner, Llew (1966), 'The Fringe Left', in Gerald Kaufman (ed.) *The Left*, Anthony Blond

Garner, Robert (1990), 'Labour and the Policy Review: A Party Fit to Govern?', *Talking Politics*, volume 3, number 1

Harris, Robert (1984), *The Making of Neil Kinnock*, Faber and Faber

Hattersley, Roy (1987a), *Economic Priorities for a Labour Government*, Macmillan

Hattersley, Roy (1987b), *Choose Freedom: The Future for Democratic Socialism*, Penguin

Healey, Denis (1990), *The Time of My Life*, Penguin

Held, David, and Keane, John (1984), 'Socialism and the Limits of State Action', in James Curran (ed.) *The Future of the Left*, Polity

Hobsbawm, Eric (1989), *Politics for a Rational Left: Political Writing 1977–1988*, Verso

Hughes, Colin, and Wintour, Patrick (1990), *Labour Rebuilt: The New Model Party*, Fourth Estate

Jefferys, Kevin (1993), *The Labour Party since 1945*, Macmillan

Jones, Mervyn (1994), *Michael Foot*, Victor Gollancz

Jones, Tudor (1994), 'Neil Kinnock's Socialist Journey: From Clause Four to the Policy Review', *Contemporary Record*, volume 8, number 3

Kinnock, Neil (1978), Foreword, in Aneurin Bevan, *In Place of Fear*, Quartet

Kinnock, Neil (1980), 'Which Way Should Labour Go?', *Political Quarterly*, volume 61

Kinnock, Neil (1984), 'Mobilizing in Defence of Freedom', in James Curran (ed.) *The Future of the Left*, Polity

Kinnock, Neil (1994), 'Reforming the Labour Party', *Contemporary Record*, volume 8, number 3

Kogan, David, and Kogan, Maurice (1983), *The Battle for the Labour Party*, Kogan Page

Labour Party (1982), *Labour's Programme 1982*, Labour Party

Marquand, David (1992), *The Progressive Dilemma: From Lloyd George to Kinnock*, Heinemann

Mitchell, Austin (1983), *Four Years in the Death of the Labour Party*, Methuen

Sanders, David (1993), 'Why the Conservative Party Won – Again', in Anthony King (ed.) *Britain at the Polls 1992*, Chatham House

Shaw, Eric (1994), *The Labour Party since 1979: Crisis and Transformation*, Routledge

Whiteley, Paul (1983), *The Labour Party in Crisis*, Methuen

Young, Ken (1985), 'Shades of Opinion', in Roger Jowell and Sharon Witherspoon (eds) *British Social Attitudes: The 1985 Report*, Gower

Questions for discussion

- Does the Labour Party's performance since 1974 show that a genuine socialist party can no longer win elections in Britain?

- How far did changes in the policies of the Labour leadership bring the party into line with continental social democratic parties?

Selected further reading (see also Chapters 1 and 3)

Benn, Tony (1981), *Arguments for Democracy*, Penguin.

Blunkett, David, and Crick, Bernard (1988), *The Labour Party's Aims and Values: An Unofficial Statement*, Spokesman.

Cripps, Francis, Griffiths, John, Morrell, Frances, et al. (1982), *Manifesto: A Radical Strategy for Britain's Future*, Pan.

Foot, Michael (1984), *Another Heart and Other Pulses*, Collins.

Foot, Michael (1986), *Loyalists and Loners*, Collins.

Gould, Bryan (1989), *A Future for Socialism*, Jonathan Cape.

Heffernan, Richard, and Marquese, Mike (1992), *Defeat from the Jaws of Victory: Inside Kinnock's Labour Party*, Verso.

Kavanagh, Dennis (ed.) (1982), *The Politics of the Labour Party*, Allen and Unwin.

Kinnock, Neil (1986), *Making Our Way*, Blackwell.

Lansman, Jon, and Meale, Alan (eds) (1983), *Beyond Thatcher: The Real Alternative*, Junction.

Miller, David (1989), *Market, State and Community: Theoretical Foundations of Market Socialism*, Clarendon Press.

Milliband, Ralph (1985), 'The New Revisionism in Britain', *New Left Review* 150.

Plant, Raymond (1984), *Equality, Markets and the State*, Fabian Society.

Plant, Raymond (1988), *Citizenship, Rights and Socialism*, Fabian Society.

Seyd, Patrick, and Whiteley, Paul (1992), *Labour's Grass Roots: The Politics of Party Membership*, Clarendon Press.

Smith, Martin, and Spear, Jo (eds) (1992), *The Changing Labour Party*, Routledge.

Taylor, Gerald (1996), *Labour's Renewal? The Policy Review and Beyond*, Macmillan.

CHAPTER 6

Nationalism in UK politics

While the fall of communist regimes in 1989–90 brought wide-spread rejoicing in Eastern Europe, many western observers expressed concern about the likely consequences. World politics were hardly stable during the period of the Cold War, and many populations suffered under regimes which existed only to serve superpower interests. The supposed 'balance of terror' established between NATO and the Warsaw Pact might have had a pleasing symmetry for statesmen and military strategists, but this feeling was mostly confined to those who could hide from the consequences of their mistakes in nuclear bunkers. Yet despite the proxy wars, puppet governments and general insecurities, the presuppositions of the Cold War had brought a few undeniable comforts. Most importantly, as new realities became clearer it seemed as though the old system had kept nationalism in check. With this restraint removed, the scope for conflict within and between states suddenly looked greater than ever.

The effects of the end of communism were quickly registered on the map. New republics replaced the former Soviet Union, Czechoslovakia split into two states and Germany was reunited. The processes were relatively smooth compared with the hideous violence that accompanied the break up of Yugoslavia – ironically, a state which had avoided Soviet domination under Marshal Tito. The effects were not confined to Eastern Europe, as refugees keen to exercise new freedoms of movement added to existing migrations into the more prosperous western countries. The result was increased support for nationalist parties in these states, which were already experiencing economic difficulties. Apart from well-publicised incidents in Germany, the Italian Northern League joined a coalition government with the new party Forza Italia (which itself benefited from nationalistic feelings), and the French National Front under Jean Marie le Pen continued to poll well. While rationalistic observers pontificated about the inevitable decline of nation-states under the impact of technological change, activists throughout the world were busy trying to establish or reassert their collective sense of identity. The prophet of 'The End of History' dismissed nationalism as a transient phenomenon, but it seemed likely to outlast the celebrity of his strange thesis (Fukuyama, 1992, 266–75)

The UK escaped the direct impact of these developments: many were relieved about this, believing that nationalism is an unsettling political force. Yet it is a highly complex phenomenon eluding neat definitions, and like other political doctrines its effects depend on the context in which it is manifested (Smith, 1995, 13–19). As events in South Africa have shown, it can be used to promote national liberation if leaders are skilful and sincere. In other cases it is exploited as a vehicle for personal ambition, and provides a token cause to legitimise the operations of thugs. Perhaps because of an imperial history in which liberation movements were inevitably portrayed as public enemies, the British (or rather the English) have tended to overlook the creative side of nationalism. As a result, it is often regarded as an unfortunate malady which only ever afflicts other peoples. This attitude has an impact in academia as well as on party-political battles. Despite the existence of popular nationalist parties in Scotland, Wales and Northern Ireland (and the important role that nationalism plays within English-based parties), books on UK politics rarely pay much attention to this awkward sentiment. If nationalist parties feature at all, they are usually lumped together in a chapter entitled 'Other Parties'.

The unjust neglect of nationalist politics in the United Kingdom cannot be rectified by a single chapter; in particular, the extent to which nationalist parties have other priorities beyond self-government is bound to be underplayed. The intention of this chapter is to explore the diversity of views associated with each party, and to offer explanations for these variations. It also looks at the response of the major parties to the challenge posed by nationalist movements. Finally, the status of nationalism will be considered – that is, whether it shares the most important characteristics of political ideologies, or should fall into a different category of beliefs.

Scottish nationalism

Scotland lost its independence through the Treaty of Union in 1707. Most Scots originally regarded this as a beneficial measure, especially for economic reasons which soon proved misleading. Despite the bloody aftermath of the 1745 rebellion, nationalist feelings were still mainly directed towards the preservation of Scottish culture rather than an independence movement. During the eighteenth century Scotland produced figures of European renown such as David Hume and Adam Smith; the distribution of power meant that ambitious Scottish politicians had to travel to London in search of glory, but separate legal, religious and educational systems offered opportunities within other professions. The feeling that a distinctive Scottish culture could thrive under the Union is illustrated by the work of Sir Walter Scott, whose nostalgia for his country's history did not prevent him from being a staunch Tory, opposed to constitutional changes of any kind.

The desire for Scottish home rule in the twentieth century has been explained in numerous ways. Some impetus must have been provided by developments in Ireland, which culminated in the creation of the Irish Free State in 1921. Just before the First World War, the Liberal Asquith government promised to allow Scotland home rule, but the necessary legislation was not passed before the European conflict broke out. After the war parliamentary support for home rule subsided, and a Scottish National Convention was called in 1926. The Scottish Nationalist Party itself was founded in 1934, during the economic slump which hit the country's industries particularly hard. The party itself arose out of a merger between the National Party of Scotland (founded in 1928) and the Scottish Party (1932).

Although the Scottish Nationalist Party (SNP) won a by-election at Motherwell in 1945, the seat was quickly lost and it was not until the 1960s that the party 'became a well-organised mass political party' (Webb, 1978, 108). As a strictly constitutionalist party, the SNP was handicapped by some well-publicised stunts performed by other nationalists during the 1950s, such as the theft of the Stone of Destiny from Westminister Abbey. By 1960 it had only 1,000 members, but in that year the siting of a Polaris nuclear submarine base on the Clyde with minimal consultation helped to inspire a rise in interest. The SNP has a long record of opposition to nuclear weapons; in addition to the arguments advanced by CND, the Scots were also aware of the danger of being obliterated in the course of an English quarrel. In 1962 the SNP performed well in the West Lothian by-election won for Labour by Tam Dalyell, and in 1967 Winifred Ewing pulled off a sensational victory in Hamilton. The discovery of oil off the Scottish coast in the early 1970s added weight to the SNP argument that the country's economy could thrive without interference from London. By October 1974 the SNP had eleven MPs, having secured over 30 per cent of the Scottish vote in the second general election of that year. This achievement has yet to be repeated in a general election, and after the 1992 contest the party was left with only three seats. However, its share of the vote (at 22 per cent) was close to that of the Conservatives in Scotland, and it remained a force to be reckoned with; in 1994 it nearly snatched the late John Smith's Monklands seat, and the following year it took Perthshire and Kinross from the Conservatives in addition to breaking the 30 per cent barrier again in the European parliamentary elections

The SNP benefited in 1974 from general disillusionment with the larger parties, but it is clearly more than a depository for protest votes. Its main problem has been whether to embrace total independence or a measure of devolution. The sensitivity of this issue was indicated by the referendum held in March 1979 on the subject of devolved powers to a Scottish Assembly. The proposed powers for this Assembly were severely limited, excluding the authority to raise taxes, for example. One commentator has described the suggested relationship between London and Edinburgh as resembling 'that between central and local government more than that between Washington and the States in the USA' (Kellas, 1989, 154). The SNP campaigned in favour of a 'Yes' vote; after all, the necessary legislation had been promised by the Labour government in return for parliamentary support. Yet this moderate measure was at best a stepping-stone for the party, which would have negotiated for full independence had it won over half the Scottish seats in October 1974 (Miller, 1981, 243). The result of the referendum was inconclusive, with 'Yes' failing to win support from the required proportion of the electorate. This was a serious blow to the party. It was difficult to predict when it might once again hold the balance of power at Westminster, and thus be able to demand concessions. Also, the vote seemed to indicate a discouraging level of potential SNP support among Scottish voters.

A possible answer to the SNP's dilemma has arisen through membership of the European Union (EU). The Union's commitment to reducing economic inequalities between and within member states, exemplified by the development of regional policies during the 1980s, offers the party an opportunity to advocate 'independence in Europe'. Just before the 1992 general election, the Maastricht Treaty set up a Committee of the Regions, which gives Scotland the chance of direct representation in the European policy process (Harvie, 1994). In particular, as nation-states looked less suitable as promoters of economic development, regional bodies were seen as their logical replacement (Marquand, 1991, 36–7). While the oil was running out and nationalists searched for another source of future economic security, this European route to independence looked increasingly attractive – despite the fact that the SNP had originally opposed European integration (Mullin, 1979, 127). This coincided with a promising shift in popular attitudes. In January 1992 one opinion poll revealed that full independence was now favoured by half of the Scottish electorate, instead of the previous desire to stop short at devolution (Butler and

Kavanagh, 1992, 73). This change of mood meant that the SNP had not suffered from its boycott of a new Convention, called in 1988 by the Campaign for a Scottish Assembly (CSA) formed from representatives of other opposition parties (McCreadie, 1991). Although the Convention produced some constructive ideas, the SNP's withdrawal showed how the nationalist cause could be hampered by rivalries between Scotland's parties; in this case, the SNP feared that Labour would hi-jack the meeting.

The outcome of the 1992 general election was a disappointment for the SNP, but the return of the Conservatives was not a disaster. Only a quarter of the Scottish electorate had supported the government (even this was better than many had expected). The Conservative's dismal record north of the border had not prevented it from using Scotland as a guinea-pig for the Poll Tax legislation; the inevitable outcry against the new tax directly benefited the SNP, which campaigned in favour of non-payment. In November 1988 Jim Sillars, formerly a Labour MP, overturned his old party's majority of nearly 20,000 in the Glasgow Govan by-election at the height of the anti-Poll Tax agitation (Butler et al., 1994, 131). The ill-considered tax also called the Union into question. The rump Scottish Conservative Party was in no state to fight back, with the supporters of the Thatcherite Michael Forsythe engaged in guerrilla warfare with the former devolutionists Malcolm Rifkind and Ian Lang. The Scottish electorate had decisively rejected the government in four successive elections; why should it suffer just because other parts of the United Kingdom had a different opinion? Those who thought that the government enjoyed democratic legitimacy in Scotland required notable inventive powers to sustain their argument, and it was a short step from denying the Conservative right to rule to accepting the case for full independence.

The increase in SNP support since 1960 has not gone unnoticed by other parties, however slightly it might have registered with political scientists. The minority Labour government of 1974–79 was forced to spend valuable parliamentary time on the difficult passage of the Scotland Act; the defection of Jim Sillars to the short-lived Scottish Labour Party (SLP) on the devolution issue helped to force the government into the Lib–Lab Pact (Drucker, 1978). Labour has consistently promised devolution to Scotland since the 1970s, a position which might become less profitable if the desire for full independence is maintained, and if the party continues to be dogged by Tam Dalyell's 'West Lothian Question' concerning the role of Scottish MPs at Westminster after their country is given an Assembly of its own. By contrast, the Conservative Party believes that maintenance of the Union is a vote-winner. In 1991 the Lord Chancellor claimed that 'the union of Scotland and England is probably the finest example of two nations freely coming together to the mutual benefits of their peoples'. The 1992 Conservative *Campaign Guide* dismissed the charge that the party had no mandate to govern Scotland as 'absurd' (Conservative Research Department, 1992, 250–1). This defiance continues, despite the fact that even the *Sun* newspaper now finds it advisable to criticise the Union in its Scottish edition. In an election of 1996 or 1997 the Conservatives could lose prominent MPs even on small swings; if this happens in spite of Major's strong pro-Union rhetoric the demand for radical change might become irresistible.

Welsh nationalism

The development of the Welsh nationalist party, Plaid Cymru, shows some striking similarities with that of the SNP. Although Welsh nationalism was hardly absent before 1914 (Lloyd George, for example, regarded himself as a supporter), the party was not founded until after the First World War. It emerged in 1925 from several Welsh-speaking groups, with particular support from the University of Wales. For many years it seemed to be destined to continue as an agreeable outlet for cultural nationalists, and contested only a handful of Welsh seats in elections. For Plaid Cymru, as for the SNP, the breakthrough did not occur until the 1960s. In 1966 its candidate Gwynfor Evans took Carmarthen from Labour in a by-election. Evans was a well-known and popular candidate; even so, he failed to retain the seat in 1970, when twenty-six Plaid Cymru candidates lost their deposits. Despite the setback, events like this ensured that the party, and the attitudes that it represented, could no longer be ignored.

The similarities between the SNP and Plaid Cymru are overshadowed by one major difference. From the outset Plaid Cymru's 'principal concerns were the Welsh language, the Welsh identity, and Christianity in Wales' (Butt Philp, 1975, 15). By contrast, although the future of the Gaelic language concerns many SNP activists, it is not their main priority. While a Scottish Parliament has been a minimum SNP demand, many members of Plaid Cymru have had mixed feelings about devolution because Welsh speakers are only a minority of the population. While this remains true a national assembly might restore Westminster's old discrimination against the Welsh language. The refusal of Welsh nationalists to become 'obsessed' by the question of self-government can be seen as far-sighted at a time when the future of the western nation-state is in question; according to Dafydd Elis Thomas, for example, 'Constitutions are . . . probably the least important ways of constituting a national or international community' (Thomas, 1991, 67).

Despite these concerns, self-government of some kind has always been an official aim of Plaid Cymru. In pursuit of its goals, the party 'is constitutional, decentralist, co-operative, Social Democratic and non-violent' (Balsom, 1979, 141). Like the SNP, it has been handicapped by association with direct action which it rejects, such as the burning of Welsh cottages owned by absentee English people. Since Wales has suffered more than most other parts of the UK during the years of relative economic decline, the party also has a record of close attention to economic subjects. It shared the SNP's attraction to small-scale enterprises as a replacement for traditional heavy industries, which enhanced a sense of community but also brought pollution and left regions economically vulnerable in a period of technological change. Plaid Cymru is also a long-standing opponent of nuclear weapons.

The years between 1974 and 1979 were as fraught for Plaid Cymru as for the SNP. The February 1974 election focused on issues such as the role of the unions, and therefore did not favour the chances of the nationalist parties, but Plaid Cymru still managed to win two seats at Caernarfon and Merioneth. The October contest was even more satisfactory, as Gwynfor Evans regained his Carmarthen seat to join his two colleagues at Westminster. Elsewhere the outlook was less favourable, and once again only ten Plaid Cymru candidates saved their deposits. Yet this was an exciting time to have even a small representation in Parliament, with Labour holding a tiny majority. For Plaid Cymru as for the SNP, the government's plight would ensure at least a referendum on the issue of devolution.

In Scotland, the 1979 referendum produced a dubious result; in Wales, it was clear-cut. Only 11.9 per cent of the total electorate voted for devolution. Plaid Cymru had campaigned hard for a 'Yes', although there was initial hesitation. Afterwards the party continued to join Labour in parliamentary votes, but could not stave off the government's defeat on 29 March. In the ensuing general election the party secured only 8.1 per cent of the poll, and Evans was defeated once again (Balsom, 1979, 139). Lacking an emotive issue such as oil to spur supporters, Plaid Cymru has never matched the electoral performance of the SNP in percentage terms. However, while the SNP now attracts a respectable vote throughout Scotland, Plaid Cymru concentrates its greatest effort on the five main Welsh-speaking constituencies. The identity of the SNP can be confused by its need to say different things in a wide range of Scottish constituencies, but Plaid Cymru's narrower targets allow for greater clarity, despite the fact that it has suffered splits (notably between socialists and the anti-socialist 'Hydro' group in the early 1980s). In the 1992 general election its percentage support in Wales was less than half that of the SNP in Scotland, but it won more seats (four compared to three). This might prove to be almost as good a performance as Plaid Cymru can ever hope for, but it still allows them to dream of a powerful role in any future hung Parliament.

The nature and level of nationalist sentiment in Wales is very different from that in Scotland, and it is not surprising that this has produced different responses from the main parties. In 1992 both Labour and Conservatives promised concessions to Welsh speakers, but while Labour advocated an Assembly of very limited powers, the government emphasised its practical achievements. The Conservatives could argue that they were already working to meet the demands of most nationalists, by promoting the Welsh language through the National Curriculum and other measures including the establishment of a Welsh Language Board. The Welsh Office (first set up in 1964) enjoyed a surprising degree of autonomy under Mrs Thatcher; this was even more unusual given that her ideological opponent Peter Walker was Secretary of State after 1987. Levels of industrial assistance were therefore somewhat higher than might have been expected, and inward investment was particularly buoyant (Gamble, 1993, 83). This conciliatory approach to Welsh nationalism proved no more successful at winning friends than the confrontational tactics adopted in Scotland; the Tories held only six Welsh seats in 1992, on 29 per cent of the vote. There were signs, in fact, that the Conservative measures might prove counter-productive in the long term. As internal discrimination against the Welsh language is reduced, Plaid Cymru has become much happier about the prospect of a devolved parliament, at the very least. Even in 1968 one perceptive commentator noted that grievances about language were 'becoming merely a part of a general resentment at the remoteness and apparent lack of concern of Whitehall' – a feeling which cannot be assuaged by the Conservative habit of picking secretaries of state who have little previous connection with Wales (Mackintosh, 1968, 149). The Welsh case might eventually show the Conservatives that the best way to preserve the Union is to attack its enemies, not pamper them.

Nationalism in Northern Ireland

The political implications of nationalist feelings in Scotland and Wales are very different, but the SNP and Plaid Cymru share a commitment to constitutional activism. With the exception of the anti-Poll Tax campaign, these parties have discountenanced illegality, and deplored the use of political violence. For various reasons Northern Ireland has been a different case. Whatever the success of current moves towards a constitutional settlement, differences are likely to remain for some time, both in the manifestations of nationalism throughout the province and in the reactions of mainland parties.

The Anglo-Irish Treaty of 1921, which officially divided Ireland into the self-governing Free State and the partially autonomous six counties of Ulster, was difficult to defend on strictly rational grounds. It could always be attacked for creating an 'artificial' Protestant majority in the north of the island. For the British government, however, it was a tolerable means of escaping the unrest which had made rational administration an impossibility. Ireland as a whole had suffered during the nineteenth century, from famine, the violent suppression of any protest, and the unscrupulous exploitation of absentee landlords. The grievances of the majority Catholic population stretched back much further, to the atrocities committed by Cromwell's soldiers and beyond. As the United Kingdom became a more democratic state the situation in Ireland seemed increasingly anomalous, but peaceful reforms such as Gladstone's Home Rule Bills came to nothing. The resulting anger among the nationalists was matched by the insecurity of their opponents, and violent outbreaks such as the 1916 Easter Rising were inevitable.

Although sporadic paramilitary activities continued, Ulster remained relatively peaceful under the compromise of 1921 until the late 1960s. In 1968 a Northern Ireland Civil Rights Association (NICRA) was formed, in an attempt to emulate the success of similar movements abroad. NICRA's main aims were the reform of an electoral system which had been skewed to favour Unionist candidates, and the end of discrimination in areas such as housing. The Unionist response was predictably hostile, but Northern Ireland's Prime Minister, Terence O'Neill, attempted to satisfy the main demands. This was the signal for the 'Troubles' to begin, and the disorder quickly over-stretched the local security forces. In August 1969 military support was requested from the British government. As the situation continued to deteriorate, soldiers who had originally been sent to protect the Catholic minority in Ulster were increasingly regarded as their enemy; the events of 'Bloody Sunday', when troops opened fire on demonstrators in Derry on 30 January 1972, could only add to this impression. Direct rule from London was established later in the same year. Since then, it has proved impossible to find a way of transferring significant powers back to the province without alienating one of the main groupings, although this situation may be changing in the mid-1990s.

In the period of the Troubles the main constitutional parties in Ulster have been the Ulster Unionist Party (UUP), the Democratic Unionist Party (DUP), the predominantly Catholic Social Democratic and Labour Party (SDLP) and the Alliance Party, which attempts to draw support from moderates on both sides of the dispute. Since the early 1980s Provisional Sinn Fein has contested elections in line with its slogan of 'the ballot paper in one hand and the Armalite rifle in the other'. Sinn Fein was legalised in 1974 in an attempt to wean its supporters away from their close alliance with the Irish Republican Army (IRA); the failure of this strategy was indicated by Mrs Thatcher's broadcasting ban on the party imposed in October 1988 (Thatcher, 1993, 406–12).

In fact, it has been difficult to draw a precise line between constitutional and paramilitary activities in Northern Ireland, at least since the time when senior Conservative politicians encouraged Unionists to arm themselves early in the twentieth century. Just as Sinn Fein speaks for those who will accept nothing short of total British withdrawal from Ireland, people who are ready to fight to maintain the Union will rarely disagree with the opinions (if not the methods) of the Reverend Ian Paisley's DUP. British governments have long recognised that these incompatible attitudes exist and must at least be listened to. As a result, the main UK parties have tried to isolate Ulster's problems from the usual party conflicts; the formula that the province will remain part of the United Kingdom until a majority decides otherwise has satisfied most mainland politicians. Although the Unionist parties have historic ties with the Conservatives at Westminster and the SDLP normally sides with Labour, the kind of tactical considerations which affect the main parties' dealings with Scottish and Welsh nationalism at election time have been subdued in the case of Ireland. Unfortunately, the problems of the Major government in the mid-1990s have coincided with a period in which Unionists might hope to win concessions in the peace process as the price of support. Ironically, a sustained attempt to bring peace in the province threatens to remove one of the few areas of UK politics which has been relatively free from opportunism in recent years.

The usual terminology applied to the Irish scene equates the Catholic and nationalist populations, and makes similar assumptions about Protestants and Unionism. This approach is understandable given the historic divisions, but it can be misleading. In a sense, all the main parties of Northern Ireland are nationalistic; Sinn Fein and the SDLP both aspire to Irish unity (either immediately or in the long term), but the UUP and the DUP are determined to preserve a culture which is very different from that found in other parts of the United Kingdom. In 1990 a survey found that 27 per cent of the Protestant population identified themselves as 'Ulster' or 'Northern Irish' rather than as British (Jowell et al., 1990). When pressed, the Unionist parties have been prepared to defy the UK government. In 1974, for example, a general strike supported by many Unionists destroyed the 'power-sharing' initiative introduced by William Whitelaw, and relations have been particularly strained since Mrs Thatcher signed the misnamed 'Anglo-Irish' Agreement in 1985. In 1979 the Unionist New Ulster Political Research Group (NUPRG) proposed independence for the province in its paper *Beyond the Religious Divide* (cited in Arthur and Jeffery, 1988, 49).

The ideological situation in Northern Ireland is complicated by divisions within the parties. For example, under Gerry Fitt the SDLP was an avowedly socialist party; since John Hume became leader, however, a more social democratic outlook has prevailed (Rolston, 1987, 60). Sinn Fein has traditionally been inspired by Marxist doctrines, but its nature has inevitably promoted power struggles based on tactical considerations. Under the leadership of Ian Paisley the DUP has been united from its base in the Free Presbyterian Church, but the UUP has also experienced tensions between those (such as Enoch Powell) who advocate full integration within the United Kingdom and others who prefer a return to the status quo before 1972. The peace process has subjected the parties to new strains, and the option of 'independence within Europe' is an additional complication (Boyle and Hadden, 1994, 135–57). Leaving aside the differences between Northern Ireland and other parts of the United Kingdom, even a brief glance at the situation there shows that nationalism is a phenomenon which eludes simplistic definitions.

English nationalism

Unlike the Scots, the Welsh and the Northern Irish, the English have not needed to debate the question of national self-determination in the modern period – at least until recent storms over the EC. This has helped to produce a supercilious attitude towards nationalism. When English people exhibit enthusiasm for their country in the yearly 'promenade' concerts, or in more unusual circumstances such as the Falklands War, they generally admit to patriotic, rather than nationalistic, feelings. Patriotism is seen as a steadfast love of one's country, which involves aggression only when the homeland is attacked by others. Nationalists, by contrast, are believed to harbour negative feelings about others rather than pride in themselves. On this reading, nationalism is a sure sign of frustrated ambitions or a country in spiritual decline. A version of this theory was expounded by George Orwell, who wanted to teach socialists that it was not wrong to love one's country (Crick, 1991, 96). As used by Orwell the distinction is important; like Edmund Burke, Orwell thought that one can love one's country only if it is intrinsically lovable. Unfortunately for the English, it has been more common for them to betray the feeling which Orwell abhorred – 'My Country, Right or Wrong'. As the English deplore the evils that can arise from nationalism in other parts of the world, they often fail to appreciate how strongly it affects their own politics.

The immigration question

The United Kingdom has traditionally benefited from immigration, particularly that which accompanied religious persecution in Europe during the sixteenth and seventeenth centuries. During the nineteenth century the confidence of British governments allowed them to give refuge to dissidents from abroad such as Mazzini and Marx. Whatever the conditions in industrial areas and workhouses, or the treatment of native populations by British colonialists, the symbolism of empire was used to evoke the idea of a nation at ease with itself. Even the criticism of Disraeli's 'Jingoism' during the Russo-Turkish War of 1878 indirectly implied that Britain was strong and righteous enough to base its foreign policy on moral concerns rather than self-aggrandisement. The nation's mission was to spread good government and unimpeachable values to less fortunate countries; when war broke out in 1914 colonies were expected to show their gratitude by fighting on behalf of their generous benefactor.

After the Second World War some colonial governments encouraged migration to the UK in response to unemployment at home. Despite labour shortages in certain industries and concerns about a possible fall in the indigenous native population, this trend was discouraged by the British government. The British were beginning their retreat from empire, and did not want the empire to come home with them. In particular both of the main parties were worried about the impact of 'coloured' immigration. Sometimes this attitude arose because policy-makers genuinely feared that racists would react violently to the newcomers; this was borne out when riots occurred in Liverpool and parts of London between 1948 and 1954 (Layton-Henry, 1992, 37). More often it simply reflected the prejudices of governments and their officials. In fact, recruitment proceeded steadily during the 1950s and 1960s (though not as rapidly as populist legend implied). Economic growth stimulated demand for unskilled labour in industries such as textiles, and cheap workers were needed in the developing National Health Service. While the economy was healthy the issue did not feature in party conflict, although riots at Notting Hill, West London, in 1958 increased public alarm.

The 1960s was the key decade for the treatment of immigration. Both parties established a dual-track approach which has remained in force ever since. Immigration was limited, but some mild legislation was also introduced to curb racial discrimination. Although the Labour Party created the Race Relations Board in 1966, both of the governing parties acted to restrict immigration during the decade. The strategy caused deep misgivings for committed multi-culturalists within each party, but they had little choice but to accept what was seen as the dictation of electoral necessity. The compromise meant that the Conservative Party could contain both the enlightened Iain Macleod and rabid members of the Monday Club, which had been formed to oppose Britain's retreat from empire and now advocated the compulsory repatriation of immigrants in addition to its conspiratorial work with elements of the secret services (Dorril and Ramsay, 1992, 224–8). In April 1968, however, this fragile unity was threatened when the Conservative Enoch Powell delivered his 'Rivers of Blood' speech. Whatever Powell's motives, his language could only inflame existing prejudices, and he was instantly sacked from the Shadow Cabinet. His defence was that he had only repeated party policy, but his assertion that most immigrants had no desire to be integrated with the rest of the population was a direct assault on the established approach. An opinon poll conducted in the following month found that 27 per cent of the electorate considered immigration to be the most urgent problem facing the country (Wybrow, 1989, 88). It was subsequently claimed that the Conservative victory in the 1970 general election owed much to Powell's personal following in the midlands. In 1971 the Heath government passed an Immigration Act, parts of which have been described as 'blatantly racist' (Layton-Henry, 1992, 89). Certainly the Act had the effect of seriously curtailing rights of entry for non-white Commonwealth citizens. The Home Secretary responsible for the Act, Reginald Maudling, betrayed this attitude when he related in his memoirs how 'immigrants had been pouring in to this country from the Commonwealth in large numbers . . . they came in numbers that were too large to be assimilated' (Maudling, 1978, 157–8). Yet when Idi Amin expelled 50,000 Asians from Uganda in August 1972 more than half were allowed to settle in the United Kingdom, despite an hysterical campaign in the Conservative press. Heath's refusal to capitulate to racist propaganda disgusted many of Powell's supporters, who began to leave the party even before their hero did in 1974.

By 1977 Enoch Powell was an Ulster Unionist MP, but his preoccupation with the immigration issue continued. On 21 January he delivered a speech that was consciously intended to test the scope of the third and most powerful Race Relations Act, which Labour had passed in the previous year (Berkeley, 1977,

87). Now that Heath had been replaced, the Conservative Party had a leader who was sympathetic to Powell's economic views. In 1978 Margaret Thatcher also hinted that she was receptive to his thoughts on race. In a *World in Action* television interview she declared that 'People are really rather afraid that this country might be rather swamped by people with a different culture'. Thatcher 'was taken aback by the reaction to these extremely mild remarks'. A simplistic reading would suggest that these views are incompatible with her later statement that 'individuals are worthy of respect *as individuals*, not as members of classes or races'. In fact, colour was probably irrelevant to Mrs Thatcher, who instinctively disliked people of any shade if they had absorbed a culture which rejected free enterprise and the minimal state. She might have thought that this applied very strongly to West Indians, but she was equally convinced that it was true of the French. Whatever the reasons for her stance, race joined the extensive list of issues on which she sensed the support of most British people; as she remarks, opinion polls after the interview showed that the Conservatives had suddenly established an eleven-point lead over Labour (Thatcher, 1995, 406, 408).

One probable effect of Thatcher's remarks was a sudden reversal of fortune for the racist National Front (NF) party. This had been formed in 1967 from three existing groups who wanted the repatriation of immigrants. By 1973 the National Front was popular enough to take 16 per cent of the vote in a midlands by-election, and was attracting defectors from the Monday Club. These recruits fitted rather uneasily with Margaret Thatcher's assertion that groups like the National Front 'were just as much socialist as they were nationalist' (Thatcher, 1995, 406). In fact, the National Front had no more to do with socialism than Adolf Hitler, who had used the word to attract a following which was purged as soon as it had served his purposes. In the 1979 general election its candidates received 189,000 votes; even this was a disappointment, after some encouraging performances in local elections (Walker, 1979, 199). By contrast, in 1992 the National Front and a splinter group, the British National Party, fielded only twenty-seven candidates, who scraped 12,000 votes between them.

This does not mean that racists have experienced a mass conversion since 1979; some groups, such as Combat 18, are more interested in direct action against the immigrant community than in the democratic process. Yet it is safe to assume that, after their disillusionment with Heath, a good proportion of NF support returned to the Conservatives once Mrs Thatcher became leader. The Conservatives did not introduce repatriation, but they certainly took every opportunity to discourage further immigration. In Peter Riddell's words, the British Nationality Act 1981 virtually removed automatic rights of entry and settlement from everyone except 'whites with close ties to the UK' (Riddell, 1991, 156). Just in case anyone else could sneak in, the government passed yet another Immigration Act in 1988; in the House of Commons the Bill was introduced by Edward Heath's old ally Douglas Hurd, who had once praised his mentor's 'disgust at colour prejudice' (Hurd, 1979, 50). This was the price that enlightened ministers had to pay for serving in Thatcher Cabinets. Unlike his predecessor, John Major has always been an outspoken anti-racist, but this has not prevented his Home Secretary, Michael Howard, from urging more restrictions on immigration, particularly affecting those seeking political asylum. As internal EU borders disappeared, other states 'set out to make it impossible for immigrants and asylum-seekers to enter Europe', but clearly this was a policy from which the Prime Minister was disinclined to 'opt out' (Wheeler, 1993). As a result of all these obstacles to potential settlers, the Conservatives could now feel complacent about the anti-immigrant vote; this is indicated by the fact that the 1992 *Campaign Guide* devoted only one out of four hundred pages to the issue. This is not to say that Labour would have behaved very differently if it had held office since 1979; after all, racism is prevalent in many of the working-class areas where the party has traditionally thrived. The record implies, however, that after capturing the racist vote in 1979 the Conservative Party has not disappointed it.

The European controversy

Despite the endeavours of Powell, Thatcher, and certain newspapers, the dual-track approach to immigration still prevailed in 1995. That is, the volume of immigration was controlled, but those already in the United Kingdom were given at least token protection from racism. The number of racist attacks continued to rise, but the political salience of the issue subsided during the 1980s. Initially, a similar compromise was established on the question of the EC in order to satisfy internal party divisions. If pro-Europeans were pleased because the UK had joined, Euro-sceptics had to be placated by means of an obstructive attitude – in Stephen George's phrase, the UK had to be at best an 'Awkward Partner' (George, 1994). Hence, Harold Wilson renegotiated the terms of entry after his return to office in 1974, and then held a referendum on the subject at the prompting of Tony Benn, Labour's most prominent anti-marketeer. Margaret Thatcher's vigorous demands for a fairer budget contribution continued the trend. Since the time of the Maastricht negotiations of 1991, however, this has become an increasingly hazardous position for the Conservative government; in time it promises to be equally troublesome for Labour.

Nationalism clearly lies at the root of these problems. Had the UK signed the Treaty of Rome in 1957 it would have become a powerful founding-member of the EC, and controversial measures such as the Common Agricultural Policy (CAP) would have been designed differently. The decision not to join was at least partly the result of a calculation that the UK could thrive outside the Community. This made the unsuccessful applications of the 1960s particularly humiliating, and continuing membership still acts as an affront to those who think that the UK could survive on its own. A negative attitude towards the Community has trapped the UK in a vicious circle; the annoyance of other European states makes it feel like an impotent outsider, and this leads to further negative feelings. In a typical manoeuvre, Euro-sceptics quickly spread the myth that the most crucial European decisions are taken by the unelected Commission instead of the Council of Ministers; even ministers who were well disposed to the EC found the Commission a welcome scapegoat for their own decisions. Thus a nationalistic hatred of power-sharing with foreigners is disguised under a more respectable appeal to democratic principles. The fact that the public overwhelmingly approved membership in 1975 (even on unsatisfactory terms) has not deterred those who see the fight against closer European union as a battle 'to save our democracy' (Gorman, 1993, xvii).

Obviously not all 'Euro-phobia' is dictated by prejudice. Some opponents of membership base their views on an assessment of UK interests which has little (or even nothing) to do with the fact that foreigners now have some influence over government decisions. Some economic liberals agree with Mrs Thatcher, and simply equate 'foreigners' with 'socialism'; if they thought that all the world agreed with their ideology, they would become cosmopolites. However, even the Chancellor of the Exchequer could not explain the depth of Conservative feeling in mid-1995 without using the word 'xenophobia'; during the Maastricht debates, John Major had privately described his opponents in even harsher terms. In fact, Major had done all he could to please these critics short of actually leaving the EU – to the extent, for example, of seriously exaggerating the scope of the Social Chapter of the Maastricht Treaty in order to justify the

UK's opt-out from it. Just as Mrs Thatcher's reference to being 'swamped' unconsciously revealed her fears for a culture in decline, the Euro-phobes unwittingly betrayed an understandable concern that the UK economy was too weak to ensure that its interests prevailed in Europe. Whatever the state of the economy, however, their tactics ensured that the UK could not hope to exercise an influence in proportion to its budgetary contribution. Of course, this did not worry the Euro-phobes: evidence that ministers were ignored in European battles helped their argument that the UK should withdraw altogether.

Conclusion: varieties of nationalism

Even a brief survey of nationalism in the United Kingdom reveals the complexity of the subject. Although it would be a mistake to concentrate on single factors in each case, Welsh nationalism is mainly cultural and linguistic, Scottish nationalism focuses on politics and economics, while religion is the most telling feature in Northern Ireland. Wales and Scotland have internal differences, but nothing to compare with the rift between the communities of Northern Ireland. Nationalism of various kinds dominates politics in Northern Ireland, whereas it is one of many important influences in Scotland and Wales. Only in Northern Ireland have constitutional parties developed an ambivalent attitude to political violence, although civil disobedience has sometimes been encouraged in the other countries. As Tom Nairn has pointed out, all these varieties of nationalism differ from the experience of the 'Third World', where national consciousness has arisen in tandem with economic development (Nairn, 1981). In fact, nationalism within the UK became a dynamic political force in the 1960s, at a time of growing disillusionment with the economic outlook. Crude deterministic explanations ought to be resisted, but the temptation in this instance is unusually strong.

In England, many would point to the unsuccessful history of the NF (following the dismal failure of Oswald Mosley's fascists) to back their claim that nationalism is of no account. This view is based on a misconception of nationalism which has arisen from previous English experiences. Nationalism is not simply a struggle to achieve self-government; it can also arise when a nation falls on hard times, and needs to sustain the feeling that it runs its own affairs. The result is a search for the reason why things went wrong in the past, and for present enemies to struggle against; myths are as necessary to governments under pressure as they are to movements for national liberation. After so many years of economic power and political influence, it is not surprising that this form of nationalism has emerged in England since the Second World War. The 1979 election gave the UK its first truly nationalist government; ironically, however, Margaret Thatcher's nationalism worked in tension with economic liberalism, an ideology which dictated that no nation should be protected from the consequences of its failure to compete. For a nation in economic decline this is a hard doctrine – but, in this sense at least, capitalism is 'colour blind', in the former Prime Minister's phrase (Thatcher, 1995, 406).

The question which remains is whether or not nationalism ought to be considered as an ideology itself. The answer provided by most books on the subject is affirmative. Ian Adams, for example, claims that it 'is the simplest, the clearest and the least theoretically sophisticated' of ideologies (Adams, 1993, 82). However, Andrew Vincent acknowledges that 'it is difficult to provide any clear and overarching sense to the diverse claims of nationalism' (Vincent, 1995, 238). Moving from general works to particular studies of nationalism, Keith Webb observes that it differs from other ideologies because 'it implies nothing specific about the internal organisation of the state or the nation' (Webb, 1978, 19). When cohesive ideological groups win power they might disagree over the details of subsequent policies, but they can at least understand the reasoning behind different positions. There is no reason why successful nationalists should be so fortunate unless their common desire for liberation is matched by agreement about the best kind of social organisation – or, as in the case of totalitarian nationalists like Hitler and Stalin, manipulative leaders can make the public confuse the enemies of state policies with the enemies of the nation.

Of course, there may be cases of activists whose political desires have been fully satisfied once national liberation has been achieved. Yet nationalism is more often a means to an end. The enemy is regarded not just as a force which prevents self-government, but as an obstacle to the fulfilment of human potential in a specific form of social organisation. On these grounds, since nationalism itself does not prescribe any social form, it cannot be regarded as an ideology in the full sense of the definition used here. Instead, it should be understood as a motivating principle which can be held by members of any ideological grouping. Once national feeling has been satisfied, ideology takes over. In short, there are liberal nationalists, conservative nationalists, and so on; fascists are not simply extreme nationalists, but ideologues who have thrived only because they are ready to exploit any emotional tool that will further their aims. Within all the ideological varieties of nationalism there is room for great variation; on close inspection, even within a single state like the United Kingdom nationalism turns out to be far from 'simple'.

List of works cited

Adams, Ian (1993), *Political Ideology Today,* Manchester University Press

Arthur, Paul, and Jeffery, Keith (1988), *Northern Ireland since 1968*, Blackwell

Balsom, Denis (1979), 'Plaid Cymru: The Welsh National Party', in Henry Drucker (ed.), *Multi-Party Britain*, Macmillan

Berkeley, Humphrey (1977), *The Odyssey of Enoch: A Political Memoir*, Hamish Hamilton

Boyle, Kevin, and Hadden, Tom (1994), *Northern Ireland: The Choice*, Penguin

Butler, David, and Kavanagh, Denis (1992), *The British General Election of 1992*, Macmillan

Butler, David, Adonis, Andrew and Travers, Tony (1994), *Failure in British Government: The Politics of the Poll Tax*, Oxford University Press

Butt Philp, Alan (1975), *The Welsh Question: Nationalism in Welsh Politics 1945–1970*, Cardiff University Press

Conservative Research Department (1992), *The Campaign Guide 1992*, Conservative Central Office

Crick, Bernard (1991), 'The English and the British', in Bernard Crick (ed.), *National Identities: The Constitution of the United Kingdom*, Blackwell

Dorril, Stephen, and Ramsay, Robin (1992), *Smear! Wilson and the Secret State*, Grafton

Drucker, Henry (1978), *Breakaway: The Scottish Labour Party*, EUSPB

Fukuyama, Francis (1992), *The End of History and the Last Man*, Penguin

Gamble, Andrew (1993), 'Territorial Politics', in Patrick Dunleavy, Andrew Gamble, Ian Holliday and Gillian Peele (eds) *Developments in British Politics 4*, Macmillan

George, Stephen (1994), *An Awkward Partner: Britain in the European Community*, Macmillan

Gorman, Teresa (1993), *The Bastards: Dirty Tricks and the Challenge to Europe*, Pan

Harvie, Christopher (1994), *The Rise of Regional Europe,* Routledge

Hurd, Douglas (1979), *An End to Promises: Sketch of a Government 1970–74*, Collins

Jowell, Roger, Brook, Lindsay, and Taylor, Bridget (eds) (1990), *British Social Attitudes: The 7th Report*, Dartmouth

Kellas, James (1989), *The Scottish Political System*, Cambridge University Press, 4th edition

Layton-Henry, Zig (1992), *The Politics of Immigration*, Blackwell

McCreadie, Robert (1991), 'Scottish Identity and the Constitution', in Bernard Crick (ed.), *National Identities: The Constitution of the United Kingdom*, Blackwell

Mackintosh, John (1968), *The Devolution of Power: Local Democracy, Regionalism and Nationalism*, Penguin

Marquand, David (1991), 'Nations, Regions, and Europe', in Bernard Crick (ed.), *National Identities: The Constitution of the United Kingdom*, Blackwell

Maudling, Reginald (1978), *Memoirs*, Sidgwick and Jackson

Miller, William (1981), *The End of British Politics? Scots and English Political Behaviour in the Seventies*, Oxford University Press

Mullin, W. A. Roger (1979), 'The Scottish National Party', in Henry Drucker (ed.), *Multi-Party Britain*, Macmillan

Nairn, Tom (1981), *The Break-up of Britain: Crisis and Neo-Nationalism*, Verso, 2nd edition

Riddell, Peter (1991), *The Thatcher Era and its Legacy*, Blackwell

Rolston, Bill (1987), 'Alienation or Political Awareness? The Battle for Hearts and Minds of Northern Nationalists', in Paul Teague (ed.) *Beyond the Rhetoric: Politics, the Economy and Social Policy in Northern Ireland*, Lawrence and Wishart

Smith, Anthony (1995), 'The Dark Side of Nationalism: the Revival of Nationalism in Late Twentieth-Century Europe', in Luciano Cheles, Ronnie Ferguson and Michalina Vaughan (eds) *The Far Right in Western and Eastern Europe*, Longman, 2nd edition

Thatcher, Margaret (1993), *The Downing Street Years*, HarperCollins

Thatcher, Margaret (1995), *The Path to Power*, HarperCollins

Thomas, Dafydd Elis (1991), 'The Constitution of Wales', in Bernard Crick (ed.) *National Identities: The Constitution of the United Kingdom*, Blackwell

Vincent, Andrew (1995), *Modern Political Ideologies*, Blackwell, 2nd edition

Walker, Martin (1979), 'The National Front', in Henry Drucker (ed.) *Multi-Party Britain*, Macmillan

Webb, Keith (1978), *The Growth of Nationalism in Scotland*, Penguin

Wheeler, Francis (1993), '*The New Europe: Immigration and Asylum*', in Tony Bunyan (ed.) *Statewatching the New Europe: A Handbook on the European State*, Statewatch

Wybrow, Robert (1989), *Britain Speaks Out, 1937–87: A Social History as Seen through the Gallup Data*, Macmillan

Questions for discussion

- Do the policies of the nationalist parties in Britain support the notion that nationalism is an ideology? Answer with particular attention to any two parties.
- Explore the English attitude to nationalism.

Selected further reading

Bogdanor, Vernon (1980), *Devolution*, Oxford University Press.

Bruce, Steve (1994), *The Edge of the Union: The Ulster Loyalist Political Vision*, Oxford University Press.

Crick, Bernard (1990), *Political Thoughts and Polemics*, Edinburgh University Press.

Foot, Paul (1965), *Immigration and Race in British Politics*, Penguin.

Gellner, Ernest (1983), *Nations and Nationalism*, Oxford University Press.

Harvie, Colin (1977), *Scotland and Nationalism: A Study of Politics and Society in Scotland 1707– Present*, Allen and Unwin.

Hobsbawm, Eric (1990), *Nations and Nationalism since 1780*, Cambridge University Press.

Holmes, Colin (1988), *John Bull's Island: Immigration and British Society 1871–1971*, Macmillan.

Holmes, Colin (1991), *A Tolerant Country? Immigrants, Refugees and Minorities in Britain*, Faber and Faber.

Kedourie, Elie (1974), *Nationalism*, Hutchinson, 2nd edition.

Laqueur, Walter (ed.) (1979), *Fascism: A Reader's Guide*, Penguin.

Marr, Andrew (1992), *The Battle for Scotland*, Penguin.

Miles, Robert (1990), 'The Racialization of British Politics', *Political Studies*, volume 38.

Mitchell, James (1992), 'The 1992 General Election in Scotland in Context', *Parliamentary Affairs*, volume 45, number 4.

Mosley, Oswald (1968), *My Life*, Book Club edition.

Nairn, Tom (1970), 'Enoch Powell: the New Right', *New Left Review* 61.

Osmond, John (ed.) (1985), *The National Question Again: Welsh Political Identity in the 1980s*, Gower.

O'Sullivan, Noel (1983), *Fascism*, Dent.

Paterson, Lindsay, Brown, Alice, and McCrone, David (1992), 'Constitutional Crisis: The Causes and Consequences of the 1992 Scottish General Election Result', *Parliamentary Affairs*, volume 45, number 4.

Schapiro, Leonard (1972), *Totalitarianism*, Macmillan.

Solomos, John (1993), *Race and Racism in Britain*, Macmillan, 2nd edition.

Stokes, Gale (1993), *The Walls Came Tumbling Down: The Collapse of Communism in Eastern Europe*, Oxford University Press.

CHAPTER 7

Principles and politics since Thatcher

Background: Thatcher to Major

Margaret Thatcher's sudden departure from office in November 1990 has been variously attributed to her style of government, her championship of the Poll Tax, the economic recession, the insecurity of Tory MPs, and the petty vindictiveness of former ministers such as Michael Heseltine, Nigel Lawson and Sir Geoffrey Howe. The question which her fall left unanswered was whether or not Thatcherism would survive Thatcher. The signs here were mixed; after all, at the time of the contest John Major was regarded as Mrs Thatcher's favourite political son, but almost all the reasons that were advanced for her unpopularity were linked in some way to her political beliefs. Michael Heseltine, whose opposition to Mrs Thatcher went beyond questions of style, had failed to win a majority of Conservative votes, but his supporters were numerous enough to suggest that some changes, at least, would be necessary to restore the party's fortunes under its new leader.

A crucial factor in the future direction of the party was the thinking of the new Prime Minister. His emergence as the person most likely to promote unity was significantly helped by the obscurity of his views. After entering the House of Commons in 1979 he had worked his way steadily through the government hierarchy, joining the Cabinet as Chief Secretary to the Treasury in 1987. In July 1989 his promotion to Foreign Secretary in place of Sir Geoffrey Howe caused general surprise, but Thatcher's decision to make him Chancellor of the Exchequer when Nigel Lawson resigned in October of the same year was an even bolder move. With a background in finance, Major was better qualified to work in the Treasury than in the Foreign Office, but he could now be regarded as the favoured candidate to succeed the Prime Minister on her eventual retirement. When that time came, the fact that he had avoided being identified with any ideological section of the party would help rather than hinder his prospects.

Major had not been Foreign Secretary for long enough to create much impression, but soon after becoming Chancellor he showed that he was more than just Mrs Thatcher's yes-man by joining with Douglas Hurd to persuade the Prime Minister that the UK should join the ERM. This ran counter to Thatcher's instincts in two important respects; it represented a move towards deeper European integration, and it also contradicted her belief that currency exchange rates should be decided by the free market. Major's only Budget provided some relief for Poll Tax payers, and introduced a new tax-free account for savers. It was not a spectacular Budget after the fireworks of the Lawson years, but it made no additional enemies for the party at a difficult time.

Major officially supported Margaret Thatcher on the inconclusive first leadership ballot, but he was recovering from a timely surgical operation when the rest of the Cabinet were asked for their views about her prospects in a second contest. After running a skilful campaign Major defeated Michael Heseltine on the second ballot by 185 votes to 131; Douglas Hurd, whose love for his new job at the Foreign Office made him a surprising challenger, received 56 votes. A notable feature of the campaign was its inverted snobbery, with the Old Etonian Hurd offering lame excuses for his privileged background. Major had gained few academic qualifications, and a great deal was made of his relatively humble origins in Brixton, South London. Labour leadership elections have never concentrated so narrowly on class issues.

In keeping with his image, Major declared that he wanted Britain to become a 'classless society' (Junor, 1993, 253–4). This was a theme which had featured previously in Labour and Liberal propaganda, although each party meant different things by it. Major, a known opponent of discrimination, was indicating his preference for the kind of equal opportunity which he had benefited from. Whether his experience in the days when governments made full employment a high priority was relevant in 1990 was another question. Old definitions of class were becoming blurred in a consumer age, but social inequalities were rising. Yet at least Major's rhetoric hinted at a change of emphasis from the Thatcher years. According to the former Prime Minister, 'Class is a communist concept' (Thatcher, 1992).

Major's selections for his first Cabinet continued to give the impression that he was above any party infighting. Michael Heseltine was brought back into the Cabinet as Environment Secretary, charged with a thorough reform of the Poll Tax. The only important casualty was Cecil Parkinson, who had been Mrs Thatcher's personal favourite, but there was no general purge. Other ministers closely associated with the old regime kept their places; even Kenneth Baker, who had been party chairman while Tory fortunes declined, was moved only to the Home Office. Baker had once been an ally of Edward Heath, but had prospered under Thatcher. The new Chancellor, Norman Lamont, was well placed as both a convinced Thatcherite and a close friend of the new Prime Minister. Lamont was a member of the so-called 'Cambridge Mafia', whose members had all been prominent in Conservative circles at Cambridge University in the early 1960s. Other Cabinet ministers from this group included John Selwyn Gummer, Michael Howard and Kenneth Clarke; in addition, Leon Brittan and Norman Fowler had held Cabinet posts under Thatcher. At Cambridge, Howard had been such an outspoken opponent of racism that some doubted whether he would remain within the Conservative Party, but by 1990 he was seen as a standard-bearer of Thatcherism (McSmith, 1994, 12–29). The others were suspected of secret 'wet' leanings, although their ministerial records showed that they had disguised their secret very effectively. Such ministers, along with the Health Secretary William Waldegrave, could be described as 'Career Thatcherites', who would probably have implemented very different policies if they had enjoyed a free hand. Christopher Patten, the chairman of the party, had made his dissent from Thatcher very public in the early 1980s, but like the Mafia he had finally succumbed to the call, agreeing to oversee the Poll Tax as Environment Secretary in 1989. The subsequent behaviour of these flexible ministers would be a useful barometer of Major's intentions.

If John Major had wished to abandon Thatcherism, there was little to stop him. One authoritative study in 1989 found that only about 20 per cent of the Parliamentary Conservative Party were convinced believers in the 1980s revolution; in 1988 half of the electorate rejected the Thatcherite nostrum that inflation was a greater curse than unemployment (Norton, 1993, 33–5). The Poll Tax was regarded as the flagship of Thatcherism; now that this was sinking to loud popular applause, why not torpedo the whole fleet? With a secure parliamentary majority, Major had more than a year before a new election to carry out a counter-revolution. In addition to the special advantages of the situation, the new Prime Minister could also count on the tradition of loyalty to the party leader, and the fact that an alternative course would be perfectly compatible with the general trends of post-war conservatism.

After the Conservative victory in the 1992 general election, some commentators claimed that changes had taken place, although the shift had not been dramatic. One seasoned observer of the Conservative Party wrote that Major 'had no distinctive ideological leanings'; he differed from Thatcher in 'being a pragmatist'. Admittedly, he had declared his loathing of inflation in a forthright manner which his predecessor must have applauded, but according to this commentator the undoubted change of style under Major did reflect substantive policy differences (Norton, 1993, 60). If the country had sought a change of government in 1990, John Major gave it what it wanted without the trouble of going through a general election.

This verdict can be accepted only on the view that ideological politics are invariably linked with crusading zeal and radical change. Between 1990 and 1992 the Thatcherite revolution did not accelerate, but when the circumstances of recession are taken into account this was always unlikely. In most areas it simply proceeded at a steady pace. The education reforms introduced under Mrs Thatcher were given extra momentum by the energetic Kenneth Clarke (whatever his private reservations). Clarke introduced a new source of controversy with the first suggestion of league tables to evaluate school performance. At the Department of Health the bruising Clarke was replaced by Virginia Bottomley, but the change of style did nothing to slow the pace of reform, despite public concerns that this was merely the first step to a private health service. The much-publicised 'Citizen's Charter' meant that state employees could now be identified by name-badges, but their numbers continued to diminish. The 'Next Steps' programme initiated under Thatcher continued to transform government departments into independent agencies, which could be regarded as a temporary halt on the road to privatisation (Giddings, 1995). The Major government seemed even more anxious to replace local government with its unelected and secretive quangos, even though such bodies had once been a target for Thatcherite criticism (Holland, 1981). By 1994 a joint study by Essex University and Charter 88 found that there were 5,521 of these appointed bodies in the UK; the government, working on a more stringent definition, found 1,345 (Marr, 1995, 78). The share of national wealth taken by the state had not diminished, but the UK now seemed to have been sold off. The idea of private prisons, which had once provoked either laughter or nightmares among non-Thatcherites, brought only muffled protests when they became a reality. Returning railways and the coal mines to private hands remained high priorities, as did tax cuts. In short, the government acted on Thatcherite principles in all of these areas, sometimes proceeding boldly when Mrs Thatcher would have hesitated. Even the misleading difference in personal style between Major and Thatcher had its limits; Major was touted as a 'listening' Prime Minister, but he could not hear the arguments of trade unions while they continued to be barred from Downing Street.

Actions which superficially suggest a retreat from Thatcherism should also be examined in context. In some cases, when the new government was asked to clear up débris left by the previous regime, it was convenient for ministers to hint that Mrs Thatcher had been personally responsible. The Pergau Dam affair, which involved the misapplication of £56 million from the overseas aid budget, illustrated the benefits of portraying the fallen Prime Minister as an erratic dictator (Marr, 1995, 248–9). The short-term success of this strategy concealed dangers. Since it demanded that ministers should disown policies which they had once helped to implement, its usefulness depended upon the short attention span of the electorate. Sometimes, as in the case of the Scott inquiry into the sale of arms to Iraq, the issues were too spectacular for the government to rely on public amnesia. Hence, rumours quickly spread that ministers were keen to delay the publication of Scott's findings for as long as possible. Sometimes the government seemed to be spending more time on damage-limitation than on constructive work; as a result, ministers were more likely to make mistakes of their own. Even the previous Labour government, living with the constant threat of parliamentary defeat, had never been as accident-prone as the Major administration. However bad the late 1970s had been, Conservative Central Office could no longer rely on voters remembering those distant years.

The best evidence that Major represented a new start was his prompt abandonment of the Poll Tax. Its eventual replacement, the Council Tax, took some account of house values and reflected a greater concern for 'the ability to pay' (Butler et al., 1994, 176–83). When the new tax is compared to the old rating system, however, its effects are still regressive. It can be argued that Michael Heseltine simply substituted a workable for an unworkable Thatcherite policy; after all, the original tax had been poorly planned and its implementation too hurried. If the Council Tax was a defeat for Thatcherism, it implied no more than a minor tactical withdrawal. These had been fairly common during the 1980s, but Mrs Thatcher's occasional fits of pragmatism were now fading in the memory of commentators. Instead of comparing Major with other post-war Prime Ministers, the media wanted to measure him against an exaggerated image of his immediate predecessor. As a result it was not surprising that public opinion polls consistently showed that Major was regarded as pitifully weak (King, 1994).

The economic strategy of the government showed no serious deviation from the Thatcherite approach. Inflation remained the chief enemy, and interest-rate policy was still the weapon used to control the money supply. Unemployment climbed back to around 13 per cent before the 1992 election, but the government took the same 'hands-off' approach as Mrs Thatcher had done. Norman Lamont caused uproar in May 1991 when he declared that unemployment was 'a price worth paying' for economic recovery. In its handling of recession, the Major government differed from Mrs Thatcher's only by being less flexible; it courted electoral defeat through its inactivity when economic problems were affecting its natural supporters in the south. The small business people who formed the backbone of the party suffered as much as anyone; 44,000 small concerns went bankrupt in 1991 (Norton, 1993, 64). If the budget deficit rose, this was inevitable at a time when unemployment was rising steeply and fewer people were paying stamp duty as the housing market collapsed.

This evidence shows that if Thatcherism was slain by Tory back-benchers in November 1990, its ghost made a very effective understudy. It is normally a mistake to draw a clear distinction between perceived style and the content of policy, but in Major's case the difference between the two was unusually vivid. Major's style brought the Conservative Party credit for a rethink that never took place. His predecessor played an important part in creating this impression; with Mrs Thatcher herself now free from ministerial responsibility it was natural that she should criticise Major when his resolution seemed to be weak. In particular, she failed to appreciate that Major's tactic of remaining as an obstructive force within the EC was essentially the same as her own. Short of total withdrawal from the Community (which she has apparently never favoured) it is difficult to see how she would have achieved different results.

In the run up to the 1992 general election, almost all of the public opinion polls pointed to a narrow Labour victory, or at least a hung Parliament which would end thirteen years of Conservative rule (Sanders, 1993). A fourth successive victory in spite of a severe economic recession was an impressive achievement, even if the majority was now down to twenty-one seats. If Major could win in such unpromising circumstances, how could the Conservatives ever be beaten? The Labour Party had already redesigned its image, and there was a limit to the further changes which it could make. Although the Liberal Democrats had recovered from Owenite distractions, they still seemed unable to win the necessary support for a breakthrough. Yet the news was not all good for the Conservatives. For the first time since 1979 parliamentary unity would be essential to maintain a relatively slender majority. The party had not been wholly united at any time since 1970, and now the issue of Europe loomed as a possible threat to Major's authority, despite the opt-outs negotiated at Maastricht in December 1991.

More worrying still, the party was experiencing a serious membership crisis. A study conducted in the election year showed that estimates of well over 2 million members in the 1960s were now well out of date, if they had ever been accurate; the figure in 1992 was not far above 750,000. Of these, less than 5 per cent were younger than 35 (Whiteley et al., 1994, 25, 42). Under similar circumstances in the 1980s Labour's weakness in the constituencies had encouraged revolutionaries to practise 'entryism'; for the

Conservatives, apart from a little-publicised row which led to the disbandment of the Federation of Conservative Students in the 1980s, there was little sign of even unwanted enthusiasts joining the ranks. While party members were becoming both fewer and older, they were also increasingly difficult to manage. The party conference, once unfairly derided as a synchronised orgy of deference, has certainly become more consistently unruly since the fall of Margaret Thatcher (Kelly, 1994, 221–60). In the Charter Movement the Conservatives now have their own version of Labour's RFMC, demanding greater democracy within the party. The triumph of inverted snobbery has helped to ensure the election of three successive leaders from outside the British social elite, but the old elitist thinking certainly helped internal discipline.

The triumph of Thatcherism?

Few people attributed Labour's defeat in 1992 to insufficient socialist fervour. Instead, the post-mortem needed to explain why the electorate were still unwilling to accept that the party had changed. To make sure that the message would not be misunderstood in future, the campaigners for modernisation believed that they must press for further changes. After Neil Kinnock's immediate resignation, his Shadow Chancellor John Smith succeeded him as leader. Smith had been challenged for the post by Bryan Gould. Gould was unhappy with some developments within the party, such as the new warmer relationship with financial institutions, and his crushing defeat showed that Labour was not in the mood to tolerate the advocates of cautious modernisation. Before long Gould left to take up an academic post in New Zealand, complaining that Labour no longer stood for 'the goals of greater equality and freedom for ordinary people' (Gould, 1995, 281). The new deputy leader, Margaret Beckett, had benefited from the campaign to deselect the moderate Dick Taverne in Lincoln during the early 1970s. Fortunately her views had changed since her Bennite days, and unlike Taverne she saw no reason to leave the party.

Smith himself had joined Taverne in the 1971 parliamentary rebellion on membership of the EEC. Unlike many of his fellow-dissidents, however, he did not join the SDP. A brilliant lawyer, he had worked on Labour's plans for devolution before entering the Cabinet as Secretary of State for Trade. This governmental experience made him unusual among Labour's current front-bench team, if not in the PLP as a whole. Apart from his obvious administrative and debating skills, Smith at least gave the impression of listening to opinion from all sections of the party.

In the eyes of Kinnock's critics this made Smith a change for the better, although listening and acting on unwelcome advice are different things. Smith's shadow budget was identified by some as the main cause of Labour's defeat, but this was not enough to prevent his victory. He had also recently recovered from a serious heart attack. The size of his vote – 91 per cent – demonstrated that these handicaps were dwarfed by his popularity.

Smith immediately promised to complete the constitutional reforms of the Kinnock years, and to unite the anti-Conservative majority in the country. The most important development during the brief period before Smith succumbed to a second heart attack was a vote at the 1993 party conference which adopted OMOV (although in return for an extra £3, trade union levy-payers would also be treated as ordinary members). On policy matters Smith set up a Social Justice Commission under Sir Gordon Borrie. When this reported after Smith's death, it advocated a national minimum wage and spoke of a social security system which offered 'a hand-up rather than a hand-out'.

The emphasis was placed on opportunity, rather than dependency. This kind of language jostled uneasily with un-Thatcherite words like 'community', implying that Labour was still struggling to establish a distinctive or consistent vocabulary. The problem was not confined to the language of the report. Lurking behind some of its recommendations was the Thatcherite belief in rational individualism. For example, the report urged that young people should be encouraged to plan for their retirement. This advice could not be very impressive to people growing up amidst almost universal economic insecurity, particularly since the Borrie report did not suggest that Labour should restore its post-war target of full employment.

The independent status of the Borrie Commission meant that Labour was not bound by its conclusions, although there was no chance that the leadership would criticise them as deviations from socialism. By the time the Commission reported, the new Labour leader Tony Blair had set his sights on a new battle against the party's traditions. In the same month of October 1994 (ten weeks after becoming leader) Blair announced that Labour should have 'a clear, up-to-date statement' of its objectives (White, 1994). Since his objectives clearly did not include nationalisation, this meant that Hugh Gaitskell's attack on Clause IV (section 4) of the Labour constitution was being renewed. Unlike Gaitskell, however, Blair's gamble was successful. Despite some trade union opposition the constitution was amended in April 1995.

Blair's campaign was based on several shrewd calculations. First Clause IV itself had much more than a symbolic importance. Since the time of the Attlee government it had lent authority to damaging attacks from both Conservatives and socialists, one side claiming that Labour might one day fulfil its aspirations, the other protesting that the leadership always ignored it. Blair's supporters urged that if the party was serious about presenting a more modern image, it had to discard a commitment which dated from 1918 and had never been fully endorsed by public opinion. Secondly, the campaign gave Blair the chance to stamp his authority over the party while still enjoying the usual honeymoon period for new leaders. If this meant defying the trade unions, so much the better; Blair and his advisers shared an 'extraordinary fixation' on the idea that the connection with the unions was a major cause of Labour's election disasters since 1979 (Minkin, 1992, 678). Finally, ditching Clause IV maintained the impression that Labour was not complacent about its electoral chances; while John Major's attempts to relaunch his tired party backfired, Blair would press on to seize the initiative. The impression of dynamism was particularly useful, since Blair's strategy demanded that he should avoid constructive commitments until as late as possible.

Before Blair took over the leadership, it seemed as though a decisive swing in electoral opinion had really taken place. In the June 1994 European elections, Labour scored a clear victory, winning sixty-two out of the UK's eighty-four seats with 44 per cent of the vote. This was not just a sympathy vote after the death of John Smith; the trend continued after Blair became leader, as the Conservatives lost almost all of their local government councils and Labour performed well in parliamentary by-elections. Labour's recovery in the south was particularly chilling to Conservative MPs. Meanwhile, the drive for new members which had begun under Kinnock was now succeeding. A Labour victory in the next election seemed certain, and Blair was anxious to prevent any mood of complacency within the party.

Labour's ideological battle over the period since 1970 had produced one definite result: socialism had lost. What had won, exactly? The answer would have been 'social democracy' before the arrival of Tony Blair, but afterwards it was not so clear. As one astute critic observed in July 1995, during his first year as leader Blair had proved more adept at 'reassuring the exponents of the status quo than at inspiring those who detest it' (Young, 1995). In the European elections, the Conservatives registered the same level of support as Labour had achieved in its disastrous year of 1983. Surely this evidence meant that caution was no longer necessary? Or was the imprecision of Blair's rhetoric merely a camouflage for his lack of practical ideas?

Labour's experience in the 1992 election campaign showed the dangers of exposing policy ideas to detailed criticism, but the new leader's problems went deeper than this. Blair's chances of constructing a distinctive philosophical platform were undermined by developments within the Conservative Party. After the 1992 election, Mrs Thatcher had launched an explicit attack on John Major, in which she denounced any suggestion of a compromise between One Nation conservatism and her own position. Between 1990 and 1992 Christopher Patten had tried to show that this was possible by drawing on the arguments of European Christian Democracy (Patten, 1991). Patten lost his seat in the 1992 election and departed to govern Hong Kong; in his absence David Willetts, the former head of the CPS and newly elected as MP for Havant, prepared a different version of this unlikely synthesis (Willetts, 1992, 1994). In particular, Willetts attempted to show that Thatcherism was quite compatible with a sense of community. Willetts had been taught at Oxford by John Gray, a disciple of the conservative philosopher Michael Oakeshott; his skilful argument was undermined when Gray suddenly decided to denounce Thatcherism as heresy (an opinion which Oakeshott had privately established much earlier) (Gray, 1993). After this realisation, Gray wrote a powerful series of articles in the *Guardian*, in which he showed that communitarian rhetoric would mean nothing unless it tackled the economic roots of social breakdown (Gray, 1995). Despite this setback, the kinds of views publicised by Patten and Willetts filtered through into John Major's speeches (Major, 1994). This meant that the social philosophies preached by Blair and Major had almost converged. Since neither was anxious (or able) to announce startling policy innovations, the struggle between the party leaders would now be conducted at the level of rhetoric, rather than substance. The prize would go to the leader who managed to convince voters that support for the free market could be squared with a sense of social responsibility; meanwhile nothing was done to reverse the Thatcherite reforms which had provoked the new concern with community in the first place.

Skilful advocates like Willetts could make the rebuilding of community seem plausible in books, but the experience of the 1980s suggested that it could not be done in practice. The mobile workforce which the free market seemed to demand (at least in its British guise) was unfriendly to social cohesion. As the police found during the riots of 1981 and the miners' strike of 1984–85, expressions of communal solidarity were generally hostile to the operation of 'market forces'; under the Major premiership even prosperous communities began to obstruct road-building projects and the free market in live calves (see Chapter 8). The beneficiaries of the Thatcher revolution seemed to be rootless individuals – notably the so-called 'Yuppies', whose main concern was their own pleasure. For the policy-makers of both main parties, the choice lay between more individualistic policies, which might divide the country further, or the end of the

Thatcherite project, permitting a new emphasis on social priorities which would go beyond rhetorical gestures.

Claims that Thatcherism had caused the social problems of the 1980s were seriously exaggerated; indeed, if community spirit had been strong in 1979 it is unlikely that Mrs Thatcher would ever have been elected. However, economic liberalism had certainly made the problem worse. If politicians genuinely believed that a country 'at ease with itself' would be easier to govern, it was in their interest to at least explore the possibility of alternatives to Thatcherism. Since Thatcherism had never impressed a majority of the electorate, this approach should have been even more attractive for both parties. After 1992, however, the two main parties learned to despise the electorate. Repeated opinion polls found that people wanted both lower taxes and more public spending; the obvious answer to this was greater borrowing, but no one wanted a return to the days of the IMF loan. Unlike Ronald Reagan, who had tried to satisfy the demand for higher tax cuts and his drive for rearmament by running a massive US budget deficit in the 1980s, British politicians chose to interpret the poll evidence as a sign that the public was confused. From this it was an easy step to decide that the electorate really wanted tax cuts, not higher spending – after all, a saloon-bar philosopher in a tight corner will always count on greed rather than altruism (Marquand, 1988, 93–5). When an opinion poll (conducted in the same month that Blair rid himself of Clause IV) found that 60 per cent of voters agreed that the basic rate of income tax should be raised from 25p to 30p in the pound to finance public services, politicians refused to take the hint (Linton and Wintour, 1995).

One of the key assumptions which underpinned Mrs Thatcher's economic liberalism was that British people would behave responsibly if left to themselves. This meant that any social problems must be due to the unwise meddling of legislators. The reforming Labour governments of the 1960s were frequently identified as the worst culprits here. Given her remarkable faith in the moral instincts of most Britons, Thatcher felt that the occasional homily on the themes of 'Victorian Values' (added to the effect of her economic policies) would do more good than direct government action. This approach clearly failed, and the impression that Britain had become an uglier place in recent years worried John Major. As a leading press supporter of the Conservatives later claimed, 'Grassroots Tories have long felt the moral ground crumbling under their feet' (Johnson, 1994). At the party conference in 1993 the theme of his speech was to urge the country 'Back to Basics'. The immediate result of this rallying call was an argument about Major's intentions: was he referring to individual moral standards, or to the rectitude of the government's programme? Whatever the Prime Minister meant, his slogan released nostalgic visions among Conservative supporters of a world in which it was safe to walk down unlit streets and back doors were always open to the neighbours.

This reaction was awkward enough, as the government had few solutions to offer beyond the negative ones of tougher sentencing and greater resources for the police. What made matters worse was that the individual moral standards of senior party figures could not withstand the extra scrutiny which the speech unintentionally invited. For the press this was particularly welcome at a time when the government looked poised to act over intrusive journalism. Spectacular ministerial resignations followed, including that of the Heritage Secretary (or 'Minister of Fun') David Mellor, who had recently warned the press that they were 'drinking in the Last Chance saloon'. One MP, Stephen Milligan, died at his home in bizarre circumstances, thus triggering off the Eastleigh by-election which gave voters a quick chance to register their disapproval of a 'sleazy' government. The campaign gradually broadened to include allegations of financial impropriety concerning donations to the Conservative Party, favours to ministers and cash payments in return for parliamentary questions. In January 1994 the *Sun*, which had boasted of ensuring Major's re-election in 1992, was warning the Prime Minister to 'wake up and get a grip'. The long-term damage of 'Back to Basics' was revealed in October, when the *Sunday Telegraph* published an opinion poll showing Tory support down to below 23 per cent, while Tony Blair was rated more highly than John Major in every leadership category.

While 'Back to Basics' was widely regarded as an own goal by the Major government, it merely unmasked the real moral ambiguities of Thatcherism. For the ex-Prime Minister worldly success and spiritual health presupposed each other. A celebrated example of this was her argument that the Good Samaritan's laudable moral sentiments were reinforced by the fact that he was rich enough to help (Riddell, 1991, 2). Throughout her premiership Thatcher was advised by moralists (such as Brian Griffiths of the Downing Street Policy Unit) who believed that markets make good citizens. Unfortunately the severity of her views on 'socialism' undermined this optimism. If post-war governments up to 1979 had really sapped the ethical strength of the country through policies designed to promote dependency and permissiveness, could the people be trusted to act responsibly now that their economic chains had been struck off? Some of her ministers had actually been young adults during the 1960s; perhaps they, too, had been tainted by the ethos of those years? In other words, if the Conservatives were right in their analysis of post-war society, some sort of direct moral reforms would be needed. If they were wrong, then their moral case against 'socialism' was wrong too. Thanks to her dauntless faith Mrs Thatcher seems not to have examined this problem very closely. As with other matters, it was left to John Major to wrestle with the consequences.

One of these left-over problems was the UK's membership of the ERM. After postponing a decision to join, Thatcher was stampeded into an application by Hurd and Major when sterling was over-valued. The economic recession was prolonged as a result. Before leaving office Mrs Thatcher had made her hostility to European developments very clear, and this created uncertainties about Britain's future in the developing Community. Most Euro-sceptics were pleased with Major's handling of the European Council Meeting at Maastricht in 1992, but other European governments were not so impressed. If the pound came under speculative pressure on the exchange markets, the necessary co-operation from Germany and France might not be available. In September 1993 the markets turned against sterling, and despite firm statements from the Prime Minister and Chancellor Norman Lamont the pound's position within the ERM could not be sustained. Ironically this gave the government more flexibility, particularly in interest rate policy, and 'Black Wednesday' probably assisted the slow process of economic recovery. Yet once again Major had been made to look weak in comparison with his predecessor. This was particularly unfair, as Thatcher had brought the UK into the ERM; she had been most reluctant to do so, but that proved only that she, too, had suffered moments of weakness. Such subtleties were ignored by the media, who sensed that Major was in serious trouble. This mood was not altered by the sacrifice of Norman Lamont, who had sung in the bath to celebrate the ERM fiasco and caused embarrassment through his personal affairs. If anything, Major's European problems grew even worse after this, technically costing him his overall parliamentary majority in late 1994 when eight Conservative MPs lost the party whip for voting against the government on a motion of confidence (a further MP resigned the whip in protest). The normal practice in such cases is for a party to let its rebels rejoin after a token period of ostracism; this time it seemed that the 'whipless ones' were themselves dictating terms, and would oppose the government again on European questions.

By this time the Conservative Party had been continuously in office for sixteen years. The popular feeling that it was 'time for a change' now prevented any good economic news from registering with the voters. Bad news proved more interesting to the media. After the 1992 election the government had extended the scope of VAT to include domestic fuels, even though there had been no indication of this during the campaign. Before the new charges were imposed, the new Chancellor Kenneth Clarke hastened to protect welfare claimants from their full impact, but the damage was done. Ministerial talk of a healthy economic revival only reminded the public that this had already been forecast, when Norman Lamont claimed to have seen 'the green shoots of recovery' prior to the 1992 general election. At that time, John Major had said 'vote for me on Thursday and the recovery will start on Friday' (Junor, 1993, 253). The Conservatives were faced with a Catch-22 situation; they needed to generate a 'feel-good factor' in order to win re-election, but it seemed that the voters would not feel good until there was a change of government. If the economy really was improving, this meant that for once Labour would win a promising inheritance, and the Conservatives might be out of power for decades.

Only one escape route looked feasible. As in 1990, the party should create the impression that there was a new government by replacing its leader. After the ERM débâcle and 'Back to Basics' a challenge to John Major before the next election looked a certainty. The only problem concerned the identity of the challenger. Major had defeated Heseltine in 1990 because he looked more likely to unite the party, and his successor would have to share this advantage. Unfortunately all the obvious candidates had strong views about Europe. A victory for either Heseltine, Kenneth Clarke or Michael Portillo would look like the triumph of one party faction, whereas Major had skilfully allowed MPs on both sides to think that he privately agreed with them. Conservative feelings over Europe had grown so bitter that this delicate balancing act could not be maintained for much longer; in particular, Euro-sceptics wanted Major to rule out in advance any prospect that the UK would join a single currency. It seemed that even the prospect of electoral disaster could not restrain the more determined sceptics from forcing a contest in 1995.

The feverish atmosphere of rumour left Major with only one card if his authority was to survive. In June 1995 he announced that he was resigning as party leader in order to precipitate a vote on his future. His opponents were preparing themselves for the usual date in November, and were caught unawares. The shock of Major's announcement looked like a master-stroke, and it immediately caused a rise in his poll rating. He had consulted the Cabinet, but one member in particular thought that this process had not gone far enough. John Redwood, the Secretary of State for Wales, announced that he would challenge Major for the vacant leadership.

Redwood was a Euro-sceptic, but his intervention meant that the election would not focus entirely on one issue. The Thatcherite legacy as a whole was at stake. As a committed supporter of the ex-Prime Minister, Redwood acknowledged that Major had done nothing to dismantle the policies of the 1980s. His campaign was motivated by a sense that Major's lack of fervour might cost the Conservatives the next election. While Major's emphasis was on consolidation, Redwood wanted the crusade to start again. Further tax cuts were needed, and waste in government departments should be attacked more vigorously.

In basing his campaign on substantive issues, Redwood was leaving himself open to the charge that he had stayed within a Cabinet which lacked direction until he saw an opportunity to strike. Yet the majority of the Conservative press supported him, and in the election itself he secured eighty-nine votes. One-third of the parliamentary party had refused to vote for Major, even though the Prime Minister had started with a significant tactical advantage. Redwood's impressive performance was due to his recognition that in contemporary British politics a lukewarm attachment to principles is not enough; the public needs to be convinced that these ideas are held with genuine enthusiasm. Major was not prepared to rise to this challenge. Whatever his real views; his performance in government showed him to be a 'Career Thatcherite'; he carried out the policies of economic liberalism, while creating the impression that his heart was not really in it. His main weapon, after all, was the perception that he was the candidate of unity, and any evidence of ideological zeal might upset that delicate position. As a result, his victory simply left the Conservative Party where it had been before the election was announced. The campaign offered a wonderful opportunity for senior figures to abuse the Labour Party on television without being challenged, but the inevitable boost in opinion polls proved temporary.

Conclusion: a new consensus?

As the major parties prepared for an election in 1996 or 1997, an unfamiliar word crept back into political discussions. Was it possible that the strife of the previous twenty years, both between and within parties, had subsided into a new kind of consensus? The leaders of both main parties agreed that full employment was no longer a realistic goal, that private enterprise was better than direct state intervention, and that the necessity of minimal welfare services did not override the requirement of efficiency and low taxation. Labour agreed that low inflation should be a high priority, and since Tony Blair's stint as Shadow Home Secretary it had been posing as the true party of law and order. Both parties sprinkled the rhetoric of compassion over the policies of tough competition.

Differences of emphasis remained over issues such as the regulation of privatised utilities, constitutional reform and minimum wage legislation. However, by this time scholars had begun to question the original notion of a post-war 'consensus'. According to Ben Pimlott, for example, the idea that the parties had once agreed on all essential matters was a myth (Pimlott, 1988). After all, this was convenient for both Thatcherites and their opponents. One group spoke of consensus in order to discredit post-war politics, while the other had become nostalgic for an era when the welfare state had been immune from ideological attack. By contrast, Pimlott thought that significant disagreement over fundamentals had always existed .

The argument of the present book supports Pimlott in so far as it shows that ideological disagreement did not cease in the years before Thatcher. Yet the vast majority within all three major parties were able to support similar policies, even if they did so for different reasons. It is unrealistic to confuse 'consensus' with 'unanimity'; as Stalin once said, that can be achieved only in a graveyard. On this reading, Pimlott's analysis is slightly overstated, although it has provoked a valuable debate. If the existence of a consensus means that a new government will not initiate radical changes in the framework of policies and institutions left by its predecessor, the signs are that we have indeed entered a new age of consensus, and that the changes brought about during the Thatcher years will be lasting ones.

Perhaps the most interesting aspect of this new consensus is the fact that it has yet to achieve the kind of public support once enjoyed by the post-war settlement. Indeed, the data suggest that pre-Thatcherite values still command greater loyalty (Taylor-Gooby, 1991). Tony Blair has defended the recent changes in Labour's philosophy by arguing that during the 1980s his party 'lost touch' (Blair, 1995). Actually, the evidence for voters' preferences from those years shows that they regarded the Conservatives and Labour as equally distant from their own thinking (Heath et al., 1991, 217). Yet the changes have supposedly been inspired by the Labour leadership's perception of electoral necessity. The reasoning is that even modest promises lost votes in 1992, and the blurring of substantive differences with the Conservatives will ensure that Labour is not vulnerable to attacks next time. In the mean time, as one commentator has observed, Blair's position 'takes the progressive vote pretty much for granted' (Young, 1995).

Labour's new leadership claims that its policies reflect a mood of 'realism' within the party. This is a word which students of politics should be wary of. The interpretation of political reality depends upon the values of the observer. Some people will always try to prove that apparent acceptance of the status quo really masks a yearning for radical change; others will demonstrate that acquiescence in reform is merely a sign that the public is desperate for a period of calm. 'Reality', for the new Labour Party, is defined by its experience since 1979. During this period ambitious people within the middle-class professions have learned to act as Thatcherites, even if their dinner-party talk is still of social justice. They believe that compassion makes friends, but competition influences people. These individuals are a small minority of the electorate, but their voices are louder than the rest, particularly when they are seconded by the clamour from the Conservative-supporting press. 'New Labour' is their natural home, and their opinions are welcome to the leadership. After all, the culture of economic liberalism has dominated UK policy-making since 1979, and Tony Blair was first elected to Parliament in 1983.

The challenge for Labour is to find a convincing vocabulary which will sell these principles to a sceptical electorate. The presentation of policy will also have to satisfy those within the party who oppose the new consensus, if Blair is to avoid the necessity of a damaging purge. Under similar circumstances the Conservatives just about managed this in 1979, but Blair cannot count on the tradition of deference to a leader which assisted Mrs Thatcher for so long. Early signs were not encouraging to him, as Roy Hattersley joined more predictable critics of Blair's reforms. Blair was also underestimating the potential threat from the Liberal Democrats, who signalled their continued allegiance to post-war policies through the Dahrendorf Commission (Elliott and White, 1995). At times it seemed as though Ashdown's party was resigned to some kind of electoral deal with Labour, but the Liberal Democrat by-election triumph at Littleborough and Saddleworth in July 1995 (against some dubious Labour tactics) reopened the possibility of another independent effort to break the two-party mould. In the longer term, it is even possible that socialists might desert Labour for those parties which have not abandoned the faith – notably the SWP, which no longer faces serious competition from Labour as a vehicle for idealists (Foot, 1993).

Whatever the result of the next election, it is unlikely that the new governing consensus will go unchallenged for long. Clever packaging of ideas can win elections, but it cannot ensure success in office. Mrs Thatcher's dynamic personality ensured that her actual record was not examined in context, but without a windfall like North Sea oil it is unlikely that her good fortune will be repeated in the near future. Even before the controversies over sleaze, critics were discussing a 'crisis of party' caused by the inability of traditional politics to represent the aspirations of civil society (Jacques, 1993). Technological developments pointed to a future in which parties could be bypassed altogether by means of push-button referenda; not surprisingly, the British leader who showed most interest in this possibility was Paddy Ashdown (Bevins, 1994). Rather than signalling 'the end of ideology', this would guarantee space in public debate to ideas which are currently ignored by 'realistic' politicians. The experiment would present dangers as well as opportunities, and perhaps it would be short-lived. It might be that the diagnosis is wrong, and that the British political system is in need of substantial reform rather than complete reconstruction. By mid-1995, however, the sense that something had to change was becoming irresistible, and if party leaders need a scapegoat for the discontent they are likely to find the system a useful shield for their own inadequacies.

List of works cited

Bevins, Anthony (1994), 'Ashdown Fights Major on Yobs', *Observer*, 11 September

Blair, Tony (1995), 'Left with No Option', *Guardian*, 27 July

Butler, David, Adonis, Andrew, and Travis, Tony (1994), *Failure in British Government: The Politics of the Poll Tax*, Oxford University Press

Elliott, Larry, and White, Michael (1995), 'Lib Dems' Vision of a New Tomorrow', *Guardian*, 26 July

Foot, Paul (1993), *Why You Should Join the Socialists*, Bookmarks

Giddings, Philip (ed.) (1995), *Parliamentary Accountability: A Study of Parliament and Executive Agencies*, Macmillan

Gould, Bryan (1995), *Goodbye to All That*, Macmillan

Gray, John (1993), *Beyond the New Right: Government and the Common Environment*, Routledge

Gray, John (1995), 'Hollowing Out the Core', *Guardian*, 8 March

Heath, Anthony, Evans, Geoff, Field, Julia, and Witherspoon, Sharon (1991) *Understanding Political Change: The British Voter 1964–1987*, Pergamon

Holland, Philip (1981), *The Governance of Quangos*, Adam Smith Institute

Jacques, Martin (1993), 'The End of Politics', *Sunday Times*, 18 July

Johnson, Paul (1994), 'How Yeo Fell Foul of the New Morality', *Daily Mail*, 6 January

Junor, Penny (1993), *The Major Enigma*, Michael Joseph

Kelly, Richard (1994), 'The Party Conferences', in Anthony Seldon and Stuart Ball (eds) *Conservative Century: The Conservative Party since 1900*, Oxford University Press

King, Anthony (1994), 'Tories Suffer from Sleaze Factor', *Daily Telegraph*, 10 October

Linton, Martin, and Wintour, Patrick (1995), 'Voters Say Yes to Tax for NHS', *Guardian*, 13 April

McSmith, Andy (1994), *Kenneth Clarke: A Political Biography*, Verso

Major, John (1994), 'Major Pledges Continuity and Stability', *The Times*, 15 October

Marquand, David (1988), *The Unprincipled Society: New Demands and Old Politics*, Fontana

Marr, Andrew (1995), *Ruling Britannia: The Failure and Future of British Democracy*, Michael Joseph

Minkin, Lewis (1992), *Contentious Alliance: Trade Unions and the Labour Party*, Edinburgh University Press

Norton, Philip (1993), 'The Conservative Party from Thatcher to Major', in Anthony King (ed.) *Britain at the Polls 1992*, Chatham House

Patten, Christopher (1991), Interviewed by David Marquand, *Marxism Today*, February

Pimlott, Ben (1988), 'The Myth of Consensus', in L. M. Smith (ed.) *The Making of Britain: Echoes of Greatness*, Macmillan

Riddell, Peter (1991), *The Thatcher Era and its Legacy*, Blackwell

Sanders, David (1993) 'Why the Conservative Party Won – Again', in Anthony King (ed.) *Britain at the Polls 1992*, Chatham House

Taylor-Gooby, Peter (1991), 'Attachment to the Welfare State', in Roger Jowell, Lindsay Brook and Bridget Taylor (eds) *British Social Attitudes: The 8th Report*, Dartmouth

Thatcher, Margaret (1992), 'Don't Undo What I Have Done', *Guardian*, 22 April

White, Michael (1994), 'So Far, So Good', *Guardian*, 27 December

Whiteley, Paul, Seyd, Patrick, and Richardson, Jeremy (1994), *True Blues: The Politics of Conservative Party Membership*, Oxford University Press

Willetts, David (1992), *Modern Conservatism*, Penguin

Willetts, David (1994), *Civic Conservatism*, Social Market Foundation

Young, Hugo (1995), 'Voters Want to Hear the Painful Truth', *Guardian*, 27 July

Questions for discussion

- If John Major has continued to pursue Thatcherite policies, why does he have so much trouble from members of his own party?
- Has a new consensus been established between the main parties? Set out the arguments for and against, and compare recent developments to earlier post-war politics.

Selected further reading (see also Chapter 8)

Anderson, Bruce (1991), *John Major*, Fourth Estate.

Catterall, Peter (1994), *Contemporary Britain: An Annual Review 1993*, Blackwell.

Commission on Social Justice (1994), *Social Justice: Strategies for National Renewal*, Vintage.

Ellison, Nicholas (1994), *Egalitarian Thought and Labour Politics: Retreating Visions*, Routledge.

Etzioni, Amitai (1993), *The Spirit of Community*, Crown Publishing.

Galbraith, John Kenneth (1992), *The Culture of Contentment*, Sinclair-Stevenson.

Kemp, Peter (1993), *Beyond Next Steps*, Social Market Foundation.

McSmith, Andy (1993), *John Smith*, Verso.

Norton, Philip (ed.) (1991), *New Directions in British Politics*, Edward Elgar.

Shell, Donald (1994), 'The British Constitution in 1993', *Parliamentary Affairs*, volume 47, number 2.

Shepherd, Robert (1991), *The Power Brokers*, Hutchinson.

Tebbit, Norman (1993), *Unfinished Business*, Weidenfeld and Nicolson.

Tritter, Jonathan (1994), 'The Citizen's Charter: Opportunities for Users' Perspectives?', *Political Quarterly*, volume 65, number 4.

White, Stuart (1995), 'The Commission on Social Justice: An Assessment', *Political Quarterly*, volume 63, number 3.

Wickham-Jones, Mark, and Shell, Donald (1991), 'What Went Wrong? The Fall of Mrs Thatcher', *Contemporary Record*, volume 5, number 2.

CHAPTER 8

A crisis of party?

So far the discussion has concentrated on political principles which have been advocated by members of UK parties represented in Parliament, with the greatest emphasis on ideas which have underlain manifesto pledges and government policies. In 1951, when the two main parties received almost 97 per cent of general election votes between them, it might have been possible to provide a reasonable picture of influential political ideas in the United Kingdom without mentioning anyone except Labour and the Conservatives. Since February 1974 support for these parties has only once climbed above 80 per cent, and a much broader view of the political scene is now essential.

Even the recognition that the UK is now a 'multi-party' state is no longer sufficient to explain the role of principles in contemporary politics. For most of the period since 1970 the parliamentary system has failed to cater for the range of views expressed by groups in society. Like most political phenomena, the resulting disillusionment is difficult to quantify. For example, it is often claimed that the electorate has become more 'volatile' since the 1970s, but the evidence for this is inconclusive (Heath et al., 1991, 10–31). Despite the political turbulence which affected the Conservatives, Labour and the Liberal Democrats between 1987 and 1992, and some spectacular by-election results, polling evidence from the 1992 general election suggests that party allegiances actually hardened among voters during these years. For example, even though the Conservative vote declined by 1.6 per cent, the proportion of those who claimed to be strong supporters of the party increased by more than 4 per cent (Sanders, 1992, 222). In addition to being improbable in themselves, these findings contradict the impression left by many significant developments since the 1950s – for example, the growth of an 'underclass', and the widely-publicised 'joy-riders' and 'New Age Travellers'. Of course, the groups which are excluded from the political process (either voluntarily or otherwise) will not feature in either electoral statistics or opinion polls. Yet there is a feeling that dissatisfaction has spread beyond them. Is this feeling simply wrong, or do the figures lie?

The latter is the more tempting option; after all, lying to the opinion pollsters became something of a national pastime between 1987 and 1992 (Crewe, 1992). If people are prepared to lie about their voting intentions before an election, they might be equally cynical when reporting their degree of party commitment to researchers. Evidence of increasing apathy was certainly available during the 1980s; between 1974 and 1986, the proportion of people who felt that they had no chance of influencing government policy jumped by 10 per cent (Topf, 1989). Furthermore, the supposed 'facts' about a particular election – the turn-out figure and the level of support for each party – cannot tell us much about the real enthusiasm of the electorate. Henry Drucker has argued that 'it is difficult to believe that highly disaffected people would bring themselves to vote for any party', but it is unlikely that many supporters of the Monster Raving Loony Party are overjoyed with the alternatives on offer, and of course there are well-known examples of revolutionary parties winning power through the democratic process (Drucker, 1979, 8). What we might be experiencing is a trend towards 'apathetic participation' – voting which is motivated by a feeling that one ought to take part in a national ritual, rather than any idealism about party politics. The Grand National or the Derby provide a parallel example; many people feel that they should follow the tradition of 'having a flutter' on these events, but this does not prove that they are very interested in horse-racing. These speculations are difficult to verify, but they lend additional support to the view that an investigation of contemporary political principles should look beyond the traditional institutions.

The principles and movements briefly examined here are feminism, the Campaign for Nuclear Disarmament and environmental movements (with particular emphasis on the animal rights movement). Obviously those who support these causes have had contrasting fortunes since 1970, and it can be argued that all of them have some keen supporters at Westminster. The broad factor which connects them is that some of their members have resorted to extra-parliamentary action, often provoked by a feeling that the urgency of their views was not sufficiently conveyed by other means.

Feminism

The first national conference of the Women's Liberation Movement (WLM) was held in 1970. The movement was inspired in part by civil rights activism during the 1960s, and coincided with the publication of notable feminist writings such as Germaine

Greer's *The Female Eunuch* (1970). This new feminist impetus seemed to produce results very quickly; 1970 saw the passage of the Equal Pay Act, which promised to end the exploitation of women in the workplace, and the Matrimonial Proceedings and Property Act, which recognised that a woman's work in the home entitled her to a share of the family property if a marriage broke up; provisions also protected women from domestic violence. The Sex Discrimination Act 1976 was designed to ensure that women were not at a disadvantage when they applied for jobs or training. Fifty years after women had secured full democratic rights, it seemed as if the barriers to economic equality would also be removed.

This picture quickly proved to be over-optimistic. For example, the terms of the Equal Pay Act could easily be evaded by employers who wrote special job-descriptions for women's jobs. The delay in implementing the Act provided a useful opportunity to discover loop-holes. Whatever the intentions of legislators, the figures verified the claim that 'we have an Equal Pay Act but we don't have equal pay' (Coote and Gill, 1974, 21). By 1981 the average gross weekly earnings of women were about half those of men. In part-time occupations women already outnumbered men by almost ten to one – a trend that would continue during the Thatcher years (Wainwright, 1984, 211, 204). Workers in these jobs had never enjoyed much protection from trade unions, and the Thatcherite attack on the unions left women employees even more vulnerable. The Sex Discrimination legislation seems to have been fairly successful, at least to the extent of changing reported attitudes about women at work. In part, however, this evidence has been influenced by the decline in the old manual occupations. By 1984, for example, 89 per cent of respondents to a survey thought that women and men were equally suited to computer programming, and only 39 per cent thought that managing a bank was more suitable for a man. Between 1980 and 1984 the percentage of respondents who thought that 'a wife's job is to look after the home and family' dropped from 46 to 32 per cent (Witherspoon, 1985, 76–8). Yet there remained a suspicion that successful women in business and politics were the exception not the rule, and those who fulfilled their ambitions – like Mrs Thatcher herself – seemed to have done so by taking on the characteristics of men. Meanwhile, women were still grossly under-represented even in supposedly 'enlightened' professions such as academia.

It is often remarked that Mrs Thatcher did very little for the cause of women. Although her rhetoric about traditional family life was never followed up with concerted action, she also failed to improve child care, which would have made life easier for working mothers. In fact, her determined assault on local government often meant that existing facilities deteriorated. The effect of Thatcherite policies did not end there; between April 1979 and April 1990, the Conservative government cut the real value of child benefit by 21 per cent, having frozen it from 1988 (Gilmour, 1992, 158). Under Mrs Thatcher, ministers also noticed the attractions of making single mothers the scapegoat for social evils, even though at least one of the Prime Minister's closest supporters had contributed to the problem himself.

Overall, the feminist movement stalled during the Thatcher years. In one respect it was a victim of its own partial success; the legislation of the 1970s made many people feel that women had already achieved equality. This contributed to the negative public perception of those feminists who pointed out that more needed to be done. However, this image problem was at least partly attributable to differences within the women's movement. Three broad strands of feminism have been identified. Liberal feminists demand equality of rights, socialist feminists interpret gender issues within the context of class, while radical feminists celebrate the difference between men and women, and attack a 'patriarchal' society in which men are natural aggressors (Vincent, 1995, 172–207). During the 1980s black feminists added a distinctive and urgent voice to the debate, and women's participation in anti-nuclear protests illustrated the growing attraction of 'eco-feminism', which emphasised the intimate relationship between women and the environment. This diversity gives rise to questions about the ideological nature of feminism. Only the radical version seems to be a distinctive ideology in itself, since a fully consistent liberal who believes in complete equality of opportunity would inevitably support the demands of liberal feminism. The same could be said for thorough-going socialists, who logically should demand liberation for women, but would doubt that this could be achieved in a capitalist society. Liberal and socialist feminists, then, are liberals and socialists who place special emphasis on women's issues. However, radical feminists, who believe that male aggression is inevitable and advocate segregation as a result, have a world-view which cannot be squared with any other ideology.

This interpretation is only a sketch, but it suggests why unity of purpose among all these groups was never likely. In particular, once demands began to be satisfied tension was inevitable between liberal feminists (who are often accused of concentrating on the needs of middle-class women) and others whose priorities had not been met by the legislation of the 1970s. These strains came to a head at the 1978 WLM conference (Lovenduski and Randall, 1993, 360). Unhelpfully, the media gave most prominence to radical feminists, whose ideas could be used to inflame popular prejudices. This group suffered the most open attack from government policies, particularly Section 2a of the Local Government Act 1988, which outlawed the promotion of homosexuality by local authorities.

Some sections of the media had a commercial interest in arousing public hostility towards feminists. In 1986 the Labour MP Clare Short attempted to ban the use of 'Page Three' pin-ups in newspapers. During her speech on a ten-minute rule Bill she was subjected to childish heckling by Conservative MPs; one, Robert Adey, declared that the Bill 'deserves the booby prize' (Short, 1986). It is difficult to imagine that parliamentarians of the 1970s, when the image of feminism was more positive, would have indulged in this kind of exhibition. Short's campaign highlighted the continuing exploitation of women during the Thatcher decade; indeed, the introduction of the *Daily Sport* newspaper meant that standards in the press sank even lower, while television, advertising and the film industry gladly exploited the new relaxations. The anti-pornography movement drove a further wedge between feminist groups, as liberal opponents of censorship began to claim that in some cases the sex industry actually enhanced the power of women. While such abuses continued, however, it was difficult to see how men could regard women as equals at home or in the workplace. Perpetrators of domestic violence were also unmoved by the legislative protection of women in 1976, and refuges for battered partners became more common. Cases like that of Sara Thornton, who was convicted of murder after killing her violent husband, illustrated the inherent sexism of the legal system. During one week in 1980, two women who murdered a barbaric father were sent to jail for three years, while the killer of a so-called 'nagging wife' escaped with two years' probation (Sebestyen, 1985, 95).

By the early 1990s the prospects for feminism looked ambivalent. There were some important gains to set against recent reverses; notably, Labour and the Liberal Democrats both promised a ministry for women, and Labour accepted that more women candidates should be chosen in safe seats. This example of positive discrimination was controversial, yet something clearly needed to be done; after the 1992 election women still only accounted for one-tenth of the House of Commons (Lovenduski et al., 1994, 626). After an interesting and occasionally bitter debate, the Anglican church finally accepted that God could speak through both sexes, and allowed the ordination of women. Bizarrely, this helped to provoke one female member of the government into becoming a Catholic. UK society might have become a poor copy of the USA in most respects during the 1980s, but at least MPs refused to succumb to US-style hysteria about abortion, and women's rights over their bodies were secured by the failure of the Alton Bill in 1988. The fight against this measure brought many women's groups together again, but it is telling that their defensive purpose was very different from the radical days of the late 1960s and early 1970s.

Of course, an essentially defensive campaign could bring positive results, and some could draw comfort from similar movements during the 1980s. For instance, the miners' strike of 1984–85 could not have been sustained for so long without the dynamism infused by numerous women's support groups (Lovenduski and Randall, 1993, 122–5). The Greenham protest against the introduction of cruise missiles to the UK was probably the most-publicised campaign of the decade, however. Beginning with a march in August 1981, the women's peace camp at Greenham was a remarkable example of political commitment in the face of discomfort and intimidation. If it also proved easy for sections of the media to distort the nature of the camp (particularly over the decision to exclude men) this was hardly the fault of the protesters, who at least had taken action while others acquiesced in an astonishing policy. The same newspapers which thundered against the infringement of sovereignty represented by membership of the EC were quite happy for nearly one hundred cruise missiles to be deployed at Greenham, even though the weapons would remain under US control (Campbell, 1986, 259–60, 297–338). World developments might have played a greater role in removing the missiles than the civil disobedience of the Greenham women, but this example of principled protest for a moral purpose was a notable reminder that a healthy democracy cannot survive if it depends entirely on the ballot box.

The Campaign for Nuclear Disarmament

The Greenham protest was just the most publicised episode during the revival of an anti-nuclear movement which had first emerged in the 1950s (Taylor, 1970). The Campaign for Nuclear Disarmament re-emerged from obscurity in 1980 after the coincidence of several worrying developments. The Soviet Union invaded Afghanistan in late 1979, soon after the election of the fiercely anti-communist Margaret Thatcher. At the same time, plans to install cruise missiles in Europe were announced, supposedly in response to the development of the Soviet SS-20. On 22 June 1980 the veteran campaigner and new Labour leader Michael Foot joined a major CND demonstration through London (Jones, 1994, 443). Labour might be in opposition, but at least CND could be sure of principled support from its leadership for the first time; after all, it had been a Labour administration which secretly decided that the UK should be a nuclear power.

By 1986, CND membership was estimated at around 60,000 (Byrne, 1988, 55). This figure is even more impressive given that the Labour Party (along with the nationalists and the Greens) were also committed to unilateral disarmament at the time. The growth of the movement caused alarm within the Conservative government, and a propaganda war intensified after Michael Heseltine became Secretary of State for Defence early in 1983. The government's argument was that nuclear weapons had maintained peace in Europe since 1945; only the retention of the most advanced nuclear technology would continue to deter potential aggressors. The UK was a responsible power, and without nuclear weapons it would be unable to exert much world influence. Against this, CND could claim that there had always been a conflict somewhere during the 'post-war' period, whether or not it had taken place in Europe. Furthermore, the possession of nuclear weapons itself acted as a source of danger. If a dispute between two nuclear powers escalated, each side would be tempted to launch a devastating first strike to ensure that the enemy could not respond in kind. Technological developments had not been matched by a growth in human wisdom; hence, an impulsive decision could lead to a holocaust within minutes. Even worse, missiles could be launched in error.

Since nuclear weapons could not be dis-invented, there were strong arguments on each side of the debate. Given the high stakes involved, the government was not prepared to let the contest be decided by logic, and it resorted to smear tactics to discredit both the cause of unilateralism and individuals within CND. Its tactics succeeded; in 1981 public support for the objectives of CND stood at about 33 per cent, but by the 1983 general election this figure had slumped to 16 per cent (Byrne, 1988, 211). Perhaps the Falklands War had reassured the public that Britain could rule the waves without actually detonating any warheads. The war also caused some disruption within CND. The movement was opposed to weapons of mass destruction, rather than being committed to complete pacifism. This position was wholly logical, but many members went further in their objection to violence, and there was some dismay when Michael Foot supported the government's decision to recover the Islands. At least a hard-core of supporters remained loyal, and even after the war the 1983 annual demonstration organised by CND in Hyde Park attracted an estimated 300,000 people (Byrne, 1988, 152).

Nevertheless, 1983 was a bad year for CND. In the general election the Conservatives succeeded in convincing voters that Labour was an extremist party; since unilateralism was included in the party's manifesto, the policy became identified as an example of the 'loony left' in action. This perception was enhanced when CND responded to Labour's national defeat by encouraging local authorities to declare themselves 'nuclear free zones'. By 1987 Neil Kinnock was forced to compensate for his continued commitment to unilateralism by promising additional expenditure on conventional weapons. Even this did not prevent the Conservatives from sensing a vote-winning issue, and they damaged Labour by claiming that the party would simply surrender if attacked (Shaw, 1994, 78).

The 1987 controversy over nuclear weapons looks even more unreal in the mid-1990s because by that time world developments had made a disarmament programme much more practicable, even on the government's premises. The rise of Mikhail Gorbachev had ensured a thaw in East–West relations, and President Reagan's 'Star Wars' initiative promised to make nuclear weapons (or at least those possessed by the Soviet Union) obsolete. At the Reykjavik summit in 1986 Reagan startled Thatcher by rivalling CND in his enthusiasm to rid the world of the nuclear threat. Yet the issue caused more mayhem in 1987 than in any other election year; in addition to the Labour–Conservative clash, it brought underlying disagreements within the Liberal–SDP Alliance to a head. While most pressure groups are delighted to win support from political parties, CND discovered that the irrational conflicts of a modern election campaign only obscured the real message they were trying to convey. When the cruise missiles departed after the fall of communism in 1989 and 1990 the Conservatives tried to claim this as a triumph for their deterrence theory; however, when the public is reminded of the nuclear threat in future, CND might be better placed to win the propaganda war.

Environmental movements

Nuclear weapons were not the only perceived threat to the survival of the planet. Concern about environmental damage caused by industry grew during the 1960s. Rachel Carson's book *The Silent Spring* (1962), which drew attention to the use of chemicals in agriculture, is normally cited as the starting-point of serious modern thinking on the environment. A UK branch of Friends of the Earth (FOE) was set up a year after the organisation had been founded in 1969. This helped to publicise the growing feeling among researchers that the developed world's obsession with economic expansion would quickly become unsustainable. In 1972 a group of scientists and industrialists who called themselves the Club of Rome met to consider the problem; their report, published as *The Limits to Growth* (Meadows et al. 1974), aroused public attention, and in this year the Paris European Council responded to concerns by laying the foundations for future EC action on the environment. In the UK a Department of the Environment (DOE) had been set up in 1970, but originally this owed more to Edward Heath's desire for institutional efficiency than a determination to check environmental damage. The main tasks of the DOE concerned housing and local government, rather than the control of pollution.

The environmental groups which had arisen in response to the new concerns had three options. They could form their own parties, to win publicity and (hopefully) representation at either national or local level; they could remain as pressure groups, informing and advising the government and organising demonstrations if they were ignored; or they could combine these approaches, fielding candidates in elections while keeping up the pressure through propaganda and other forms of protest. Ostensibly, this last course was taken by the movement as a whole, although the non-hierarchical structure preferred by activists indicates that there are still mixed feelings about wholehearted commitment to the political process. A party called 'People' contested both of the 1974 general elections (without notable success), and in 1975 this group changed its name to the Ecology Party (Rootes, 1995, 66). This was the first western party of its kind, but similar groups were soon founded in other European countries. The German 'Green' party was particularly successful, winning seats in the Bundestag by 1983; in the mid-1980s the UK party also adopted the Green label.

Taking the name of the German Greens was one thing, but it was much more difficult to repeat their success. The proportional electoral system in Germany, and its thriving local democracy, meant that it was far easier to achieve meaningful representation there than in the UK. The most spectacular achievement of the UK Greens came in the 1989 elections to the European Parliament, when their candidates received nearly 15 per cent of the vote. Admittedly turn-out at the election was low, but the fact that the Greens won no seats for their efforts made the UK system appear unjust. The Greens were able to pick up some council seats, but with the powers of local government being eroded these victories could serve only as temporary boosts to morale.

In fact, there was a danger that the frustrations of the Green Party might detract from the growing popularity of the cause itself. The late 1980s saw a surge in membership for environmental groups; between 1988 and 1989 FOE attracted almost 100,000 new supporters (Rootes, 1995, 71). At the same time pressure group activity seemed to be paying off at last. A MORI opinion poll conducted in April 1987 showed that 81 per cent of respondents wanted the government to do more to protect the environment (Porritt and Winner, 1988, 62). This message was apparently heeded in Whitehall; in September and October 1988 Margaret Thatcher delivered speeches which seemed to indicate at least a partial conversion to environmental awareness. This new departure was followed up in February 1989 by her active participation in a London conference on the ozone layer (McCormick, 1991, 2). At the time Nicholas Ridley, whose credentials as custodian of the environment were dubious, was Secretary of State at the DOE; in July 1989 he was replaced by Christopher Patten. As an economic liberal Ridley was bound to be antipathetic to the collectivist remedies demanded by the environment lobby, but as a One Nation conservative Patten had no such reservations. This appointment was a step forward, but the Prime Minister was primarily concerned to have a good communicator in charge of the department which handled the Poll Tax (Thatcher, 1993, 602). Whatever Thatcher's motives, the advocates of pressure-group activity could now claim that the government would be more receptive in future to environmental arguments; it could also point to the environmental agenda of the EC, which was producing strong directives on issues such as the pollution of beaches (Judge, 1993). By contrast, the Green Party was earning itself bad publicity through the antics of David Icke, the former sports commentator and party spokesman, who revealed in 1990 that he was 'the son of God'.

The tactical split within the movement between party-oriented leaders such as Jonathon Porritt and those who regarded such narrow political activity as a waste of resources mirrored a theoretical disagreement which had been signalled as early as 1972 by the Norwegian philosopher Arne Naess (Dobson, 1990, 47). Naess distinguished two broad categories of environmental commitment, namely 'shallow' and 'deep' ecology. Shallow ecologists are worried about the environment but not to the extent of agreeing to give up their life-style. They might urge that future economic growth must be sustainable, but growth remains a priority for them. Deep ecologists have escaped this kind of thinking, which still insists that the needs of the human race ought to be considered before the rest of the eco-system. Instead of providing possible solutions to the crisis which faced the planet, shallow ecologists are seen by more radical thinkers as forming part of the problem; despite their good intentions, they reflect the type of arrogance which has put the earth's future in jeopardy. By contrast, deep ecologists place human interests on a par with those of animals, and even plants and rocks; some have gone further, and laid themselves open to the charge of hating human beings by advocating sweeping measures of population control. The potentially damaging implications of this theoretical split are illustrated by experiences in France. In 1990 Brice

Lalonde, the former presidential candidate of the green party 'Les Verts', formed a new group called Génération Écologie. Lalonde accused Les Verts of ecological fundamentalism; since he later refused to condemn the Gulf War, even 'shallow' ecology must have seemed extreme to him (Cole and Doherty, 1995). Like the divisions between radical feminism and its other variants, this quarrel seems to originate in the fact that deep ecologists have a distinctive world-view, while it is possible for members of all other ideological families to show a 'shallow' commitment to the health of the planet. In short, this reading would suggest that deep ecology is a separate ideology, while the shallow view will be held by conservative ecologists, liberal ecologists, and so on.

Deep ecologists have sound arguments to back their claim that all life on earth has equal value, but nutritional difficulties might arise from the logic of the proposition that lentils and human beings deserve equal consideration. The most prominent leader of the UK Greens, Jonathon Porritt, once described such views as 'really a bit dotty'. Porritt pointed out that it is impossible for human beings to submerge their identities in nature; even if one seriously tries to 'think like a mountain', one cannot avoid thinking like a human (Porritt and Winner, 1988, 238). The UK Green Party has followed a consistent deep ecology line, but Porritt's own views were pragmatic. In 1988, for instance, he expressed a preference for policies 'which will not entail everyone donning hair-shirts or sacrificing the "good things" in life' (Irvine and Ponton, 1988, x). Unfortunately, even his highly pragmatic approach to environmental questions can appear 'a bit dotty' in a consumerist world. The success of moderate 'light-Green' ideas can be measured from the new concern of manufacturers to appear 'environmentally friendly', and the success of businesses such as The Body Shop; by the mid-1980s polls were showing that a majority of the population were more interested in preserving the environment than in economic growth (Wybrow, 1989, 140). By 1990 80 per cent of the population were either using environmentally-friendly aerosols or intending to do so (Young, 1991, 122). Yet politicians and industrialists retained their obsession with votes and profits, and the knowledge that a serious clamp-down on pollution would cost money for taxpayers and consumers added weight to the argument that only cosmetic improvements ought to be introduced. After all, environmental damage is a global phenomenon, and vandalism could always be excused on the grounds that the guilt of other countries was even worse.

The danger that the environment might be used mostly for party gain was highlighted when Patten unveiled a government White Paper (*This Common Inheritance*) in September 1990; despite the glossy presentation, this document was most notable for its omissions. For instance, it was rumoured that a DOE proposal for a tax on fossil fuels had been vetoed by the Energy Secretary (McCormick, 1991, 171). While the priorities of individual departments conflicted with Patten's plans, the ethos of the government as a whole opposed the sort of regulation of industry which an effective environmental programme required. In this climate, Patten was certain to lose ministerial battles. Where the government could point to genuine successes, these often turned out to be measures enforced by the EU, which ministers usually tried to portray as an intrusive and alien organisation. Like the EU, the United Nations' Conference on the Environment and Development held at Rio de Janeiro in June 1992 served as both justification and excuse for the government. When Norman Lamont introduced VAT for domestic fuel in his March 1993 Budget, he claimed that this was intended to discourage consumption in line with the Rio goal of stabilising carbon dioxide emissions by the year 2000. He bluntly told the Commons that 'it is crucial to avoid taking measures that will have a disproportionate impact on the competitiveness of British industry' (Lamont, 1993). Since the UK had been obstructive during negotiations on this subject, Lamont's appeal to green principles in order to deflate criticism was breathtaking (Skjaerseth, 1994, 32). In the face of such cynicism, even Porritt's limited demands may not be realistic.

By July 1993 membership of the UK Green Party had fallen to 4,500 (from a peak of around 20,000 only three years previously) (Rootes, 1995, 86). In the general election of 1992 the party received only 0.5 per cent of the popular vote; in the European Parliamentary election of 1994 it fought every seat, but still attracted only 3.2 per cent of the electorate. Internal disagreements have continued to dog the party, and its best-known leaders have abandoned their attempts to manage the unruly membership. Perhaps the UK Greens will have to wait until the electoral system is changed before parliamentary representation becomes a realistic possibility; as Robert Garner has pointed out, the electoral prospects of the party also depend on the clarification of its relationship with other parties and sympathetic pressure groups, which the German Greens have managed with greater skill (Garner, 1996). In the mean time, the best chance of influencing UK government policy lies with 'the oldest, strongest, best-organized and most widely supported environmental lobby in the world' – a lobby which is backed by around 4.5 million people (McCormick, 1991, 34). However, even this faces daunting handicaps in its attempt to bring about significant changes.

The campaign for animal rights

Apart from lobbying in Whitehall, environmentalists can exert pressure through direct action. Greenpeace's attempts to disrupt nuclear testing have been widely publicised, and in 1986 they rattled the French government sufficiently to provoke the sinking of the movement's ship, the *Rainbow Warrior*. In 1995 Greenpeace's protests against the sinking of Shell's Brent Spar oil platform led to a Europe-wide boycott of the company, which eventually gave in to this pressure even though it had the support of the UK government. It is doubtful whether this stunning triumph will be the last of its kind, although directly challenging the policies of a government, rather than those of a commercial company, will continue to prove more difficult.

While Greenpeace has revenues which allow it to mount spectacular international campaigns, the importance of local movements should not be overlooked. In the UK during the 1990s protesters against new roads (for example, the one planned at Twyford Down) won widespread publicity, and contributed to the rethinking of the government's transport strategy despite the power of the motoring and road-building lobbies. At the same time demonstrators began to target the trade in live veal calves. These diverse campaigns, which spawned a large number of local groups, were particularly notable for the range of supporters they attracted, and the violent scenes that were often associated with them. Some traced the origins of this kind of protest to the clash between police and 'New Age Travellers' at Stonehenge in June 1985 (Grant, 1995). The Travellers, whose whole lives were a determined protest against the spiritual void in modern society, were certainly able to provide the organisational skills needed for sustained action. However, by themselves they cannot explain the new mood.

Britain is traditionally an animal-loving nation, although this reputation is not easy to square with its long history of bear-baiting, cock-fighting and other cruel sports. Many animal protection organisations date back to the early nineteenth century; the Royal Society for the Prevention of Cruelty to Animals (RSPCA), for example, was founded in 1824. Anticipating much modern thinking, humanitarians such as William Wilberforce supported this body in a logical extension of his campaign on behalf of slaves. Other long-established movements, such as the British Union for the Abolition of Vivisection (1898), have concentrated their efforts against sadistic and unnecessary animal experiments. In the 1970s these groups received an important boost from the writings of the Australian philosopher Peter Singer; his *Animal Liberation* not only provided vivid illustrations of animal sufferings in the laboratory, but also elaborated a sophisticated moral theory to explain why most of these experiments were wrong (Singer, 1975). Singer based his argument on the fact that animals resemble humans in their capacity to feel pain. This means that only experiments which lead to significant benefits can possibly be justified; as Singer showed, this criterion was unsatisfied in the vast majority of cases. Tom Regan's *The Case for Animal Rights* asserted that animals have inalienable rights, and thus should not be used to satisfy human purposes under any circumstances (Regan, 1983). These powerful claims applied to other activities, such as hunting and the use of animals to provide food and fur. Whatever the intentions of these authors, their work implied that something had to be done to stop the torture and killing.

The Animal Liberation Front (ALF) was founded in 1975, and began to receive media attention in the 1980s. Apart from releasing laboratory animals, the Front was blamed for the arrival of letter-bombs at the addresses of all four main party leaders in 1982, and the planting of incendiary devices in stores which sold animal fur. Later in the decade, it was accused of planting car-bombs and blowing up the Senate House of Bristol University. These tactics certainly won attention for the animal rights movement, but there was a danger that this publicity would prove counter-productive. In reply, activists could point out that more traditional forms of protest had been ineffective (Garner, 1993, 218–19, 224).

By contrast, the protests against the export of live veal calves were based on non-violent civil disobedience. Even so, one activist was killed in a protest at Coventry airport, which was used by exporters in the face of effective action at the south-coast ferry ports of Shoreham and Brightlingsea. On an average night, these Conservative strongholds would be invaded by 1,000 police officers, often confronting members of the public who had not previously been involved in demonstrations of any kind (Erlichman et al., 1995). The veal trade was particularly emotive, because in addition to the brutal treatment they receive in transit, calves are also separated from their mothers after only a day or two; however, the protesters soon moved on to blocking the export of live lambs, which remain with their mothers for longer.

The nation-wide publicity given to these protests was understandable, particularly since they coincided with a violent demonstration against the government's Criminal Justice Bill (October 1994). However, the demonstrations against animal rights, like the road protests, represented something new. The government, which had now won four successive elections, seemed to have lost its ability to select the right enemies. The recession of the early 1990s had hit the south of England, which had previously escaped the worst effects of economic hardship. Now road-building and animal exports provoked anger among government supporters, yet the response was either inactivity or grudging concessions. It was as if the Conservative Party now felt that it could take the whole electorate for granted. However, this strategy ran the risk of creating a constituency which could never be reconciled.

Conclusion: the politics of alienation?

By 1995, after sixteen years of a government which promised to restore British pride, many commentators sensed that the political system was failing. Almost every established institution had suffered damage in recent times. The troubled marriage of the Prince of Wales had destabilised the monarchy, the Anglican church had been split by the ordination of women, parliamentarians had accepted money in return for asking questions, members of the government had resigned for various improprieties, and the legal system was discredited by several well-publicised miscarriages of justice. Even Conservative commentators were beginning to record their discontent; when the *Daily Mail* serialised Paul Johnson's book *Wake up Britain*, it began with the headline 'What's going wrong with Britain?' (Johnson, 1994). His lamentations could not have been louder if the Labour Party had held office for the previous decade and a half.

Of course, the system had been in this plight before, particularly in the early 1960s. Harold Wilson's rhetoric about the 'white heat of technology' was perfectly timed to rescue the state from the impact of scandals that marked the end of the last sustained period of Conservative rule. Even so, irreverence towards established institutions, expressed in television satire and new magazines such as *Private Eye*, carried unmistakable warnings for the future. During our period, celebrations of the Queen's Silver Jubilee of 1977 had been overshadowed by the popularity of the Sex Pistols, whose single 'God Save The Queen' was banned by the BBC in a desperate attempt to create the impression of unanimous respect for the monarch. The Sex Pistols' message of despair found a receptive audience, although their belief that British youth had 'No future' was ironically contradicted by the energy and creativity of the punk movement. What this cultural phenomenon lacked was any agreed constructive channel for this vitality. For example, Nazi symbols were adopted by the Sex Pistols and their following; this originally demonstrated their rejection of all modern ideologies, but could easily be misunderstood by those who still clung to the old politics. In fact, punk groups were prominent in the fight against the National

Front. Many of them performed under the banner 'Rock against Racism', in collaboration with the Socialist Workers' Party. Yet even this was an essentially negative campaign, working to stave off further decay rather than pursuing an idealistic goal.

The punk movement coincided with the most depressing days of the 1970s, when the IMF dictated to the Labour government. On the fringes of the establishment unbalanced journalists and spies plotted to replace the elected government with a junta headed by Lord Mountbatten. When the Liberal Party leader Jeremy Thorpe was publicly implicated in a sex scandal the parallels with the last years of the Macmillan government seemed irresistible. To make matters worse, the pervasive mood of economic 'realism' after the oil shock meant that young people were even deprived of the futile dreams which enlivened the 1960s. As the hopes generated by the 1964 Labour government evaporated, Vietnam had offered that generation something tangible to lash out against; by contrast, the Sex Pistols were only left to explore their love/hate relationship with boredom. In this atmosphere, at least Margaret Thatcher provided a sense of purpose; as Jon Savage has remarked, the relationship between her policies and punk was complex, but rootless individualism was at the core of both (Savage, 1991, 480). When disillusionment culminated in the Winter of Discontent, there was one politician on hand to rejuvenate the body politic. The emergence of Thatcherism placated those young people who sympathised with her ideas, and provided her opponents with a refreshing new target for their hatred.

The situation in the 1990s is quite different. Again, popular culture can be used as a convenient barometer. Punk performers of the 1970s had either searched for a message, or discovered profundity in their regret that life had no obvious meaning. Recent fads in popular music, such as 'Acid House' and 'Rave', celebrated a disengagement from the world. The futility of things was seen as a reason to escape, not to get angry. Punk groups had been individualistic; their successors were simply anonymous. It took a while for profiteers to eat away the original motives of punk, but the new crazes arose from a culture in which elevated feelings were met with incomprehension.

These developments might be regarded as a cause for gloom, on the grounds that even purposeless energy is better than nothing. In September 1995 a survey by the think-tank Demos seemed to confirm that young people had no appetite for engagement with a society and political system which was alien to them (Wilkinson and Mulgan, 1995). However, the disenchantment of the 1990s is not exclusively a generational phenomenon. The signs are that after years of disorientation since the collapse of the familiar 'big' solutions, those who grew up in the years before 1976 are finding new inspiration in local campaigning; instead of being the single motor for new ideas, younger people are equal collaborators. The desire to change the world piecemeal rather than in one majestic sweep is easily ridiculed – the acronym NIMBY (Not In My Backyard) was quickly coined to question the motives of those who protested against new roads – but more charitable observers will see this as the best possible response to a world in which government seems increasingly distant and abstract. In this context Jonathon Porritt's attempt to embrace several established pressure groups under the umbrella organisation 'Real World' might be both premature and counter-productive (Keeble, 1995). Even bodies like FOE and Greenpeace are now regarded as being tainted through years of contact with the establishment, and it might be best to wait and see what local movements can achieve for themselves. The non-party campaign for constitutional reform, 'Charter 88', handicapped itself at the outset by choosing a name which commemorated the Glorious Revolution of 1688. This was bound to make its demands seem anachronistic; in addition, even sensible institutional reform seemed to be an abstract and indirect alternative to the grass-roots spirituality of the new movements.

If this trend continues, there is a real chance that the old parties will become irrelevant. Some believe that economic forces outside the control of national governments have brought this about already. Yet incidents like Brent Spar suggest that if governments are not prepared to annoy the giant corporations, the public (as citizens and consumers) might be willing to take up the challenge. The potential has not gone unnoticed by government; after the Brent Spar incident, John Major chastised Shell for having succumbed to popular pressure. Coming so soon after the Conservatives capitulated to public anger against the Poll Tax this was a bizarre and significant political moment. Meanwhile elements of the Conservative Party raged against the developing EU, oblivious to the fact that most of the electorate were already sick of the subject. The Labour leadership concentrated on getting rid of a constitutional clause which the party had disregarded in practice for years. Others decided that everything would be transformed by the abolition of impotent institutions like the monarchy or the House of Lords. Of the party leaders only Paddy Ashdown, for the Liberal Democrats, noticed the growing threat to the supremacy of parties; predictably, his important book *Beyond Westminster* was generally written off by the media as a stunt (Ashdown, 1994). Ironically, despite Ashdown's willingness to befriend the future, his party had abolished the Young Liberals in 1992. The Young Socialists suffered the same fate in the following year (Beckett, 1995).

It is tempting to describe most of the developments discussed in this chapter as products of a post-modern (or post-materialist) age. This reading is particularly seductive in relation to the environmental movement; it would suggest that only societies which no longer need to struggle for existence can afford to take stock of the destruction wrought by the previous two centuries. A complex mixture of guilt and concern also can help to explain the charitable movements of the 1980s, such as Live Aid; this was another example of people seizing the initiative from a government whose overseas budget was intended to secure arms contracts as much as to save lives. There is much truth in such speculation, although it would be wrong to belittle environmental concerns as mainly the offspring of contemporary comforts. The general post-modernist diagnosis, that the old ideological 'narratives' have broken down, also seems persuasive at the moment. Yet too often this kind of thinking, with its associated jargon, is an alibi for social philosophers who have now even given up on interpreting the world.

Whatever the underlying reasons for contemporary developments, the alternatives offered by today's political leaders will not suffice for much longer; even if they continue to win elections on their present programmes, disobedience against world markets will be increasingly forced on them by pressure groups. In some respects the situation seems ideal for the emergence of a charismatic leader who can win power without the support of established parties, but the British precedents for this are inauspicious. In the long run the most likely solution is the establishment of new ideologies, as ambitious as the old ones were and even sharing some of their characteristics. Although they will arise from politics at the local level, these beliefs will also have to be applicable on a wider scale, whether their forum is the nation-state or some other kind of larger community. Philosophers who follow Hannah Arendt in searching for clues in ancient Athenian practices are close to the truth; when any system is in trouble it is usually best to return to its originating principles. As usual, however, these musings will be pre-empted by activists on the ground. When this occurs the closing years of the present century will be regarded not as 'The end of history', but as an inevitable and relatively brief period of flux.

List of works cited

Ashdown, Paddy (1994), *Beyond Westminster*, Simon and Schuster
Beckett, Andy (1995), 'Power to the (Young) People', *Guardian*, 19 June
Byrne, Paul (1988), *The Campaign for Nuclear Disarmament*, Croom Helm
Campbell, Duncan (1986), *The Unsinkable Aircraft Carrier: American Military Power in Britain*, Paladin, updated edition
Carson, Rachel (1962) *Silent Spring*, Houghton Mifflin

Cole, Alistair, and Doherty, Brian (1995), 'France: *Pas comme les autres* – the French Greens at the Crossroads', in Dick Richardson and Chris Rootes (eds) *The Green Challenge: The Development of Green Parties in Europe*, Routledge

Coote, Anna, and Gill, Tess (1974), *Women's Rights: A Practical Guide*, Penguin

Crewe, Ivor (1992), 'A Nation of Liars? Opinion Polls in the 1992 Election', *Parliamentary Affairs*, volume 45, number 4

Dobson, Andrew (1990), *Green Political Thought: An Introduction*, Unwin Hayman

Drucker, Henry (ed.) (1979), *Multi-Party Britain*, Macmillan

Erlichman, James, Vidal, John, and Keeble, John (1995), 'A New Political Animal is Born', *Guardian*, 7–8 January

Garner, Robert (1993), *Animals, Politics and Morality*, Manchester University Press

Garner, Robert (1996), *Environmental Politics*, Harvester Wheatsheaf

Gilmour, Ian (1992), *Dancing with Dogma: Britain under Thatcherism*, Simon and Schuster

Grant, Linda (1995), 'Just Say No', *Guardian*, 3 June

Greer, Germaine (1970) *The Female Eunuch*, Granada

Heath, Anthony, Evans, Geoff, Field, Julia, and Witherspoon, Sharon (1991), *Understanding Political Change: The British Voter, 1964–1987*, Pergamon

Irvine, Sandy, and Ponton, Alec (1988), *A Green Manifesto: Policies for a Green Future*, Optima

Johnson, Paul (1994), 'What is Going Wrong with Britain?', *Daily Mail*, 23 April

Jones, Mervyn (1994), *Michael Foot*, Victor Gollancz

Judge, David (ed.) (1993), *A Green Dimension for the European Community: Political Issues and Processes*, Frank Cass

Keeble, John (1995) 'Time is Right to Get Real', *Guardian*, 12 July

Lamont, Norman (1993), 'Green Measures', Budget Statement, *Parliamentary Debates*, volume 221, 182–3

Lovenduski, Joni, and Randall, Vicky (1993), *Contemporary Feminist Politics: Women and Power in Britain*, Oxford University Press

Lovenduski, Joni, Norris, Pippa, and Burness, Catriona (1994), 'The Party and Women', in Anthony Seldon and Stuart Ball (eds) *Conservative Century: The Conservative Party since 1900*, Oxford University Press

McCormick, John (1991), *British Politics and the Environment*, Earthscan

Meadows, Donella, Meadows, Dennis, Randers, Jorgen, and Behrens, William (1974) *The Limits to Growth: A Report for the Club of Rome's Project on the Predicament of Mankind*, Pan

Porritt, Jonathon, and Winner, David (1988), *The Coming of the Greens*, Fontana

Regan, Tom (1983) *The Case for Animal Rights*, Routledge and Kegan Paul

Rootes, Chris (1995), 'Britain: Greens in a Cold Climate', in Dick Richardson and Chris Rootes (eds) *The Green Challenge: The Development of Green Parties in Europe*, Routledge

Sanders, David (1992), 'Why the Conservative Party Won – Again', in Anthony King (ed.), *Britain at the Polls*, Chatham House

Savage, Jon (1991), *England's Dreaming: Sex Pistols and Punk Rock*, Faber and Faber

Sebestyen, Amanda (1985), 'The Politics of Survival – While the Work Goes On', in Robin Morgan (ed.), *Sisterhood is Global: The International Women's Movement Anthology*, Penguin

Shaw, Eric (1994), *The Labour Party since 1979: Crisis and Transformation*, Routledge

Short, Clare (1986), Speech Introducing Indecent Displays (Newspapers) Bill, 12 March, *Parliamentary Debates*, volume 93, 937–40

Singer, Peter (1975) *Animal Liberation*, Thorsons, 2nd edition

Skjaerseth, Jon (1994), 'The Climate Policy of the EC: Too Hot to Handle?', *Journal of Common Market Studies*, volume 32, number 1

Taylor, Robert (1970), 'The Campaign for Nuclear Disarmament', in Vernon Bogdanor and Robert Skidelsky (eds) *The Age of Affluence 1951–1964*, Macmillan

Thatcher, Margaret (1993), *The Downing Street Years*, HarperCollins

Topf, Richard (1989), 'Political Change and Political Culture in Britain, 1959–87', in *Contemporary Political Culture*, Sage

Vincent, Andrew (1995), *Modern Political Ideologies*, Blackwell, 2nd edition

Wainwright, Hilary (1984), 'Women and the Division of Labour', in Philip Abrams and Richard Brown (eds) *UK Society: Work, Urbanism and Inequality*, Weidenfeld and Nicolson

Wilkinson, Helen, and Mulgan, Geoff (1995) 'Can We Really Afford to Grow Old?', *The Independent* 25 September

Witherspoon, Sharon (1985), 'Sex Roles and Gender Issues', in Roger Jowell and Sharon Witherspoon (eds) *British Social Attitudes: The 1985 Report*, Gower

Wybrow, Robert (1989), *Britain Speaks Out: A Social History as Seen through the Gallup Data*, Macmillan

Young, Ken (1991), 'Shades of Green', in Roger Jowell, Lindsay Brook and Bridget Taylor (eds) *British Social Attitudes: The 8th Report*, Dartmouth

Questions for discussion

- Is there anything that links contemporary protest movements beyond their discontent?
- Give the cases for and against a continuance of the present party political system in the United Kingdom.

Selected further reading (see also Chapter 7)

Canovan, Margaret (1992), *Hannah Arendt: A Reinterpretation of her Thought*, Cambridge University Press.

Crick, Bernard (1992), *In Defence of Politics*, Weidenfeld and Nicolson, 4th edition.

Garrett, John (1992), *Westminster: Does Parliament Work?*, Victor Gollancz.
Green, David (1993), *Reinventing Civil Society*, Institute of Economic Affairs.
Haworth, Alan (1994), *Anti-Libertarianism: Markets, Philosophy and Myth*, Routledge.
Hutton, Will (1995), *The State We're In*, Jonathan Cape.
Lenman, Bruce (1992), *The Eclipse of Parliament*, Edward Arnold.
Mount, Ferdinand (1992), *The British Constitution Now*, Heinemann.
Mulgan, Geoff (1994), *Politics in an Anti-Political Age*, Polity.
Symonds, Matthew (1994), *The Culture of Anxiety: The Middle Class Crisis*, Social Market Foundation.
Wright, Anthony (1994), *Citizens and Subjects*, Routledge.

Principles and Politics since 1970

The history of UK politics since 1970 shows the consistent importance of principles, yet it also proves the dangers of neat generalisation. The main political parties and the wider public remained divided in their views before and after the supposed 'breakdown of consensus'. Harold Wilson and Edward Heath were both criticised even from within their respective parties before 1975; Mrs Thatcher's victory in the Conservative leadership election of that year did not cause the mass conversion of her party. Thatcherism was never accepted by a majority of the population, but people outside Westminster were far from unanimous in their support for any alternative principles. Commentators often talk of a 'climate of opinion' as if such a uniform phenomenon could be discovered, but anything more than a cursory examination of the evidence reveals the diversity of views held at any time during our period.

With this essential proviso, some broad themes may now be recapitulated. Between 1970 and the advent of Mrs Thatcher, Conservative party policies were broadly compatible with conservative ideology. By 1970, this essentially meant a mistrust of human nature, which necessitated purposeful national leadership in a quest for social stability. Until 1979 Thatcher was on her probation as party leader, but once she had been elected Prime Minister a new approach was quickly established. Economic policy was now under the exclusive control of nineteenth-century liberals, whose views had previously been ignored. Identifying closely with only a vigorous minority within the population, Thatcher prioritised inflation rather than unemployment; warnings about the likely impact on society went unheeded. This brand of liberalism remains the ruling dogma of the Conservative Party, since the internal opposition has been unable to change the government's course even since the coup which toppled Thatcher. The only change is that the present leadership lacks the crusading zeal of the former leader. Commentators who claim that policy is based on greater 'moderation' have simply mistaken style for content.

In 1970 the most influential thinking within the Labour Party came from its social democratic wing. Theorists such as Anthony Crosland owed their inspiration to the ideas of 'New' liberalism rather than to any recognisably socialist premises. The New liberal conviction that the state must intervene to provide economic security for individuals fostered the key reforms of the 1945–51 Attlee government, and the Labour leadership was anxious to defend this settlement until 1976. Nationalisation of certain utilities was an essential part of this programme, but economic growth depended on a vibrant public sector. Unfortunately for Labour, world conditions, and the deplorable record of domestic UK investment, meant that growth was not forthcoming during their years of power after 1964. Harold Wilson was unable to pursue any consistent policy line, and his successor James Callaghan explicitly rejected social democratic priorities after the IMF moved in. Socialists attempted to fill this ideological vacuum within the party, achieving most success in 1970–74 and 1979–83 – significantly, the years immediately following the loss of office. Harold Wilson's victories of 1974 scuppered the first of these efforts, while Michael Foot and Neil Kinnock ensured the defeat of the second. Between 1983 and 1992 Labour returned to a social democratic position, but this development did not carry conviction with the electorate. Since the election of Tony Blair, thinking has moved even further away from socialism, to the extent that the economic policies of a future Labour government might be hard to distinguish from Thatcherism.

Throughout our period, the Liberal Party has retained its allegiance to New liberalism, having discarded most adherents of the nineteenth-century variety during the 1950s. This loyalty to the welfare state and the mixed economy should have ensured easy collaboration with the social democrats who left the Labour Party in 1981. The attempt to break the mould of British politics foundered on the personality of Dr David Owen, who quickly ceased to be a social democrat once he had escaped from a party which attacked him for holding those views. Under Paddy Ashdown the Liberal Democrats are more receptive to public opinion than the other main parties, but in the absence of proportional representation the prospect of power remains distant for the party.

For various reasons, the range of political views espoused by the main parties is now more restricted even than it was during the days of 'Butskellism'. This has left a useful opening for other groups, including nationalist parties which have also been helped by the concept of independence within Europe. While Marxists still wrestle with the implications of developments in Eastern Europe, the Green Party has tried to tap growing disillusionment with a society lacking in spiritual direction. The fact that green ideas seem more suited to pressure-group activity need not be a handicap for those who wish to influence government policies; as discontent with political parties continues, non-parliamentary action combined with enthusiastic lobbying is an increasingly attractive model for future politics. Currently political principles are less diverse and ambitious than they were at the beginning of our period. Yet they remain as important as ever; the requirement now is for new forms of belief which can restore political commitment at all levels of society.

Of the general themes which have emerged from this study, the most important is that the politicians who have fared best since 1970 are those who have convinced the public that their convictions are deeply held. This is always important, but it has become vital at a time when perceived economic realties place limits on the creativity of party thinking. It also needs reasserting at a time when party strategists are apparently unanimous in the view that elections are inevitably decided by economic factors. Clearly economic appeal must be part of a successful platform, but if views are expressed in a suitable idiom they can make people think that they are better off even when the hard evidence is questionable. This certainly helps to explain why (for instance) Margaret Thatcher won three elections on a platform which was culled from thinking that was over a century old, and provoked fierce opposition from some sections of the electorate. It might also have contributed to John Major's surprising election victory of 1992; Major's personal views remain obscure, but his decision to preach his message from a soap-box provided a more sincere impression than the glitz of Neil Kinnock's campaign. Although Kinnock undoubtedly retained his humanitarian objectives, he had ditched many of the detailed policy ideas which had brought him into politics; in view of this the confessional soap-box option was not really open to him. The implication of this finding is that parties which advocate policies merely because the public apparently likes them cannot hope to succeed – unless, of course, their competitors are doing the same. Elections fought on these lines could only be insincerity contests, and even parties which feel that they have been out of office for too long can hardly think that the shrinking power of the UK state is worth winning at this price.

A P P E N D I X

General election results, 1970–92: % of votes cast

	1970	1974 (Feb)	1974 (Oct)	1979	1983	1987	1992
Conservative	46.4	37.9	35.8	43.9	42.4	42.3	41.9
Labour	43.0	37.1	39.2	36.9	27.6	30.8	34.4
Liberal Democrat*	7.5	19.3	18.3	13.8	25.4	22.6	17.8
SNP*	0.6	2.0	2.9	1.6	1.1	1.3	1.9
Plaid Cymru†	1.1	0.6	0.6	0.4	0.4	0.4	0.5
Others (GB)	1.4‡	3.4	0.8	1.2	0.6	0.4	1.3
Others (NI)	–‡	2.3	2.4	2.2	2.5	2.2	2.2
Turnout (%)	72.0	78.7	72.8	76.0	72.7	75.3	77.7

*Until 1979 read as Liberal. For 1983 and 1987 read as SDP/Liberal Alliance.
†For 1970, and February 1974 the vote for these parties is included in Others (GB)
‡Figures for 1970 are distorted because Northern Ireland Unionist and Northern Ireland Labour have traditionally been included into the major party vote for this election

INDEX